RESOURCES & RESOLUTIONS

TAROT COUPLING

Gina G. Thies

Schiffer Publishing Ltd

4880 Lower Valley Road • Atglen, PA 19310

Disclaimer
The material in this book does not replace therapy by a licensed professional.

Schiffer Books are available at special discounts for bulk purchases for sales promotions or premiums. Special editions, including personalized covers, corporate imprints, and excerpts can be created in large quantities for special needs. For more information contact the publisher:

Published by Schiffer Publishing, Ltd.
4880 Lower Valley Road
Atglen, PA 19310
Phone: (610) 593-1777; Fax: (610) 593-2002
E-mail: Info@schifferbooks.com

For the largest selection of fine reference books on this and related subjects,
please visit our website at
www.schifferbooks.com.

We are always looking for people to write books on new and related subjects.
If you have an idea for a book, please contact us at
proposals@schifferbooks.com

This book may be purchased from the publisher.
Please try your bookstore first.
You may write for a free catalog.

DEDICATION

For my husband Daniel
For my sons Jeremy and Jordan
For all my Tarot Friends near and far

Author Note

A word: Most of what I am discussing here works in the realm of people who do **NOT** have some sort of severe mental disorder.

Tarot readings are guidance in terms of soul evolution.

Unless you are licensed, please make reference to a licensed professional when the situation calls for it.

Contents

CHAPTER 10. THE MAJOR ARCANA: THE FOOL THROUGH THE WORLD

CHAPTER 11. THE MINOR ARCANA: ACE THROUGH TEN

CHAPTER 12. THE MINOR ARCANA: COURT CARDS

CHAPTER 13. CORE VALUES SPREAD 242

PREFACE

Tarot Coupling provides details of my professional work. Trying to understand human behavior as explained through card meanings and spreads, I have explored different possibilities that seemed to "ring true," both for myself and for my clients.

These possibilities began to emerge as I noticed a link when I applied psychoanalytic theories to Tarot card readings. I became aware that other Tarot users corresponded personality types and psychological functions, too. Nobody, though, seemed to be clear in its usefulness in helping the querent.

If you're new to Tarot study, does it all seem overwhelming?

I thought so when I was learning, not to mention that all of the information in those little white books did not help much in practical terms of explaining human interactions.

Humans are complex creatures. I began "testing the waters" with my findings while reading for clients experiencing crisis in love relationships.

For me, Tarot started as a tool for predicting the future. Through it, I discovered that many people are concerned with the existential facts of life: the reality of living and staying alive, which is why most people want to know "what do you see in my future?"

My goal in writing this material is to engage you, the reader, in considering Tarot through the lens of an insight-oriented counselor who oversees an introspective process.

The intention is not to write another "how-to-read Tarot-cards" book, but write one with the purpose of conveying information about intimate relationships and dilemmas that emerge within the context of Tarot consultations.

Tarot perfectly explains the human emotional experience and seems naturally integrated with psychological perspectives. However, intimate partnerships are the platform where characteristics and dynamics of human nature are acted out in transformational theatrics.

Performance is not always perfect. When emotional turmoil disrupts the flow of happiness, people reach out for direction. We, as readers, are often called to the task, so I also felt it beneficial to write from the perspective of the professional reader and in the spirit of those who guide others as agents of change, while also avoiding prescriptions for guaranteed success.

My hope is to appeal to those who may consider Tarot consultation as a career path, new readers, and seasoned professionals. For those who seek an "advanced" approach to reading the cards, *Tarot Coupling* aspires to meet that need.

One of the biggest challenges in the topic of relationships would be to avoid offending a select group, or establishing generalities about human sexuality in all its diverse arrangements. I think I have done this nicely as will be evidenced as you read further.

Acknowledgments

This book would not have happened without the great patience and love of my family and friends. I would like to thank Ruth Ann and Wald Amberstone of The Tarot School for being the greatest Tarot teachers in the world.

Thanks to the students who took my study group at the 2010 Readers Studio and to the BATS Queen Thalassa.

To the wonderful PJ Gunter, who graciously worked hard with initial edits and manuscript preparation.

To my friend, Tammy McInnis, for all of your encouragement and the shoulder I cried on for a long time.

To Beatrice Scaffidi, my mentor and the most gifted reader in the universe! Thanks for all the readings and guidance you have given me since 1994.

My cousin, Donna Brazile for being a role model to me now and while growing up in Kenner, Louisiana, and to her father, my late great-uncle Lionel Brazile, for opening the door I entered that awakened my gifts.

I would like to also thank my clients who have shared their lives, allowing me to give guidance and trusting me.

Many special thanks to Katrina Wynne, M.A. and Dan Pelletier.

To everyone else who helped in publishing this book and to the many masters of Tarot who taught me so much about the cards; and a heartfelt thanks to everyone at Schiffer Publishing, Ltd.

INTRODUCTION

Love looks not with the eyes, but with the mind, therefore
is winged Cupid painted blind.

~William Shakespeare
Mid-Summer Night's Dream, 1595

Many of life's essential lessons may be drawn from the writings of William Shakespeare. The above quote from one of Shakespeare's famous plays seemingly describes Major Arcana card 6 – The Lovers.

The Lovers card is traditionally depicted with two or three figures along with an angel, Cupid or Eros, as the Romans called him, hovering above and poised with an arrow ready to be released, its goal the unsuspecting victim. This winged boy, armed with his "love weapon," was a very familiar figure featured in Hellenistic and Roman art. In some depictions, the figure sometimes carried a torch.

In literature and art, Cupid is painted as blindfolded, but it is not meant to imply that he is without eyesight.

The ancients considered the god of fertility, desire, and love to have blind reasoning, just as lovers are blind to the defects or faults of the one whom they love.

The allegory of The Lovers card featuring this winged creature, which became an angel on most modern decks, symbolizes Divinity's union with humankind. While assumed to represent harmony, relationships or union through marriage in the exoteric context, The Lovers in esoteric circles are explained by dualism rather than ordinary human love.

Falling in love is such a natural act of emotional expression; we don't tend to think of it as a "choice." Certainly, there's free will and right in choosing a mate to date or marry in the majority of cultures, but how often have you heard, "you can't help with whom you fall in love"? Certain psychological perspectives propose that a person can't resist whom they love based on a number of factors.

The way we come to fall in love has a great deal to do with the heart, but also the mind. When this happens, people tend to question the mind and, because of the emotions involved with falling in love, often find it difficult to rationalize their own affections objectively.

This material was based on many readings that I, and, with certainty many of you, have experienced. Intimate partnership, individual personal well-being, fears, and success are long-term explorations, which are commonly examined in a Tarot reading.

Undoubtedly, relationships can be challenging to all of us. Even those of us in satisfying partnerships can have bumps that in a moment's notice would leave the most emotionally healthiest of us unsettled by doubts.

The purpose of relationships is to appease our social inclinations. Various interconnections assist us in learning about others and ourselves with intimate relationships contributing greatly to the process of reflecting our inner selves. Relationships act as transformative catalysts for transcendence through joy and inevitable pain.

There is a tendency to empathize with traits or qualities we admire in others and reject the ones we hate. These are difficult to recognize and are the unconscious traits theorists tell us have come from our parents or primary caretakers. These are subconscious patterns that shaped and molded our behaviors.

It is believed that insight emerging from our unconscious through the use of Tarot is boundless. The Tarot reader should be able to give important revelations along with clear direction of possibilities on how to avoid or transcend life's complications. Tarot explains human behaviors, emotions, mind frames, motives, and most probable actions, as well as other psycho-spiritual processes. This could explain its allure to those in the depth psychology and alternative health fields.

Generally, people are more curious about others, rather than holding up a mirror for self-inspection because of the possible ugliness in that reflection.

In relationship readings, you are likely to have an inquirer who is more interested in finding Mr. or Ms. Right, rather than know or ask why they are attracting Mr. or Ms. Wrong.

This is how my use of Tarot has successfully helped my clients unravel the mysteries of relationships. Tarot can be used to examine and articulate the hidden aspects of what drives our choices and gives fascinating insight regarding human attraction and interactions.

This book, therefore, demonstrates how Tarot can assist in your understanding of intimate partner choices, compatibility, and adult attraction, by exploring Tarot in conjunction with psychological theories specifically regarding relational issues. The ultimate hope is that you find the information immensely valuable and that this book becomes one reference source you reach for in deepening your understanding of Tarot's language. I hope it helps educate you in your pursuit of that perfect love or enhances your current relationship.

Within is the culmination of my interests in historical Tarot, divination, psychology, and my own personal trials in relationships. Two previous failed attempts at marriage led me to understand WHY I was choosing difficult, inappropriate partners via deep self-study. Needless to say, I suspected it had to do with factors of my lack of a proper relationship model.

It took courage, and a willingness to understand the magnitude in which my childhood contributed to the theme of my relationship struggles. I began the journey of healing, which is by no means complete, years ago. While I've learned plenty along the way, the result of confronting my past has been a blessing in disguise.

In the sections that follow, I shall present very basic information on the inner workings of love, attraction, and partner choice that may be familiar to some, uniquely used in conjunction with Tarot to explain certain aspects of romantic partnering, while demonstrating their successful use in relationship readings.

I have given interpretations for each card from what is based on the structure of four relationship stages, which will be introduced in a later chapter.

Using the information in *Tarot Coupling* provides an exploratory map with pieces and parts of the relational experience. With such a map you are guided to ways of analyzing what's happening in your relationship and will yield vital insights regarding the nuances of relationships.

I am a big fan of movies, shopping, and romance. I am sure you'll enjoy the suggestions provided with the intention that you'll use them not only to enjoy your love life, but as a way to experience the cards.

Whether you have been in love for twenty-five minutes or twenty-five years, dates are important. You'll enjoy the ideas for outings and gift giving suggestions, too.

And Two Shall Be Joined...

What is coupling? Coupling as defined in *The American Heritage® Dictionary of the English Language*, Fourth Edition (©2000 by Houghton Mifflin Company), is defined as:

1. The act of linking together or forming couples.
2. The act of uniting sexually.
3. A device that links or connects.

In this book, it applies to Tarot's "coupling" with perspectives and theories formed in psychology as it applies specifically to relationship readings. Similar to the method of integrating various approaches in analysis, the Tarot reader pulls in various methodologies for the querent's consultation.

From early in our lives we are taught to see the world in pairs: day and night, male and female, sun and moon, cold and hot. The list goes on. So this book shows insight to human interaction and particularly the dyad in love relationships.

Coupling and pairing brings harmonious symmetry to the world and allows a better understanding to all that surrounds us and those we love. Tarot is the "device" that helps bridge understanding of human interactions and emotions to the questioner. The Tarot as a language proficiently communicates the subtleties of emotional life.

Over the years, many novice readers have focused on card meanings and techniques, which are void of counseling support tactics. "Therapeutic'" divination, assumed to attend to the spiritual health of the querent, has no clear definition as it varies from practitioner to practitioner.

While Tarot has attempted to distance itself from the clandestine grip of velveteen parlors, many struggle to legitimize Tarot. Being a Tarot reader is like being a social worker, tons of education and study in order to do something that earns little and very few appreciate.

Just as Tarot is corresponded to other disciplines of mystical thought and aligned with everything from kitchen recipes to the latest fashion trend, I've found a pragmatic approach in understanding attraction and love through the cards.

The adage "life didn't come with a manual," could well apply to relationships. To some, the only "manual" needed has tenets established millennia ago that apply to civil and domestic life. Most people have a romanticized, idealistic conditioning about their love journey in life.

It is rare, perhaps in my own limited experience, to find that gem of a partner, well educated in proper relationship functioning.

Humanity is capable of proper relational functioning indeed. This does not mean that all will be done perfectly, but it is possible to excel beyond mistakes, accept others and whom they choose to love.

It is necessary to protect those who cannot fend for themselves, preserving young souls from ruin through abuse and neglect.

Dysfunction spreads like wildfire. Considering the magnitude and the limited or costly access to medical/mental health care, perhaps spiritual practitioners with the right training need to take up some slack, so to speak. To those willing, let this book inspire you.

CHAPTER 1

THE LAND OF MYSTERY, OF THE UNKNOWN YET KNOWABLE[1]

The fortune-tellers are the moralists, as well as the consolers of the lower classes.
They supply a want that society either cannot or will not do.

~The Book of Days, ed. R. Chambers[2]

Meeting with a Stranger

We sat across from each other, strangers, awaiting our hostess, in a dimly lit room with the scent of Nag Champa incense and the floral essence of lavender.

Anticipating an introduction, I adjusted my weight, sitting in a high-back chair of soft, dark leather, noticing the table draped in a black tablecloth with layers of colorful silk scarves on top as two newly lit candles on the tabletop formed pools of heated wax.

The stranger across from me, neatly attired in crisscrossed hues of blue, was unmoved by my growing expectation and curiosity.

I had seen this stranger before, irresistibly attractive and popular with the ladies (and men); I could not have imagined mutual interest.

This stranger was rumored to be a teacher, a master, and a magus with a long pedigree of royal lineage. I could certainly understand the attraction: traveled, worldly, fluent in multiple languages, and a bit devilish. What more could a gal ask for? A wedding? I didn't want to be premature about the situation, but I could tell it was love. You know the feeling?

Our lovely hostess arrived. Noticing my anxiety, she said, "Please take a deep breath." I exhaled, letting my shoulders fall. I exhaled while gently releasing the air through rounded lips and pulled the air steadily back in. "Is this your first time?" she asked. Sheepishly looking from side to side, embarrassed, "First time?" I asked. "Yes, having a reading with Tarot?"

I had learned the stranger's name. The curiosity didn't end there. I wanted more. I wanted to know its secret. I wanted to know its beginnings and so the affair began.

A Colorful Past

How did you first start your relationship with Tarot? Do you remember playing card games as a child? I sure do. I recall having to learn all the rules of Spades; I think this is what I played the most. No matter what was played, I had to know what the cards meant in terms of number or rank within the context of the game.

The history of cheap playing cards never crossed my mind. Unless they make it their business to know, most people are not even vaguely aware of playing card history.

It is particularly beneficial to know which cards have a purpose that allows victory over the opponent in any card game, even if played alone like in Solitaire. I wanted to learn the best tactics and how they could help my chances of winning. Do not misunderstand that it's all about winning. On the contrary, it is all about knowledge and intelligent tact. Learning Tarot as a way to tell fortunes was for me, much like learning to play cards in the sense of using all the shortcuts.

I (and perhaps you can understand) became more interested in deciphering the meanings of the cards so that I could see a person's future, just as I had experienced in my own first Tarot reading. Alas, Tarot became much more than I could imagine.

The history of the cards was not on my radar at the time that I began learning to read with them. Of the history of Tarot, I say, "Oh what a web we've weaved!"

Honestly, considering my esoteric interests, up until a recent 2011 Tarot History tour in Italy, I struggled to reconcile occult origin theories, esoteric principles, and historical evidence regarding Tarot's origins.

Over the decades, a plethora of theories have been presented, but the one Antoine Court de Gébelin, alleged, in 1781, of Tarot's ancient Egyptian origin, has been agreeably debunked. But he wasn't that far off in a cultural sense.

An early set of playing cards, said to be the model of the Italian suits, were found in a Turkish museum by L.A. Mayer whose embellishments he suggests closely matches the Circassian (Sunnite) artistic style in Egyptian documents, and a fragment of another card discovered which possibly predates the Mamlûk decks have Islamic-Egyptian decoration.[3]

Antoine Court de Gébelin, who believed the Tarot's Major Arcana genesis to be ancient Egyptian, wrote one of the first works on Tarot in one of nine volumes of *Monde primitif, analyse et compare avec le monde moderne* (*Primitive World, analyzed and compared with the modern world*).[4]

It's an honest assumption, given that this ancient culture (believed to be the source of mankind's wisdom at the time) transcribed in symbols or hieroglyphs encased by an elongated frame (cartouche) royal names of their rulers.

The burning of the library of Alexandria possibly destroyed an invaluable connecting discourse from sagacious priests, but the hieroglyphs were deciphered, and so, unfortunately, de Gébelin infamously fantasized Tarot's Egyptian origin.

Many have added that his theories were ridiculous because there are no existing Egyptian images that resemble Tarot images. However, the Egyptian hieroglyphic symbols illustrated in Sir E. A. Wallis Budge's *An Egyptian Hieroglyphic Dictionary (Volume I)* resemble some of the trumps, including The Chariot, from a Jungian collective unconscious (archetype) point of view, but in no way constitutes or confirms an ancient Egyptian origin for Tarot. I know many Tarot enthusiasts and historians don't have a sense of humor about the Egyptian stuff.

Interestingly, the hand-painted set of playing cards discovered in the Topkai Sarayi Museum of Istanbul in 1939, which dates from the 15th century, had no trumps, so technically is not a Tarot deck.

Helen Farley in *A Cultural History of Tarot* mentions the discovery of other Egyptian cards, one of which dates to the 12th century and thinks this shows that card making in Egypt was in existence long before the Mamlûk deck in the Istanbul's museum.[5]

The Mamlûks were racially diverse military warriors imported to Egypt as slaves, acquired by the Ayyubid dynasty.[6] They rose to power in 1250 through 1517 and were considered "no less than tyrannical leaders to Egypt's French invaders in 1798," notes Darius Speith in his work, *Napoleon's Sorcerers*.[7]

The four suit designs of the Mamlûk playing cards with the exception of the polo sticks, inspired the European card maker's design when they made their own playing card decks. The Mamlûk deck's court card figures of King, a Governor, a Viceroy, and Second Viceroy are not illustrated with human figures. This was believed to be due to the Muslim religious ban against human portrayals.[8]

Nassar D. Khali explains in *Islamic Art and Culture: Timeline and History*:

> Contrary to popular assumption, figural imagery plays an important role in Islamic art. The hadith (traditions) prohibits the representation of human beings and animals in the religious context. This rule does not extend to secular art.[9]

Although it's probable that playing cards reached Europe through Spain or via ports of Venice, Islamic-styled playing cards were mentioned in the *History of the City of Viterbo* in 1379 describing the "nayb" (naib), a game brought to Italy by Saracens. *Naib*, translated to "naibi" in Italian, was a term used for playing cards, and Tarot historian Michael Dummett concluded these words as a possible reference to one of the Mamlûk court cards.[10]

Tarot distinguishes itself from regular playing cards in that it adds 21 trumps, The Fool card, and four royal court cards instead of three. Determining the original purpose of Tarot cards is difficult without knowing who designed them in the first place. Another theory is that cards were the invention of the Chinese. The Chinese were captured in 751 by Arabian armies, and while in captivity, taught the Arabs how to produce paper.[11]

There is evidence that the cards were being played in Belgium and Switzerland circa 1379, but the Chinese cards of the late 1370s do not bear any resemblance, says card artist Brett A. Jones of White Knuckle Playing Cards.[12]

What has been established through historical record and mention by several Tarot historians is that games and gambling are referenced as how playing cards were used in several documents as far back as the late 14th century, with a particular mention of Tarot found in documents from the D'Este court in Ferrara, Italy from 1442.[13]

Tarot was a specific type of game enjoyed by the populace of Europe. Eventually, Tarot cards gained popularity with early occultists. By the latter part of the 18th century, significant interpretations stemmed from occult France and was laced with elements of Qabalah, Astrology, Hermeticism, and Medieval philosophy provide the framework for today's Tarot card meanings.

Exactly where, who, and when the Tarot card system we have today originated is relatively colored by its "mysterious" origins.

The truth is lost somewhere out in East Jesus, a reference to an invented fairytale-like place that you'll get the gist of while living in the South, but I should make clear that it in no way speculates about the "fairytale-ness" of Jesus Christ.

Both the history and theories of playing cards and Tarot origins would make up unusually large volume(s) with many twists, turns, and offshoots, not to mention that there are several already penned.

It is safe to say that present research yields playing card designs can be traced to a combination of European and Arabic influences weaved with elements of a variety of Mediterranean cultures.

An important distinction made about the inventions of cards is that playing cards may not originally have been European, but Tarot and the idea of the trumps, once called triumphs, were a European invention.[14] Italians commissioned decks that were painted for the noble classes, much like the art of the period, as symbols of their wealth.

Freemasonry and other secret societies with their constant study of the cards contribute to what we see in Tarot studies today.

Many members of these societies made up part of The Hermetic Order of The Golden Dawn. The Golden Dawn was an occult society founded in England that devoted itself to the study of many esoteric topics, including Tarot. One of the most famous Tarot decks was a collaboration of two members: author Arthur Edward Waite and illustrator Pamela Colman Smith.

Smith, under the patronage of Waite, based her design, Stuart Kaplan tells us, in *The Encyclopedia of Tarot (Volume II)* on the Sola-Busca cards in which pictures were married to the quantity of suit objects.[15]

In addition to the Golden Dawn, Tarot was the object of serious study by occultists Ettelia, Eliphas Levi, and Papus, among others. An excellent resource for the occult origins of Tarot is *A Wicked Pack of Cards – The Origins of the Occult Tarot* (Ronald Decker, Thierry Depaulis and Michael Dummett, 1996, St. Martin's Press, New York).

Over the years, much has been written about Tarot and its popularity is still growing along with its combined use of other systems of thought much like when it was attached to Qabalah. Today, we have access to more information than theorists did in the 18th century. The longer you use Tarot, you'll come to understand many insights, whether they are esoteric or exoteric.

Tarot's reputation for cartomancy remains well-known around the globe. It also is easily integrated into systems of alchemy, magic, and astrology. It is useful to look into mythology, philosophy, art, history and symbols from different cultures, not just that of one particular element to determine the nuances in Tarot meanings.

Tarot tells the story of many cultural perspectives and ideas. Certainly a number of different meanings can be applied to its symbols. Symbols of course do evolve, and so does the iconography of symbols.

In the beginning, I myself traveled the same route that so many novice occultists take on the quest to learn Tarot. In the meantime, many unanswered questions remained, one of which became, "Where did they get that?" This has taken me on a journey, literally, that expanded my understanding of each card.

Once, while discussing Tarot with my husband, I told him that I was thinking of covering the walls of our game room with poster paper in order to work out some of the dots I was connecting with Tarot. How does Tarot lead someone, who left the woes of math to high school, all ramped up about the Fibonacci sequence?

When I began to read everything I could get my hands on about Tarot, it was pretty overwhelming. As an example, I wondered about things like, "Should Justice be numbered 11 – or is that just wrong?"

A few years back, during my study of the cards, an "aha" moment came. I could see how Justice could be Key 8 instead of Key 11, and it made more sense too. With that observation, I began to understand how some conclude that The Magician is better suited to Aleph rather than The Fool.

Which way is correct? "Even Crowley did not agree with Waite," I explained to my husband while we chatted one evening as I stood in front of the bathroom mirror doing my nightly ritual of prepping for bed. I continued a little discouraged, "It's as if they made up all these correspondences." As I entered the bedroom, I stopped in my tracks when my husband looked up from his *Scientific American* and said, "It is all made up!"

My coming to terms with the origins and meanings of the cards aligns with the authors Decker, Depaulis, and Dummett in writing:

> The earliest exponents of Tarot occultism did not even pretend to be privy to any secret tradition: they claimed to have discovered the truth about Tarot by the power of their own intuition.
>
> ~*A Wicked Pack of Cards – The Origins of the Occult Tarot*
> **Ronald Decker, Thierry Depaulis,** and **Michael Dummett**
> 1996, St. Martin's Press, New York[16]

It matters not that the cards were used for trick-taking or other games. What matters is that it works (in theory for some) in spite of the proof of its origins. It works as a form of entertainment and as a tool that stimulates wisdom, self-exploration, and ideas.

But history and facts do matter. Yet, it should not go unnoticed that the cards have been more than a game to thousands of people that see its value and worth in Tarot's rich iconographic history.

Images that are consistent with Tarot are painted on many frescos that were common to the Middle Ages and Renaissance people of Italy with no apparent occult meaning.

But at the same time, when I was there constantly surrounded by these images, I have come to know through immersion in the Tarot, I did get the sense that the images, symbols, and icons had an undercurrent of meanings that is in every sense of the word, esoteric.

This book was not written to satisfy all components of possibilities in the origins of Tarot. I did not take for granted the historical perspective, but nor could I ignore the viewpoint of many who are dedicated in using Tarot as part of their magickal tradition.

After all, these enthusiasts are not immune from relationships issues, whether it be those of their own or of anyone to whom they offer advice.

From Card Game to Occult Tool

The centuries-old Tarot with its shrouded beginnings does not originate as used in cartomancy. In terms of Tarot's European presence, historian Michael Dummett tells us, "fortune telling with playing cards of any kind is in fact a rather late development."[16a] Tarot derives its name from a French term of the Italian word, *tarocchi*. Il tarocchi was a card playing game used by many nobles who could afford to have them painted for pastime activities or group gathering entertainment. Evidence of this is shown in an early depiction of card players of the 15th century in what came to be titled, *The Tarocchi Players*, a fresco on the wall of the Casa Borromeo located in Milan, Italy.[16b]

The arrival of woodblock printing allowed the cards to be inexpensively replicated for the use of other members of European peasant order and very profitable to papermakers. A belief that the Divine intervened in human affairs had been carried into early medieval religious practices. God's will and guidance were sought through such means as prayer, bibliomancy and sortilege.[17]

Sortilege, the practice of drawing tickets or lots, was commonly used as a "decision-making" aid explains Keith Thomas in *Religion and the Decline of Magic*. Thomas also mentions that "divisory" lotteries were used to settle matters between conflicting parties and eventually on a more national level for fundraising, just as a state-operated lottery is used today.

Lots drawn by Church fathers and laymen alike were used for predictions on mundane activity. At some point, the use of prayer before drawing the lottery ticket was performed as an assurance of God's opinion. Lot drawing was held to spiritual reverence.[18]

The drawing of lots and its divinatory use could be considered a precursor to the drawing of playing cards for insight or cartomancy. It was quickly realized that the cards could be used to describe aspects of what is experienced daily in life, love, work, and community.

DESCRIPTION OF TAROT

A complete Tarot deck will traditionally consist of seventy-eight cards divided into two sections: the Major and Minor Arcana. The Major Arcana has twenty-two cards that are always illustrated with universally recognizable archetypes. The Minor Arcana is made up of the four suits: Swords, Cups, Wands, and Pentacles containing fifty-six cards in total. The word "arcana" for the division of the trumps and pips is a termed coined by one of Eliphas Levi's contemporaries, Paul Christian.[16c] Papus, one of Tarot's occult champions, called these two sections of the Tarot "arcana." We will look at these in the chapters ahead.

Research on the history of Tarot has concluded that the trumps, which were recognizable personifications, were most likely added to the minor pips, or Minor

Arcana, independently. The symbols and images on the cards can be thought of as hieroglyphs that make up language. Certain images were used because they were practical.

In *The Tarot*, author Richard Cavendish tells us in his composition on the origins of the Tarot, that teaching was also an important use of cards. Similar to the modern use of elementary school flash cards, Cavendish cites a reference to a special pack designed in 1509 by Thomas Murner that was intended for educational purposes.[19]

At most, Tarot has come to represent an allegorical journey, each card defining personal experiences or unique perspectives by meditative contemplation and self-analysis.

Today, Tarot cards, as a divination system, provide a stream of practical insight and enhance problem-solving possibilities. Tarot for some is their "voice of reason" often validating inner knowing.

I personally do not avoid predictive readings. To do so would neglect my ability to see patterns, use logic, learn from experience, and use the power of deductive reasoning.

Many of today's Tarot enthusiasts have increasingly embraced the use of Tarot strictly as a means of therapeutic exploration of self and counseling others, abandoning oracular foresight.

Despite the many critics of those who pioneered the systemization of the use of occult Tarot, we can be grateful nonetheless for the framework they provided; one that adopted traditions which had little or nothing to do with Tarot or playing cards, but instead had great relevance to the process of self-actualization, spiritual work, and progress.

One of the premises for writing this material stems from Tarot's flexibility and adaptation to systems alien to the intuitive arts. It aspires to show that in every relationship exists the possibility of union with Divine Source and how to drill down on the issues that cause a troubled love life.

In the following sections that concern the Major and Minor Arcana, I somewhat align with occult tradition for the sake of ease. There's no need to reinvent the wheel but we can certainly give it an upgrade. ◎◎

CHAPTER 2

WHAT IS DIVINATION?

*Divination is one of the most revealing of all religious phenomena: Embedded in
the questions asked and the advice given are a society's fear and desires.*

~Religions of the Ancient World.

Divination

Divination has been interwoven in the fabric of many cultures since antiquity.
The Merriam-Webster Dictionary's defines divination as:

> The art or practice that seeks to foresee or foretell future events or discover
> hidden knowledge usually by the interpretation of omens or by the aid of
> supernatural powers.[1]

Divination is most commonly defined as a method to obtain insight or wisdom
through oracular or supernatural means. Some believe divination systems
are associated with magic, sorcery, witchcraft, voodoo, and other religious
phenomena.

In ancient Egypt, priests who had minor positions were low in the hierarchy of
temple personnel. Some in the role of dream interpreters called *oneirocrites* by the

Greeks, were at the disposal of those seeking meanings or omens in their dreams.[1a]

Oracular consultations during rites or temple services gave worshippers the opportunity to hear Divine advice. Serge Sauneron in *The Priest of Ancient Egypt* notes that the "custom of recourse to the oracles in the New Kingdom grew to such importance that the priests as 'carriers of the divine word' played very esteemed roles in society".

Sauneron also describes other divinatory techniques used by the ancient habitants of Egypt. One of the consulting methods "consisted of presenting written requests to the god."[1b] He describes how two written statements were presented to the god Amon. The high priest acted as intercessor in selecting which of the statements became verdict. The small fragments of pottery or limestone found during excavations were evidence of this custom of written petitions and responses.[1c]

I would define divination as the art of interpretation utilizing a specific tool(s) whether it is natural or man-made, for the purpose of revealing information unknown to the questioner and as an aid in counseling others.

Divination methods are separated by these classifications:[2]

INDUCTIVE DIVINATION uses interpretations in which the diviner employs an induced state of awareness in which meaning is given to natural occurrences. Inductive practitioners receive information through visions or hypnotic methods.

ANALYTIC DIVINATION involves investigating symbols and drawing conclusions about their meanings to make predictions.

DEDUCTIVE DIVINATION moves a general inquiry to specific knowledge or advice based on what symbols are known to mean or certain rules or laws. So for instance, if all Aces are reasoned to mean first or beginning, then in readings, any Ace could therefore be interpreted as the beginning regardless of the context.

INTROSPECTIVE DIVINATION occurs when information would be gained though impressions based on self-reflection and self-generated insights or mental impressions.

MEDIUMISTIC DIVINATION is a psychic impression or insight by means of a natural psychic gift used in conjunction with any tool of the intuitive arts.

Divination tools like Tarot are more personal in that it provides insight on a microcosmic level. Tarot cards are not specifically oracular in nature but advice dispensed from the reader could be considered "oracle." Diviners are not necessarily prophets and they do not subscribe to any particular religious beliefs. In order to read or "divine," any insight should encompass knowledge of symbolism, philosophy, Western and Eastern thought, cultural myths, psychology and the science of things divine and human.

In some cases, divination includes forecasting. Crystal balls, tea leaves, and bones are all valid ways of tuning into psychic awareness. You may recall performing your first divination through a simple form by plucking the petals of a daisy in an adolescent game of "loves me, loves me not."

Divination versus Fortune-telling

If you asked the average person what the differences are between a psychic, a Tarot reader, or a medium, you are sure to find that many consider them one and the same, or they have very subtle differences.

While the answer varies among the general population, most occult practitioners set themselves apart, distinguishing divination and fortune telling.

There are a few licensed counselors who incorporate Tarot with their practice and are paid for their services, yet clearly are not fortune-telling.

I believe every practitioner has ownership of what they do. However, there are certifications you can get as a Tarot reader, should you have the need to validate what you do as a reader.

For those in a beginner's seat, you will no doubt have to explain what you do as a reader. Use the opportunity to educate your client in a positive way.

Unfortunately, Tarot will not lose its association with fortune-telling and any negative connotation that Tarot may have anytime soon. Fortune-telling is not the problem; it's how people use fortune-telling that is questionable.

If you are a professional, be mindful of the fortune-telling ordinances in your local area. When you tell some individuals that you "read'" Tarot cards, they most often make assumptions of psychic ability, even though you do not consider yourself psychic. I've had people mistakenly think I am a palm reader, automatically holding out their hands to show me their palms.

As a suggestion for anyone pursuing Tarot as a way to earn a living, avoid using phrases like "psychic reading" or "see into your future." There are better descriptions that you can use, such as Tarot guidance, Tarot reader, practitioner, and others.

Many Tarot enthusiasts today are interpreting the cards from a philosophical or psychological premise. They are of the opinion that what they do is therapeutic and see themselves as "way-showers" for the questioner.

My Experience as a Tarot Practitioner

I can recall over eighteen years ago in a New-Age bookstore in a suburb of New Orleans, a reading by a local resident psychic who made a prediction that one day I would do readings for others.

My first thought was, "Yeah right! I don't even own a deck." I was intrigued by the ESP phenomenon and many of the topics that lined the shelves of this bookstore.

I returned for readings a few times after, in order to see what else I had coming in my future, even though parts of me discounted much of what was said. I certainly did not see myself as a French Quarter psychic!

Eventually, I did purchase my first deck and read all sorts of books on Tarot and other topics that are under the New Age/Metaphysical/Occult umbrella. I didn't consider myself a "psychic."

I witnessed many predictions in my personal readings that came to pass and thought, "Okay, this is real. I want to learn how to advise others and assist with their soul's evolution."

I did reading after reading for friends, my sister, and myself. My first "professional" reading was amazing! I was prepared, but naturally nervous. The seeker asked, "Could you look at my relationship?"

I didn't have a lot of time, less than eight minutes, and was praying that I would impress her. I know you're thinking that this was egotistical, but I'm sure most rookie readers experience ego issues at some point.

I drew three cards and told her that I saw many issues that caused distress in the relationship, and, from what I could sense, had for some time. I sensed indecision on her part.

It was difficult to tell her what I foresaw, but alas, she came to me for help. After about five minutes, I could sense she was distancing herself in the reading.

I was not telling her anything that she mostly needed confirmation on. I told her I would draw one last card for clarification.

"Oh dear!" I thought silently. I had drawn the dreaded Death card. In this particular reading I used the Rider-Waite deck. I went on with the reading, and in an instant, one tiny innocuous detail became the biggest part. On this card is a very tiny boat on the river in the background. I asked, "Does a boat mean anything to you?"

She gasped and replied, "Oh my God! He owns a boat and that boat has been a huge problem in our relationship. He spends all his money and time with that boat."

I sighed with relief. "Yes, from what this shows, it's you or the boat, and he has made his choice."

She said she had enough of the boat and she was now clear on her decision to go no further in the relationship. This reading sealed my destiny as a reader. I was hooked!

I quit my steady job of five years and began to work as a "1-900 psychic" because it was impressed upon me that I could make the same amount of money or more and be a stay-at-home mom while earning more than I had working nine to ten hours a day.

I gained lots of experience. That first job was akin to getting your first job at a fast-food restaurant. I was good – heck I was great – but my bank account didn't reflect the accounts of making good money in the psychic business.

Then the "Miss Cleo" fiasco happened. "Miss Cleo" was the psychic persona of a spokesperson who did commercials for a popular psychic line. You may remember the "Call me now!" television line with the Jamaican accent. The company went under for a number of issues, and not to mention the discovery that the famous "Miss Cleo was just an actress and not a real psychic. The calls dropped off and business slowed to a halt. Who says there is no such thing as bad publicity?

The world of Tarot has changed just over the last twenty years: No longer confined to the Occult, it has slowly crept into the field of psychological examination, if only for knowledge of the self.

Many readers now claim they are doing "therapeutic" readings. Licensed psychotherapists are beginning to use Tarot to help frame client issues in a way that compliments traditional therapy.

My interest in Tarot psychology brought me a whole new way of reading the cards for myself that yielded in better readings for my clients.

This book is the result of a class that I developed to teach my clients that there was more to life than waiting around for a telephone call from Mr. (or Ms.) Right.

The basic philosophy of what I taught and begin to realize after my own failed marriages was that there is a method to the madness of how and why we choose our partners. ◎◎

CHAPTER 3

TAROT COUPLING

If we know the divine art of concentration, if we know the divine art of meditation,
if we know the divine art of contemplation, easily and consciously we can unite the
inner world and the outer world.

~Sri Chinmoy

Today's Tarot Story

In discussing the use of Tarot today, it is clear that Tarot is widely perceived as a game that has inherited an occult purpose. On the contrary, others feel that even centuries after those early cartomancers, this generation has and will continue to contribute to the evolution of Tarot and its uses.

Tarot is more popular today than it was 100 years ago, and thanks to the tireless efforts of numerous Tarot authors, researchers, historians, and fantastic deck creators, the cards are finding their way to the mainstream, emerging from a clandestine past and into a brighter future.

Divination tools like the Tarot continue to fascinate and I do not foresee that ending anytime soon. Tarot readers of today are as author and reader Mary K. Greer says, "midwives to the soul."

Tarot, with it rich symbolism, has the uncanny capability to uncover specific psychic talents of its user (if previously unaware) helping to identify your strongest faculties as clairvoyant, clairaudient, clairsentient, empathic, etc.

Tarot Coupling: How It Helps

The cards' interpretations are separated into four categories considering four stages of the relationship:

1. The new relationship or seeking single person
2. The established stage of committed or married partners
3. The Expanded Awareness stage is for expert-level advice
4. The deteriorating stage for those relationships that are not functioning well

Tarot Coupling Keywords offer a breakdown of the relationships and quickly outlines for the reader important information about the couple and the relationship.

Anyone Can Use Tarot Coupling

Tarot Coupling integrates a number of theories on relationships with Tarot as an investigative tool. It considers variables much like a clinician when considering all experiences of a client's life within the context of the whole.

I must mention that the information within deals with relationships that are adult romantic love partnerships regardless of living arrangement or sexual orientation. Tarot as a tool for self-reflection is neutral and boundless seeing all of combined male and female energies.

Few heterosexual and LGBT (lesbian, gay, bisexual, and transgender) individuals are immune to the woes of intimate partnerships. I am sensitive to the tendency of many books that address issues as if it only relates to heterosexual people. Written here are dilemmas that run across the board, applying the experience to groups of dyads, not exclusively to one preference over the other.

I do not believe my approach to helping people is any different in regards to whomever they choose to love.

While there are alternative types of love, polyamory should be mentioned too. Individuals in polyamorous relationships are hopefully not offended by this book's title and are not assuming exclusion because of it.

My approach in reading for polyamorists is to treat their issues as "family" or group issues, hence approaching the reading from the perspective of family first, couple second, then individually. I don't presume to be an expert in sexual orientation, but only speak from my personal experience and feedback from my clients.

This book will provide a framework for learning how to "read" people. Since ruptures to relational bonds are a huge part of the many questions people ask when consulting Tarot, my approach to reading is multilevel and utilizes various aspects of the schools of thought in psychology combined with Tarot as a psycho-spiritual guidance system. Arthur Rosengarten, Ph.D. wrote in his book, *Tarot and Psychology: Spectrums of Possibility*:

> Tarot's light shines through all quadrants of the psychological universe and may be applicable in varying degrees to the diverse theoretical persuasions.[1]

No matter where you are on your Tarot journey, this book will give you valued techniques that will improve your readings.

The focus is specifically on the love life of the seeker. It speaks to issues of partner choice, compatibility, love triangles, etc. It demonstrates common themes through the narratives of stories out of myth and modern-day movies. Hopefully, you like movies as much as I do!

Using Tarot for Self-Analysis

Tarot provides us with insights about concepts of who we are as humans, why we do the things we do, and how to better manage our relationships and structure our lives.

The Tarot images are boundless in how they can be used to articulate unspoken issues that may not be at the level of conscious awareness. It can be combined with several systems to deepen knowledge on the path of self-discovery.

Understanding each of the needs and the dynamics of the individual experience is a necessary component of relationship counseling. Tarot Coupling gives a method to access the background of individual relationship models and of the unconscious process of seeking love.

Some are naturally more aware and intuitive than others. If unsure of your own intuitive gifts, you can be assured that your intuitive knowing through the regular use of Tarot will strengthen. Certainly learning to trust your senses becomes an integral part of advising others, but it begins with self-trust.

If you have been unlucky in love and are skeptical about a potential partner who has entered your life, you can learn to trust your own instincts and utilize your readings to explore your concerns and/or evaluate the dynamics of your connection.

Development for Advising Others

Your interest in Tarot may only be that of self-help. However, Tarot draws many people because of the urge to better not only themselves, but also others. There is a call to serve and help those who struggle through life and for transpersonal awareness.

Do not presume that you will be prepared to deal with everyone who comes to you for a session. Also you may at some point experience what many seasoned readers are familiar with as "burnout."

Burnout doesn't just occur because of sheer exhaustion from doing an abundance of readings. It suggests a lack of awareness in understanding limitations as an agent of change, as well as a lack of preparedness of the challenges that affect any counselor or therapist.

Some questions to consider in this respect would be:

- *How are you going to navigate your questioner/querent through a partner's infidelity?*
- *How do you turn down a paying client who appears to be dependent on your readings?*
- *How do you handle reading on the "ridiculous" day after day? (i.e., When will he call? Is he/she thinking about me? What's my future? How's my future? etc.)*
- *How should you defend what you say/don't say in a reading?*
- *What would you say if your client is dealing with a dangerous situation?*

Finding your niche as a reader will come with time but (and I can't stress this enough) basic knowledge of counseling is essential in helping others whether you go pro or not.

Choosing A Deck

The interest in decks comes largely from enthusiasts' lasting fascination with Tarot and the vast amounts of art and creative processes involved in a deck's creation.

With options ranging in the thousands, decks can be surreal, traditional, or themed. Ultimately, the deck you choose will reflect that which is appealing and pragmatic.

It proves most difficult to recommend a traditional deck because of the differences in what constitutes a "traditional" deck. In some parts of the world, it depends on the standard pattern of playing cards.

WHAT IS A TRADITIONAL DECK?

From an occultist point of view this would most likely be the standard Tarot de Marseilles or the ever popular Rider Waite designed by Arthur Edward Waite and illustrated by fellow Golden Dawn member Pamela Colman Smith.

If you are at the onset of your Tarot journey, the traditional cards will be your introduction to the traditional "occult" meanings given for the cards. The more seasoned reader will graduate to decks that expand upon what they already know about each card, and provides an opportunity for further self exploration through "different" eyes.

CONSIDER THE DECK SIZE

This is important for handling the cards. When reading for others, decks with illustrations that are inviting and clear would be a great choice.

Not all decks follow the same traditions. Some creators design decks that follow the Western traditions. Others will interchange elemental correspondences. You may have to incorporate the legends, mythology, or cultural theme used in a particular deck before you can get comfortable with explaining its significance. Again, while there are traditional card meanings, each deck and the story it tells open the potential for an enormous amount of interpretations. The goal for a skilled reader will be to make the reading relevant and useful for the questioner.

I am an avid deck collector. I am working on my own deck; something you may eventually also have as a goal. Once you immerse yourself into Tarot, you will see its images and symbols everywhere.

There are many dealers, shops, and websites that sell or promote decks. I personally love going to the various Tarot events where you can meet Tarot deck creators, vendors, and publishers.

Housekeeping

How readings are implemented is likely to vary according to many factors including the oracular gift of the practitioner. To begin, a consideration for atmosphere for both questioner and reader should be in mind.

A calm, clutter-free space without distraction would be ideal. I do most of my readings by phone and live with very territorial Miniature Pinschers who bark only when I'm on the phone (or so it seems), so my reading/office place is where I can close off from noise and interference.

Protecting and respecting your client's privacy should be a high priority in terms of the nature of the session and the forms of payment you'll accept for the Tarot readings. The use of spreads will become your source of information as a diagnostic platform.

The Tarot undoubtedly has mystical and practical applications, but as I have explained to my students, "we read people," and in many instances, you are not just considered a diviner, but may become a life coach or counselor.

The language and symbols of Tarot are of the upmost importance for interpretation of course; however, keep in mind that what you are doing as a reader is translating these into processes, needs, wants, behaviors, and actions.

Later, I will give specifics on what I call the Therapeutic Reading Structure. It demonstrates a defined approach to the elements of what is essential to readings.

When you conduct your sessions, you will develop what is comfortable for your own process. There are elements to conducting a reading that will help in your performance.

I do not believe that one method of reading the cards is better than another. What matters most is how effectively the insight gained is delivered and, more importantly, understood by the receiver.

Preparation Rituals

Before a reading that requires our full attention, some have rituals of preparation. Some practitioners use a method of "grounding" prior to and/or immediately following their readings.

Grounding or other meditative processes are to relax and gain focus. This allows for attunement to whatever source of intuitive knowing or guidance that comes into being.

This depends on your personal reading style, which could be intuitive, contemplative, therapeutic, ritualistic, or analytically based. There are many ways to ground yourself into your body and let go of distractions.

The first step is to release ego and relax, concentrating on the importance of the moment, breathing deeply. I recommend six to ten deep breaths pushing the air slowly in and out. Begin by inhaling through your nostrils and exhaling out through the mouth.

Many practitioners find meditation before a session useful. If time does not permit, I sometimes concentrate during the shuffling of the deck as a "meditation" while emptying my mind, if in a noisy setting, like a party or restaurant. It often helps for me to think only about one thing, for instance, the intent of the reading or simply the deck itself.

I enjoy organizing and placing things in order. I'm analytical by nature, and while I profess that I am not a neat freak, my Libran aspect desires balanced.

Another method is to reorder the deck. I take all 78 cards and sort through them, placing all the Majors together in numerical order, followed by the Minors in numerical order followed by the Page, Knight, Queen, and King.

You can also choose to use the historically correct order, which has the suits of Swords and Wands in descending order King, Queen, Knight, Page and then 10 to Ace, while the suit of Cups and Pentacles has them in ascending order of King, Queen, Knight, Page and then Ace to 10.[2] ◎◎

CHAPTER 4

CONSULTING AND COACHING DYNAMICS AND DILEMMAS

In the beginning, there were the leaves of the Sibyl...

~Dante's *Paradiso*

Questioners: Who Gets a Reading?

Let's consider who seeks answers or resolution – the Querent. The term querent is used to identify the person getting the consultation. "Querent" refers to the questioner, questor, or seeker, and is used interchangeably in this book. The individual receives the reading from a practitioner, reader, seer, or diviner, also used interchangeably.

More than anything, people are concerned about their future or securing a place in the future, with vision of a life of plentitude and love. I have found that most people tend to seek answers about life during crises or distress.

Others require considerable attention or "mothering," and seek answers outside of their own source and wisdom. Questioners bring to a session their personal takes on life and emotional systems. Never assume that because a client desires a reading that it resonates with any particular beliefs or needs.

You may find that individuals, and often couples, seek guidance particularlyon issues regarding self-limited thoughts or behaviors, frustration with being alone or single, advice on a particular suitable mate or establishing harmony within a committed relationship riddled with complexities.

These are complex themes that end up in questions, such as, "What do you see in my love life?" or When will I meet someone?"

I took notice when they became routine or, let's say, repetitive in the same client and noticed that people were drawn to me for advice on romance and dating. I believe people choose readers as they would when reviewing their options for any important service.

In the May 1, 2010 *Tarot Tips*, I wrote an article in the "Best Practices" column about specific types of questioners. Here is a summary of those types:

THE REPEAT CUSTOMER

This is someone who is currently a loyal client doing repeat business with you.

THE TRY IT BEFORE BUYING TYPE

This customer makes a purchase after, if they have sampled your readings free.

THE CRISIS CUSTOMER

This customer will only get a reading during a crisis or emergency. They may or may not be loyal and often "shop" for the better deal.

THE REFERRED CUSTOMER

This type has been recommended by a current or former client.

Basic knowledge about the type of questioner in this regard is of course more about the dynamics of marketing and sales, but potentially will be necessary to know when it comes to learning about your niche and your audience.

Another dynamic to knowing a questioner is an understanding in individual differences of how we take in information. As you are reading this book, you are processing the information based on a number of functions ranging from procedural memory, storing what you read, and the information having some significance to you personally.

Belief Systems

This is an issue that is not particularly focused upon in Tarot books, but comes up constantly with new and seasoned practitioners alike.

The Tarot School's *Tarot Tips* newsletter subscribers frequently ask for solutions about being confronted with disbelief in Tarot cards, for whatever reason, but usually in a religious context.

To some, card divination is taboo and ignores the will and mind of God. Predictive readings portend to know what God is thinking and is thus frowned upon by church leaders.

A belief in the supernatural, something that transcends humanness and the sacredness of certain texts is not uncommon. Religious beliefs particularly have helped structure the world, frame guidance on moral issues, and serves to ascribe meaning to a person's life.

Belief systems are interpreted in the context of cultural backgrounds that color a person's experience. Common experiences lead to similarly shared beliefs that allow people to feel included and connected. While a person can have an individual belief independent of his or her group, the cultural practice tends to guide what actions are taken due to beliefs.

Religious beliefs explain natural phenomena. Natural occurrences have been omens or symbolic of divine interventions.

Some cultures believed that the gods had an active role in the cosmic process, while others were involved in human affairs. In the ancient world, contact between different gods and belief systems were frequent.

"In ancient Rome for example, every citizen belonged to several other religious communities, starting with the household religion," as pointed out by John Scheid in *Religions of the Ancient World.*[1]

Scheid explains that "members of specific groups like military units, each practiced their own religion...specific forms of religious practices like magic, divination, and sorcery flourished even then, despite occasional episodes of external persecution."

Religious beliefs are not the only system to address. Tarot readings can also have an effect on a person's philosophical perspective and ideology.

In general, an individual or group's beliefs and their resistance to psychic ability are often at the heart of disbelief, not to mention the persecution of thousands from the church's dark past. These stereotypes and superstitions still exist within society.

Many practitioners have had to defend the use Tarot cards and know what a daunting, uncomfortable position this may be under certain circumstances.

Some religions are intolerant of medical treatment. If this is happening to you, don't feel alone in the challenge.

For some, discussing religion is as uncomfortable as talking about sex. Many people are openly proud of their beliefs, while others fear retaliation because of their faith.

In the distant past, as cultures merged and people moved from place to place, religious customs also merged. Scheid also relays how when political or military conflict arose, any one accepted religion would suddenly become quite unpopular. One of the most convenient tactics of those in power is to make religion the "object of accusations and repression."[1a]

Challenges are possible due to beliefs. However, do not take it personally. Just as there is a psychological premise to what makes humans love, the same is true for prejudices. When this occurs, I explain to people that I am not trying to get them to believe in anything. It is a simple response. I do not recommend debating.

If someone struggles with their beliefs and is hesitant to go forward with a reading, perhaps the best solution is to avoid getting a reading at that time.

Another challenge for the Tarot enthusiasts is clashing with family or cultural belief systems. This leads to conflicts that can be stressful. Personally, I think you should treat reading the Tarot like a guarded secret you would only reveal to those you trust and who won't judge you.

One other consideration is personal belief. There will not always be clients who share your similar beliefs. A questioner may have a desire to look at past lives, while you may not support reincarnation. Perhaps you believe in angels and fairies, but the questioner may have a differing slant on what is, or is not, real in terms of supernatural beings.

A great deal of subtlety should be used in approaching belief systems. Avoid impressing personal beliefs upon your client. This is a rule of thumb for most counselors and therapists, common to the dilemmas they face in their practice. Of course, one has to learn ways to deal with challenges according to the people one may encounter.

The best defense is an offense. Understand your personal beliefs and learn how to defend them in a positive way. There is a saying in sales, "educate your customer." Often, this is not a something to take on lightly. The best you can do in most situations is not to engage the opposing person. Be assured that you can trust what you are doing and the reasons for your actions.

I think it is crucial to keep an open mind and loving stance about differences. Ego has no place on the path of soul evolution. Many times there is great pride in what is known and little tolerance for what is not known.

Many people have limited exposure to Tarot, and as much as Tarot has grown in popularity, it is not that old in terms of its use as a tool for self-determination when you consider its long history.

Much like having fear of the dark, some are predisposed to the negative opinion regarding mantic tools and the practitioners who use them. I can attest to the fact that many people I have encountered – educated or not – rarely know anything about Tarot cards, know even less about divination, and are naturally prejudiced about things they do not understand. I can appreciate even more that once I "preach the gospel" of how Tarot is a tool for helping us to understand ourselves and how it is a complementary tool for any spiritual path, people show their interest, and at the very least, have an opportunity to reconsider their beliefs about the Tarot.

*It does not make much sense to ask the cards the same question
over and over again without allowing some sufficient time to pass.*

~Eleonore Jacobi
Tarot for Love and Relationships, 2000

Challenging Relational Issues

Consider where you are personally in terms of a romantic partnership at this point while reading this book. Right now there is someone just like you probably going through a similar experience. Relationship and match-making experts are on the rise. There appears to be relationship advice on every bookshelf, blog, magazine, and talk show. There is no doubt that love and relationships are important to us, but ironically, they are also troubling to us.

Below is a list of the top 20 issues in which both single and committed partners seek help or advice. (This is not a complete list but touches on the most common.)

THE ISSUES

- *Finding love*
- *Keeping love*
- *Information about a partner's thinking*
- *How genuine are the partner's feelings?*
- *How long will it take to become serious?*
- *Uncertainty about getting involved with him/her*
- *Commitment*
- *Secrecy*
- *Relationship success*
- *Answers on why the relationship dissolved*
- *Splitting up and uncertain on how to proceed*
- *Closure*
- *Dealing with former partners*
- *Infidelity*
- *Abuse (emotional, physical, verbal, sexual)*
- *Time frame/possibility of engagement or proposal*
- *Whether to marry or not*
- *Rekindling an old flame or spark*
- *Emotional distance*
- *Love – sex magic charms*

Common Pitfalls of the Relationship Reading

The last segment introduced you to the questioner. This segment will discuss primary dilemmas. The goal is to bring an awareness of issues you may find potentially challenging in the consulting process and how to work through them.

One of the mistakes I made as a new reader, was feeling personally responsible for the outcomes of the readings, more so if the questioner wanted time frames concerning whether a person would call, show up, or ask them out.

I would lie awake anxious about the time frame I'd given during the reading. The first pitfall you may encounter when reading for others is a pressure to be accurate. Contributors to this issue are both ego and confidence in your divination skills.

However, you may not want to do predictive divination versus "insight-oriented" divination. When there is a prediction that something will occur in two weeks, you can rest assured that the questioner clings to your words with bated breath. It is reasonable to consider the lack of exact science in predicting time frames, but the associations are there for a reason, if not synchronistic.

The questioner often has a subtle awareness of a conflict. However, they might not grasp the context or be far enough along on their developmental path to resolve the conflict and would prefer to make it someone else's responsibility to fix. I propose considerations below if you suspect that your client may be the difficult partner in the relationship.

Never assume a person is on a path of enlightenment, although in a sense, we all are. Do not be surprised to encounter one who has an assumption that there is a magic pill and you are its administrator.

Be mindful that the client could potentially be the difficult partner in a difficult relationship. In that case, the reading may inadvertently provide "ammo" against their partner. For instance, the client returns to the boyfriend and tells him, "The psychic said you are cheating!" Of course, you do not want to inadvertently provide these types of excuses.

Infidelity is one of the greatest distresses to all exclusive relationships. Open relationships and marriages are still troubled by infidelity.

If your client is in an affair, you could by default find yourself in the midst of triangulation. This is best avoided through taking a position of neutrality. The following section discusses neutrality in more detail. Neutrality as used here, does not mean an absence of compassion, but unbiased emotion or vagueness.

It may be ideal to look at issues that are less threatening to the relationship, without minimizing the concerns of the questioner, for instance, possibilities based on the symbolism of the cards, which nurture the "soul" of the relationship.

The spreads in this book are for inner issues as well as those that cause distress. Upon lifting the veil, the main concern may be larger than suspected or rather non-existent.

A breakthrough may not be immediate, but may occur several weeks later. I recommend making notes of the spread for later reference.

Strategies

NEUTRALITY

Recently, I have been on a long journey of what is known to clinicians as differentiation of self[2], the details of which would make a great book or a movie on Lifetime. One of the great challenges in helping others in a therapeutic sense is managing your own emotions and reactions. It is important to disconnect and release a client's reading. Why is it important?

Neutrality is important in terms of objectivity. As previously stated, this is not about a lack of compassion or caring about the circumstance of the client.

You want to remain as an outsider to any client's emotional issues. This could be why some readers find it challenging to consult for close friends and family members.

Some of you may have a Tarot business and need to consider your time. Charge accordingly while still providing empathic attention to your client and sensitive observation of matters.

Troubleshooting Common Dilemmas

In the couples' readings, even though they are both present during the consultation, there may be a need to distinguish which of the two is actually getting the reading. For instance, one partner has dragged the other along as "hostage" and you may find the unwilling participant totally disinterested.

Potentially, there could be "score keeping" in attempts to get the upper hand in the relationship. Perhaps your client who may have booked the reading wants someone outside of the relationship to take sides.

Perhaps a client is dealing with the complexities of an abusive relationship. Be aware that there are five to six stages to leaving an abusive situation and in some cases it can take years for the ending. Thus, if your client is in this dilemma, he/she may be in need of long-term sessions, or you can refer them to a licensed professional.

The first two stages deal with vacillating denial and admitting the abuse. The third stage could involve the continuation of episodes, while trying to define abuse or finding someone to trust. The fourth is taking actual action. The fifth and sixth stages are about letting go and healing. See Additional Resources. (For more on domestic violence, visit http://www.thehotline.org/.)

You need to decide if you are comfortable with couples' readings. Should you choose to, then I would suggest learning some counseling /coaching techniques.

Here are some specific issues where pitfalls occur:

THE ISSUES

- *Co-dependency*
- *Dependence on readings, period*
- *Psychic Spying – especially in love triangles, divorcee, exes*
- *Denial – questioner says: "That doesn't sound like me."*
- *Living vicariously through the readings*
- *Multiple readings on same question or person*
- *Questions – trouble coming up with one or rephrasing*
- *Unfamiliarity with questioner's thinking and decision-making process*
- *Vague information or irrelevant – involves finding the root cause*
- *Questioner takes no responsibility for roles or action in the relationship problem*
- *Disassociate from a client – neutrality*
- *Couple breakup readings*
- *Magical Thinking /Anxiety Relief (knowing future)*
- *Encouraging a partner to leave when they aren't ready*

Uncomfortable Topics

During Tarot readings, a plethora of issues can be investigated, but failures in love, abuse, drug addiction, or sex may be uncomfortable topics for the querent and reader alike. Many people with these issues desire resolution for a balanced, fulfilling, and harmonious life. Unfortunately, there appears to be a void on guidelines for Tarot readers to address uncomfortable issues that may be occurring in client relationships.

Many practitioners are uncomfortable talking about intimacy and sexual issues, and thus fail to create an environment in their sessions that would give questioners the sense that they can address taboo topics. In the context of personal or professional ethics, there are those who endorse avoidance of specific issues like third party or medical readings.

Ironically, people are comfortable inquiring about infidelity and reproductive issues. Only qualified individuals should advise on sexual health, psychological, or medical issues. Use caution in diagnosing illness (a no-no for unlicensed practitioners). Here are suggestions that may be useful when dealing with uncomfortable topics:

Great Communication Skills

Talk to the questioner about levels of comfort in discussing certain topics. If the session focuses on an issue that may potentially not be helpful to your client, then communicate this in advance.

Reason/Intention of Topic

If a questioner brings up a topic that is uncomfortable and seemingly their intention is personal arousal or gratification, stop the session and ask to refocus. If it seems unusual, it probably is, and I would recommend terminating the reading.

Pre-Reading Assessment

A good session begins by assessing the goal of the reading with the questioner. You can use this time to discuss beliefs, but it is not necessary.

Prepare for the Unexpected

Sometimes, things will come up in readings that are not part of what the questioner asked or that may be discovered in a reading. Ask the questioner if they are okay with exploring further. If you are not comfortable with the issues, tell them what you suspect it to be and move on.

Don't Assume It's a Spiritual Matter

Some sexual dysfunctions, for instance, are biological or related to medications. If you become aware that your client falls in this category, you should refer them to a physician.

The Multi-Question Session

Most people have more than one issue that they'll want to examine during a time-constricted reading. It may start out by only one convoluted question of many issues, or uncertainty of what to specifically ask.

Perhaps, it is a general reading about their love concerns. In some cases, what is shared or uncovered may open the door to subsequent questions or my personal favorite, throwing in a question about an unrelated topic.

In many instances, issues in readings emerged where the questioner needed to pay attention to matters that had no relation to the original focus, but in the end, proved to be significant in their life.

One solution is to start with a very general reading. A highlight of the cards used in the spread often points to the obvious. A moment of quiet reflection on the spread prior to discussing allows for the unconscious to speak first.

On a practical note, a reminder of time constraints should be mentioned, so ask the client to decide which issue requires their immediate attention. After the main issues are satisfied, then you can move on to other pressing matters.

Another way to manage multiple questions is by designing spreads that accommodate various topics or through a method I call "short burst" readings. These are one- or two-card side spreads, apart from the main spread that quickly answers off-topic concerns.

MENTAL DISORDERS

Generally most Tarot readings are suitable for clear-minded and rational adults. Should you become aware of any seeker's psychiatric or psychological impairment, proceed cautiously.

It may be impossible to know this information prior to a reading, and this is highly sensitive information. So is your querent's state of mind. Know your limitations and boundaries.

For instance, I once had a client who in the midst of a reading casually mentioned having been diagnosed as schizophrenic and on medication, but had not taken them in weeks. This client was desperately trying to find out information on a woman who worked with her live-in girlfriend. To make a long story short, there was no other woman!

Dealing with Infidelity

Cheating is at the top of the list when it comes to the reason that people get readings, at least in my practice.

"I saw you with that other woman!" she says.
"Baby, no, you didn't!" he says.
She insists, "I saw you with my own eyes. You liar!"
He denies it. "Nope, that was not me you saw."

After listening to his continuous denial, she thinks to herself maybe it wasn't him.

In the age of the camera phone, this scenario is not likely to turn out favorably. When I have conducted classes, the number one issue discussed concerns handling infidelity.

It is natural to want to know if a partner is cheating, but many readers consider this third-party-type reading highly unethical, while others have no desire to be the bearer of disappointing news, period.

Contributors Frank S. Pittman III and Tina Pittman Wagers in *Clinical Handbook of Couple Therapy* write that "the definition of 'infidelity' varies widely among professionals, nonprofessionals, and marriage partners." Like them, I agree that when one partner breaches the mutual agreement of sexual exclusiveness, it is considered for most, infidelity, or more familiarly, cheating.[2a]

In some committed partnerships, infidelity is not about the act itself, but seen as crossing the line from whatever each partner agrees as acceptable. How infidelity differs from "adultery" is classified according to the act of sex by religious or legal bounds.[3]

While some individuals may never encounter infidelity in their romantic life, it is sometimes a repeated experience for others. Second to money, infidelity is a serious factor as to why relationships end. One of the most difficult aspects of infidelity surrounds secrecy, another complex issue that, according to Pittman III and Pittman Wagers, "causes confusion for couples" and is in most times detrimental to relationships, but can also be necessary and catalytic, depending on the circumstance.

Some do not consider an innocent flirt as cheating, while others do. When a partner discovers the other's indiscretions, the relationship enters crisis mode. Completeness becomes fractured. Partners can often effortlessly look past the physical aspect, but the emotional devastation is harder to overcome. A seeker desires to restore the structure, confidence, and wholeness of life. Thorough contemplation of Tarot imagery is useful to orient a wounded soul(s) towards healing.

Many are uncomfortable dealing with overly emotional issues, but in order to be an effective reader, you have to "toughen your hide" and maintain emotional neutrality.

I am reluctant, as a matter of personal ethics, to suggest to a client any inkling of potential cheating in their relationship, even when undoubtedly the "storyline" in the cards (or my spider senses) emphatically indicate the possibility.

Why? Well, I could be mistaken and also the questioner's "denial" or subconscious ignorance of the partner's cheating may be a coping mechanism. The last thing you want to do is rattle a person's foundation. You could make matters worse by fueling high anxieties.

One approach is indirectly describing a third party in the relationship. This opens the door for the querent to potentially acknowledge the infidelity, if this is the case. The response may be asking if the partner is cheating. The querent may believe it is something else that has nothing to do with the relationship. This clue shows how conscious they are of a cheating situation.

State your ethics up front to the questioner regarding policies and sensitive topics. Consider when dealing with infidelity, that reputations, lives, and families are at risk.

If you are not qualified to counsel, it is always safe to rephrase the question to tackle something that you are more qualified to address.

While working as an online video chat reader, one member of the site asked for a reading in regards to her boyfriend. There was a question regarding his odd behavior. Now you have to understand that in the video chat environment, fortune-telling is par for the course.

I began the reading by shuffling the cards, laying them out in a spread, and told the client from what I could intuitively sense, there was an issue of another female contributing to her boyfriend's behavior.

In a hostile reply, the client refuted that there was no other woman in his life save for his mother. I did not blatantly mention cheating, but given the anxiety of the client, it was obvious. Not to mention that I had the card of the "other woman," the Queen of Wands in the spread.

The client, who seemed furious, informed me that I was a "fake" and incorrect about her boyfriend, and moved on to another reader. By then, I knew the importance of allowing a client to bring up cheating as part of their own conclusion of their circumstance. Unfortunately, in the age of the Internet psychic, a difficult adaptation is required for therapeutic approaches in a market that is predisposed to Tarot as fortune-telling.

The client, who I expected to never see again, did return a few weeks later. She reported that I, in fact, had been correct about a female causing angst in the relationship after all. Unbeknownst to client, the boyfriend had been intimately involved with someone (a.k.a. the female), while the client and he had briefly split. During this time apart, the boyfriend's brief affair resulted in a pregnancy, which, of course was kept secret from my client.

This was the cause of the odd behavior and suspicion. My client probably used the reading as a way to verify her feelings, but faced denial of an inconvenient truth.

As it turns out, the newly pregnant "other" woman's threats to relocate gravely distressed the boyfriend, who feared the prospect of never having a relationship with the offspring of their union.

Infidelity is considered a moral issue, often dealt with in secret. Moral issues linked to spiritual beliefs render Tarot useful in exploring important moral codes regarding the questioner. Within this context, a reader must also be conscious of his/her personal feelings regarding the relationship with one's own client, commitment, and cheating. This requires an attitude of non-judgment.

The way boys and girls are socialized, discussed in a later chapter, also plays a role in morality. Some researchers have indicated that gender differences contribute greatly to the individual gender "thinking"and justification regarding infidelity.[4]

Evidence can be witnessed in certain rites of passage – for instance, the bachelor/bachelorette party prior to marriage in which a last ditch effort of sexual freedom for some women and men is celebrated with everything from exotic dancers (male/female), drunkenness, and other acts of gender-related bonding.

With infidelity, any relationship deteriorates rather quickly and thus your client's safety and stability should be a priority if necessary.

All is not lost. This could be a transformative growth opportunity for your client. The reading could focus on self-nurturing for the querent, rather than focusing on the offending partner. I have learned from experience that a reader's best role in dealing with a client's infidelity issue is to never make suggestions of leaving or dissolving the partnership. The most effective option is to leave the client optimistic about overcoming the incident, regardless of their choices. ◎◎

CHAPTER 5

INTERPERSONAL PROCESSES

Love, Intimacy, and Relationships

Our problems were created in relationship,
and only through relationship can they be corrected.[1]

~Harville Hendrix, PhD.

A Review of Interpersonal Processes

Why is love such a popular topic in readings? Do you find that your clients desire to know how they can change their partners? What do you want from a love partner?

First of all, we are social creatures who strive through emotional bonding. As humans, it is natural for us to connect and have concern for one another. Every thing in the natural world is permeated by two principles, one positive or masculine and the other negative or feminine.

We need love relationships that are specifically "committed long-term" relationships to "heal and grow."[2] Also, relationships are important for sustaining a family. Relationships help us in our magical practices as well. Relationships also give us hope and fulfillment. We get to understand and experience balance.

The first thing we do in order to have an intimate relationship is to look for a suitable mate. The mate selection process is as varied as we are, and a multitude of tactics are used to gain the attention of a special someone.

One of these factors is motivation. Motivation is an area of psychology that involves three major components: activation, persistence, and intensity. Activation is a need, wanting, or goal; persistence is a continuation of the efforts in obtaining the goals and intensity is the strength or concentrated energy in their efforts.[2a]

We are all motivated by a number of things, like the need to survive , the need to belong, and the need to have power or to love. Love as a strong motivator, allows us to care for offspring, mates, kin, and friends explains Drew Westen in *Psychology: Mind Brain & Culture* (2nd Edition). Westen also explains how many species have biological needs that include sex or reproduction. He writes that "sex is a basic motivation from a psychodynamic perspective." Motivation, the activating force that "energizes behavior" has two parts described by Westen comprising of what people want to do and how strongly they want to do it.[2b]

Sexual desires can reflect other motivational units, including fears and wishes. Westen also writes that "sex is a basic human motivation where people tend to practice risky behavior and are prone to wishful thinking."[2c]

Modern researchers found that early, intense romantic love has to do with motivation, reward, and "drive" aspects of human behavior rather than with the emotions or sex drive.[3] Westen informs us that social psychologists have intensely studied the reasons people choose to spend time with other people, which he also calls "interpersonal attraction." These are further identified by several factors such as proximity, similarity, and physical attractiveness.[2d]

Social psychologists have intensely studied the reasons people choose to spend time with other people. They have identified several factors such as proximity, similarity, and physical attractiveness.

In recent years, more research has focused on long-term relationships and how love is more than just an emotion, but an instinctive reaction that is part of our neurological makeup.[4]

There is much to look at concerning the psychology of love, which is beyond the scope of this book. I do refer to some theories in psychology in shedding light on my approach to relationship readings.

Lessons From The Past

Childhood memories impact our current and future love relationships. Harville Hendrix impresses this concept in his *New York Times* bestseller, *Keeping the Love You Find*. In it, Hendrix proposes that through self-surveying of "clues from your childhood memories," many critical questions are answered about desires of a relationship and reasons why we choose particular mates.

If you reviewed your own childhood through introspection with the cards, you could most likely see the possibilities from inquiries such as, "What do I truly desire from a love partner?" "How is my partner helping me evolve?"

Examining past nurturing, socialization, and the effects these experiences produced helps us discover our "injuries" or "brokenness." These blocks have driven choices, fears, and emotions in intimate relationships.[4a]

Parental influence remains the primary driver of romantic choices in young adults, regardless of background. From birth to late teen years we go through certain experiences that we carry into our adulthood.

Unfortunately, many of us did not get what we needed in terms of healthy coping behaviors. The good news is things can be repaired; completion and wholeness does happen.

This is not the only valuable perspective; it is beneficial to take into account the heart essence (soul) of the relationship. How does a person know if they are marrying the right person? Why is the longing for love felt so deeply?

For some it is about all the right criteria, the right looks or maybe even the right income. It is interesting that I have had many clients that say they married for love the first time around, but for the second spouse, they were going to do it for money or security.

What many people fail to realize is that we often attract the same types, no matter how careful we think we are about choosing a good partner. Yes, some people are very lucky to have perfect relationships. The assumption is that perfect relationships minimize the risk of harm to the heart.

If you read professionally, your displeased, unhappy clients may be dealing with overwhelming negativity, while looking to resolve issues or gain optimism through a reading with you.

Of course, readings are not a magic wand that can be waved to solve problems. Is Tarot useful in helping to find your soul mate?

Few realize that the soul mate connection is a form of intimate relating. Soul mate relationships go beyond that of star-crossed lovers and can be found within the family unit, and long-term friendships.

Statistically, younger generations believe that they are destined to meet and fall in love with someone who was created especially for them, and a hefty seventy-one percent of modern online daters believe in love at first sight.[4b]

When you are reading relationships, you have to take into account what a person believes, what they value about relationships and whether they are in a crisis stage.

We spend a lot of time talking and interpreting the cards but we should also take more time to listen to the needs, feelings, and expressions of our questioners.

Listening also give you some direction on what you may need to explore. A while ago, my client Katie (alias) really wanted to explore the possibility of marriage in a relationship she had rekindled. My first reaction was to ask, "What good does my telling you that you will be married or what would help you feel more secure about the relationship?" Part of what I recognized from listening to this client tell me how much she cared for this guy, after only a short time of dating, is that she really wants to love. She doubled down on this guy being *the one*, and nothing I told her could persuade her differently. She was feeling a threat of losing his love before she knew she truly knew he loved her. They were both at different stages.

Interpersonal Attraction

Before a relationship begins, there is the desire to interact with and link to others for several reasons. In many cases, individuals feel drawn to each other as if by some magical force and often will attribute this "reaction" as a connection to the notion of "love at first sight." They find themselves attracted to a person of interest, but at the same time, they are often reluctant to act upon it.

What's interesting is that these are among factors identified by researchers as the underlying causes of interpersonal miscommunication. Attraction is often explored in the reading. The inability to cite specific reasons why we are attracted to some and not to others makes us seem to be a shallow bunch. These factors could be said to answer the question, "Why am I so drawn to him/her?"

These factors of the attraction have much to do with proximity (physical location), interpersonal reward (enjoyment/gain), similarity (same attitudes, interests, and values) and not surprisingly, physical attraction (handsomeness).[5]

It makes sense too because anyone who has ever had a long distance relationship knows how that can suck, and it is very beneficial to be involved with someone who brings an asset to the relationship, like their own house. Also it's a plus that you'd both be vegan and incredibly hot! We won't get into how much people compromise on these factors in order to avoid loneliness. Besides, we need room to discuss other things, which we have yet to cover.

Exercise 1

EXPLORING YOUR ATTRACTION FACTORS

For this exercise, you need your deck, along with a notebook, or journal for note taking. Working in a place and at a pace that is comfortable for you, begin with a few deep breaths as you shuffle and focus on your personal requirements when it comes to why you are drawn to people.

For this single-card reading, select one card that will represent a specific component of attraction regarding your love relationship(s). Record your thoughts, observations or insights in your notes. Use the following associations as guidelines for the card that is selected:

SWORDS
Like-mindedness or similar intellectual beliefs or philosophy

WANDS
Similar interests in activities, projects, or creative pursuits

CUPS
Similar emotional expression or needs, sees inner and outer beauty

PENTACLES (DISKS)
Physical proximity and/or rewards

MAJOR ARCANA
Spiritual values are similar or could have combined factors.

What does this card teach you about the circumstances of how you are drawn to others?

Record your insights.

Drew Westen, Ph.D., author and professor in the Departments of Psychology and Psychiatry at Emory University, writes in *Psychology: Mind, Brain and Culture* (2nd Edition, 1999) that the capacity for love has its roots in the innate tendency of infants to develop an emotional attachment to their caretakers.[6]

(Attachments and my theory of how I relate the theory to Tarot will be discussed shortly.)

At this point, I think it is useful to mention that it's beneficial to have some inkling of the stage of the relationship. By doing so, you may be able to highlight the positive aspects of the relationship rather than focusing on its dysfunction. For instance, in the story of Katie, earlier, she and her partner were barely between the acquaintance and build-up stages.

Before we get into that, I would like to point out that maintaining a satisfying relationship is a goal for all involved parties. If relationships are to be and remain worthwhile, they require work. In the mildest sense, it can be likened to initiation rites.

When a person decides to end a relationship, what they were getting out of the partner and the perks to the relationship lacked severely. The duration of time maintained in a relationship depends on the pros and cons of the relationship.

The length of time and the amount of emotion that a person invests in the alliance also determines their desire to leave or stay in a relationship, especially if legally bound.

In the *Twilight* movie trilogy, Bella was willing to lose her humanness for the love of Edward. The threat of dangerous enemy vampires and the promised protection from the vampire lover seemed irresistible to Bella's own sense of lack in her disconnected family. One of the benefits to a long-term relationship is a willingness to look past each other's faults.

Bella and Edward's relationship certainly passed through many stages in three successful books/movies. What are the stages in a relationship? It helps to be aware of what possible stage your questioner lies in their relationship. For instance, a couple in the new attraction stage: one partner being emotionally unavailable from the start could make the other prone to illusions of their emotional unavailability.

So, if the reading is centered around why this person is not returning phone calls or texts and the cards seems to indicate lots of unsettling wand energy, the questioner may challenge you on saying that the other person has issue with commitment. The questioner may attribute the lack of contact as the person being too busy or other excuses.

Interpersonal Relationships and Classifications of Love

Although it is beyond the scope of this book to wade too deeply into every detail of relationship science, I would like to touch on another important aspect.

The natural progression from attraction is to develop a relationship, with a prior decision about the nature of the relationship itself.

While interpersonal attraction looks at the "whys" concerning our preferences, interpersonal relationships looks at the context of the association between two or more people. Interpersonal relationships can be short-lived or ongoing, and those that concern us in this material are the ones that involve romantic coupling or dyads with the added complexity of love.

Love is expressed in many ways. No one can deny that having a person say, "I love you" is quite exhilarating and memorable. In contradiction, sometimes love feels awkward and causes a great deal of stress in some people's lives.

While some find it difficult to articulate the emotion of love, it has found expression through creative outlets such as music and poetry.

Love and relationships are so important to our human existence that entire branches of psychological and scientific research have been devoted to it. Researchers, however, are not able to study love in the abstract terms, much like it is difficult to study ESP.

Models of interpersonal relationships are examined through behavioral, psychodynamic, cognitive, and evolutionary perspectives. Love has also been classified through religious, philosophical, and political views.

Tarot is the perfect transmitter of expression for all of these perspectives. Often confused about love, partners hardly ever define what it means to say, "I love you."

Continued loyalty in the guise of commitment or "sticking to vows," while enduring years of covert or obvious abuse, packaged as "love'" by a partner, is not love, but negative reinforcement, which is rewarding bad behavior, in my opinion.

Harville Hendrix, Ph.D. and Helen Lakelly Hunt, Ph.D. in *Receiving Love – Transform Your Relationship by Letting Yourself Be Loved*, writes that relationship troubles stem from a partner's incapacity to receive love, citing this incapacity as deterring the success of relationships, particularly in marriage or other deeply committed relationships.[7]

The incapacity to receive love, which they argue results from mishaps in childhood rearing, means not only poor partner choices, but extends further than our closest relationships.

I'm uncertain that we are incapacitated in receiving love, but we do not have clarity in defining ourselves in love. Literally. All the time I hear people say, "I love him/her, but I'm not IN love with him/her."

Another mysterious component: While a committed, exclusive relationship is desired and typically pursued, further complications to love are being in love with multiple people. This is the plight of polyamorous connections, which differ from "swingers," involving a different set of rules. All rules, of course, are ethical and consent is a must.

However, while these relationships do have successes (even if temporary), they are still threatened by the same woes of love suffered in two-partner relationships. One's "openness" to love doesn't negate the inherent inclinations of jealousy.

It does not resolve the issue of finding a "'perfect love." There is probably even more of the never-ending, possibility in pursuit of love. Partners feel neglected, need privacy, break rules, have differences in parenting, and all the same other issues in which they seek help from readings.

Exercise 2

WHAT THE CARDS SAY ABOUT LOVE

1. Using your favorite deck, while shuffling, focus your intent and ask: "What is love?" You may choose up to two cards to obtain the narrative. Do not rush the process. Make your observations in your notebook.

2. Spend some time going through the entire deck of 78 cards and observe the cards that seem to symbolically represent your take on love. For instance, if you choose The Lovers, you'll assign meaning to this card based on your own introspection. For instance, The Lovers may have meaning for you that speaks to union. You may use keywords or short phrases. I recommend writing a thorough list of interpretations.

Relationship Stages

Psychologist George Levinger proposed that relationships pass through five stages that are referred to as the "ABCDE model."

In addition to relationship phases, Levinger put forth theories on the durability of marriage based on a partner's willingness to remain or leave a relationship based on attractions and barriers to the connection.[8]

Stage theories look at the positives advantages and negatives disadvantages during the life cycle of romantic relationships. Levinger's ABCDE model can be used as a guide to explore where your (or your querent's) relationship lies and to determine motivating strengths or weaknesses. Thus, understanding these stages and where they shift can help you know what works and doesn't work in your relationships, as well as help you progress or maintain the more desired stages.

This following model is based on a model proposed by psychologist George Levinger. It shows the stages of relationships. These stages can happen in all types of relationships.

Levinger's Relationship Stage Theory

A = ACQUAINTANCE

Meeting others and having interests based on proximity and physical attractiveness or great first impressions. Friendship motivation.

B = BUILD-UP

Partners reveal more of themselves and begin to build emotional bonds or build on common grounds. Positive feedback or evaluations are mutually exchanged.

C = CONTINUATION

Spending more time together, sharing more of oneself or longer-term commitments are made, such as cohabitation or marriage.

D = DETERIORATION

Relationship becomes less rewarding. Withdrawal, distance, or decline seeps into connection.

E = ENDING

Partners weakly invest in relationship or completely fail to invest time or emotions. High expectation for ending. One or both partners agree to terminate the relationship.

Relationship Stages Chart

For example: "Will he call?"

I feel this could be a first or second stage scenario. A Tarot reader could be sought out at either stage.

Relationship stages are not linear; they are cyclical. These stages vary and change depending upon life circumstances or crises. For instance, if a couple is involved in a power struggle at the Deterioration stage, then a lifestyle change, like the announcement or birth of their child, can place them back at the Building/Build-Up stage. At the first stage, Acquaintance, becoming familiar with a potential mate depends on mutual associates, physical proximity, first impressions, and a variety of other factors.

The Build-up stage has similarity with close parental bonding and allows couples to find mutual ground while growing closer.

At the Continuation stage, partners continue to deepen their bond due to the satisfaction both experience in the connection; the relationship is viewed as possibly included in a partner's future.

The Deterioration stage is when things become unbalanced and where one or both partners are frustrated as they try to meet the demands of the other's expectations. Partners start to show negative traits. These traits often mirror the undercurrents of what we have been embodied subconsciously from our caretakers.

During the Ending stage, partners usually negatively respond to one another. Contempt, superficial excuses or resentment, and displeasure are common. The expertise of a counselor may be enlisted to repair struggling relationships. However, exiting or breaking up is often seen as the only solution to unresolved problems. The second and third stages are viewed as crucial to the survival of relationship. If one or both partners decide to move forward, this is when some type of therapy, or perhaps a reading, could prove beneficial. Relationship training could provide the single person an opportunity, before they are involved, with information on how to handle what may occur in relationships.

Just as children go through normal, predictable stages of development, so do relationships. And just as it is helpful for parents to understand their children by understanding the phases of development, it is also helpful for couples to be conscious of the stages of their relationships.

Intimacy

Intimacy has different meanings according to the context in which it is used. In the broadest sense, it defines confidential closeness to another human. A Tarot reading is a highly intimate activity between reader and recipient of the reading. Most notably, to be intimate with someone implies a physical or sexual closeness with a partner.

Generally, through intimacy, we experience a level of sharing, mutual support, and warmth. Adult attachment relationships or other deep connections are the environments in which intimacy needs are typically met. The first place, (or the last we'd expect) where intimacy begins is within the individual. In *Soul Mates: Honoring the Mysteries of Love and Relationship*, author Thomas Moore expresses how pointless it is to try "to find intimacy with friends, lovers, and family if starting out from alienation and division within yourself."[9]

Within scholarly research, four types of intimacy are distinguished: physical, emotional, cognitive, and experiential.[9a] These forms seemingly correlate to the magical functions of the four suits of the Minor Arcana.

COGNITIVE INTIMACY occurs in the intellectual arena where ideas, opinions, and thoughts are shared, establishing familiarity. Cognition, as a mental expression, would correspond to Swords.

EMOTIONAL INTIMACY involves connection through feelings or empathy for another. Emotional intimacy is corresponded to the suit of Cups.

In EXPERIMENTAL INTIMACY, couples experience closeness through mutual activity, taking part in activities perhaps without talking about feelings; for example, quietly preparing a meal together. The action in this form of intimacy is corresponded to Wands.

In PHYSICAL INTIMACY, the physical body is involved; that is not exclusive to sexual intercourse as one might assume. It includes activities in which physical proximity is involved, such as kissing or holding hands. This form is corresponded to the suit of Pentacles.

Moore said that those who experience disconnection to their inner self are most likely to find intimacy difficult, finding no place for it in their relationships.[10]

As mentioned before, many of us feel some tension about our desire for love. These tensions become "blocks" to experiencing deep intimacy in relationships. Moore further states that when we experience tension in life and make the assumption that the problems are related to someone else, that these outer tensions may be an echo of inner conflict.[11]

To understand intimacy and its four stages in correlation to Tarot, let's look at how these correspondences work in a reading.

Karen's Reading

Karen, a 30 year-old consultant who was previously married and has a young daughter, booked an evening phone reading regarding how she and her boyfriend, Jerry, were doing and to learn what she could do to help her chances of marriage to Jerry.

Keeping in mind what was possible for each partner and what was possible about a marriage to Jerry, I chose a simple three-card spread.

CARD 1

The first (1) position, represented how Karen presented herself in the relationship.

CARD 2

The second (2) position represented Jerry and how he presented himself in the relationship.

CARD 3

The last position (3) three represented the possible lesson or action to take to increase closeness in the relationship.

The three cards consecutively drawn were:

Card 1: 10 of Pentacles
Card 2: The King of Wands
Card 3: The Fool

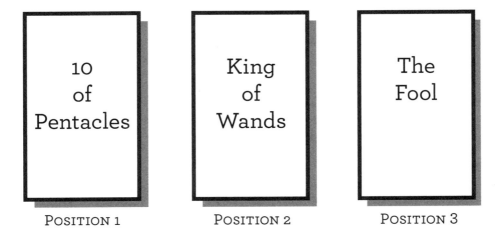

10 of Pentacles	King of Wands	The Fool
POSITION 1	POSITION 2	POSITION 3

Karen insisted that Jerry was "the one." She felt that he could offer her the life she had always dreamed about. Jerry, a successful architect, traveled quite a bit for work.

The first card, 10 of Pentacles, indicated that Karen's priority in the relationship was feeling secure in the relationship and she mentioned to me that she loved the fact that Jerry was able to meet her needs for a financially successful partner.

The King of Wands, I explained to Karen, suggested that Jerry was very focused on his business and seemed to enjoy socializing with friends and was often the life of the party. I also had the sense that he was planning a fabulous weekend trip for the two of them, adding that she would really enjoy the outing.

The Fool, in this case, suggested that the relationship in itself was a journey of self-reliance.

Looking at the 10 of Pentacles, I suggested to Karen that, at some level physical, closeness was how she felt love in the relationship, while Jerry felt closeness when they were doing things together. The Fool indicated some uneasiness on both their parts in obtaining a comfort level and sense of permanence in the relationship. Karen agreed, stating that Jerry was very uncomfortable with intimate touching.

In view of the possibilities of moving the relationship into marriage, I asked Karen to make up a little story about The Fool's behavior in a romance. I asked her to imagine what The Fool would say about her relationship.

Unsure of her confidence to make up stories on the fly, she said, "I think of The Fool as a joker or maybe someone who is not serious or does a lot of dumb things," she joked. "I don't think these things are necessarily bad; maybe he misbehaves!"

I then asked Karen to transfer statements in the story to her life and make a possible connection to what she senses about Jerry.

Karen paused for a moment, and chimed in, "I'm not sure I'd take a fool seriously, but I'd probably give him a chance to be serious. I'm not sure."

I replied, "Okay, that's fine. Do you see a relation to how you feel about your situation?"

Karen responded, "Maybe Jerry is a fool for not marrying me, and soon! I won't wait around forever!"

I interjected by saying, "Or, maybe you, Karen, should take the stance of the Fool and not be so serious about marriage at this time and allow Jerry to seriously consider marriage as a potential path."

Pausing for a moment, Karen concluded, "I guess I can do that. I really want him to fall in love with me."

In the next few chapters, you will learn about other correspondences and how to use the cards in pairs that will explain specific types of attractions.

Since the sixteen court cards are traditionally representative of personalities and real people, I will give you a neat way of interpreting combinations of the court cards. You'll also learn about elemental coupling in the cards.

For now, I want to cover how we develop socially and the effect it has in our romantic lives. Whenever there is a discussion of romance, dating, and love, psychologists like Dr. Drew on HLN News will reference attachment.

What he and others are referring to is attachment theory. You will be amazed at how adding a little knowledge of the workings of the human brain, and as Dr. Drew Pinsky says, "why they act they way they do" helps in Tarot readings. Interested? Well, read on!

A Look at Pairings and Opposition

Dichotomy in its most basic meaning is taking a whole and dividing it into two equal parts. In relationships, this is summed up as "opposites attract" or "you are the Yin to my Yang." The most recognizable dichotomy would be masculine and feminine polarities, which are integral to coupling.

There are claims that the first thing sought in terms of a relationship is centeredness. This refers to a sense of wholeness, a sense of finding someone who is a complement that both nurtures and supports us.

In Tarot, like other intuitive arts, there are two polarities frequently mentioned. They are the masculine and feminine or positive and negative aspects. This is not related to male or female in the classic sense.

Qabalistically, male and female polarities exist in all manifestation. In *A Practical Guide to Qabalistic Symbolism,* Gareth Knight explains how this duality is represented by the "Pillars of Manifestation" that are superimposed on the Tree of Life. It relates to forces – the push and pull or magnetism – involved in pairing.

Let's examine some of the oppositions in the following table. I have listed a few for you. Make notes in your notebook, adding some of your own.

Feminine and Masculine

FEMININE	MASCULINE
Cold	Hot
Negative	Positive
Inward	Outward
Creative	Productive
Circular	Linear

Know Your Deck: Polarity in the Tarot

Masculine and Feminine archetypes and roles are present throughout the Tarot. They are assigned according to the nature of commonly accepted social standards. You can easily see what these are by looking at each card and getting a sense of the energy that is reflected to you.

Find a space, preferably somewhere quiet. Take out your Tarot deck and separate out the Major Arcana cards (numbered 0-21). Place the Minor Arcana cards aside.

Look at each card of the Major Arcana individually. In your notebook or journal, make two columns, one titled masculine and one titled feminine.

Notice what you feel about each card. Do you sense whether it is masculine or feminine?

Place each card in the corresponding column as you designate each according to your sense. There is no right or wrong answer. Some of the cards are obvious and others may surprise you. After you have done the 22 Major Arcana cards, you can continue the exercise with the 56 Minor Arcana cards.

CHAPTER 6

PSYCHOLOGY PRINCIPLES AND TAROT

Tarot practitioners must continue to creatively use
Tarot's own wisdom and method upon itself in order to adjust to the
changing demands of this age and the next.[1]

~Art Rosengarten, Ph.D.

I am not a clinician, nor am I advocating newfound expertise in psychology by writing this book. My personal quest for understanding has led me to "correlate" certain schools of thought (given as introductory overviews) to Tarot.

In spite of our modern understanding of how things work, some clients need to be informed that no matter the possibility of the end result, discoveries during a reading never override free will.

From the perspective of classic philosophy, free will is the ability to freely choose actions and behaviors. On the flipside of this philosophical notion are external influences that may determine our course of action.

I don't want to discount the air of mystery surrounding unexplained accurate information given in a psychic reading, but it is important to inform your seeker about the possibility of everything changing the moment a reading draws to close. I believe this is what readers are referring to when free will comes up in discussions.

Reading Tarot for yourself, while recording your thoughts, feelings, and experiences in conjunction with journaling could be seen as a form of introspection, a method used by Wilhelm Wundt (1832-1920), who some call the "father of psychology."[2]

Wundt founded the first psychological laboratory in Leipzig, Germany, and argued that understanding the mind and behavior could be done scientifically using introspection, a high form of self-examination. He used this method with the intentions of using scientific measurement to uncover aspects of human consciousness.[2a]

Perspectives in Psychology

Many of the perspectives in psychology developed independently of one another, owing to immense ways of approaching psychology, which is almost as ridiculous as the arbitrary assignment of card meanings in Tarot.

As far as both are concerned, neither has managed to prove to be the absolute in resolving problems; but without them, it would be liked driving at night without using the headlights.

In terms of investigation, psychology contains several subfields that tend to differ and at times interconnect to one another. The following paragraphs are used to briefly review the four psychological perspectives: behaviorist, cognitive, evolutionary, and psychodynamic.

To gain a better foundation of what directs current systems of psychological views, we will explore a few branches that tend to differ, and at times interconnect, to one another. We shall briefly review four psychological perspectives: psychodynamic, cognitive, evolutionary, and behaviorism.[2b]

We will also discuss the relevance of Tarot to these perspectives. Among several pioneers in psychology, one of the most notable is Sigmund Freud, who developed what is known as psychoanalysis. Psychodynamics examines the relationship of people's unconscious motives or forces and the interplay of conscious feelings, thoughts, and actions. This perspective, like Tarot, functions on observation and interpretation of patterns. Tarot cards are akin to tools used in psychodynamics, in that they clarify or make hidden motives transparent or bring them to conscious awareness by interpretation of symbols or other content in the reading discourse.

The experiments of Russian physiologist Ivan Pavlov was associated with the onset of behaviorism, which aims to explain that mastering is a learned reaction to environmental events. Its primary significance reflects the prediction or supposition of responses relating to cause and effect from environmental events.[2c]

In Tarot and Psychology: Spectrums of Possibility, Dr. Rosengarten points out:

the map of Tarot can be seen to illustrate behavioral constructs that may be quite educational and therapeutic to a client. Conventional cause-and-effect and stimulus/response (S-R) patterns of behaviors are easily observed in Tarot primarily through a card's directional and linear sequence of spread positions.[2d]

The cognitive perspective focuses on memory or storage and recall of information. Since antiquity, budding philosophers raise questions about the mind. This perspective not only examines memory, but also mental data processing and how we arrive at decision-making.[2e]

Cognition is suggested more or less in the suit symbolism of Tarot, but is most strongly depicted in the suit of Swords due to its correspondence with the mental realm. Rosengarten also tells us that Tarot images simultaneously suggest both cognitive problems and solutions because of its natural inclination to demonstrate opposites.[2f]

In the evolutionary perspective, the focus is on evolution and how we have been able to survive and reproduce. Methods in evolution are most often deductive.[3]

Within the context of Tarot, the evolutionary perspective in psychology may be difficult to finesse. Like evolutionary psychologists, Tarot readers often use what is universal fact, presently exists in nature, or what they have personally experienced to interpret a card. Through deductive reasoning and inquiry, they are able to draw conclusions or explanations for the querent.

Social Development

*We may be deeply affected by something that happens in
another part of our life, and not realize how deep the effect is.*

~Thomas Moore
Author, *Soul Mates*[4]

We all learn how to behave and interpret social cues from our family of origin, also from religious, or educational institutions and other members of society.

From the beginnings of childhood, we soak up all sorts of information that teach us the ways of the world and our roles in it. We are taught how to live amongst others.

Social development encompasses not only cognition, but a lifetime of learning how to feel and behave. Under the umbrella of social development are attachment relationships, parenting styles, cultural roles, friendship development, peer relationships, concepts of self and others, gender roles, morality, and the stages of aging.

Attachment relationships provide our first social experiences and provide a mold for the relationships we have (or will potentially) in adulthood.

In our development, problems rising due to faulty parenting manifest as issues in our adult romantic relationships. In his work on becoming a conscious seeker in love, Harville Hendrix, Ph.D. (in *Keeping the Love You Find: A Personal Guide*) comments that:

> all of us, no matter how stable and nurturing our home lives may have been, are wounded...[5]

Social development involves adjustment in responses, feelings, interaction, and communication with others throughout our lives. Socialization is defined, according to Westen, as dynamics, in which children learn rules, beliefs, values, skills, attitudes, and behavior patterns of our society. He also adds that socialization has several processes, which are more than just a parent filling the child's mind with beliefs and values.[5a]

Where we are socialized most intensely is within gender roles. Pink is for girls and boys should only wear blue. This is an example of how we are socialized from birth. Boys learn how to be boys and girls learn how to be girls. Parental influence shapes sex-appropriate behavior in children. Socialization involves both parent and other social agents, like grandparents or other caregivers.[5b]

When they say children are impressionable, they mean it. The next time you tell your child that they are just like their dad or mom, consider socialization. My mother has a saying when I say my son is like his dad: she says, "He didn't steal it." For years I didn't understand why she made that comment, but I sure do now.

Interestingly, socialization is an ongoing, lifelong process. We also gain important cues in socialization through experiences in long-term commitments, within the marital state and in families. As children we are also born with our own unique temperament and inherit certain traits that shape how our parents respond to us.

Take some time now and think about how you were introduced to the world. Note your thoughts in your journal or notebook.

Models of Psychosocial Development

What follows next is the well-known theory of lifespan development researched by Erik Erikson.[6] He developed a model of psychosocial stages that defines personality development.

Eight stages are identified:

Stage 1. *Basic Trust vs. Mistrust*
Stage 2. *Autonomy vs. Shame/Doubt*
Stage 3. *Initiative vs. Guilt*
Stage 4. *Industry vs. Inferiority*
Stage 5. *Identity vs. Confusion*
Stage 6. *Intimacy vs. Isolation*
Stage 7. *Generativity vs. Stagnation*
Stage 8. *Integrity vs. Despair*

At each of the eight stages, a developmental crisis is normal for that period on the psychosocial journey. These crises or challenges serve as something to overcome or become a failing impairment to coping.

Of the eight stages, four occur in infancy through puberty. Each stage has two possibilities. One is healthy and the other dysfunctional. These possibilities are not a set path. Opportunities happen throughout life in which we can set new directions for our path. However, when maladaptive failure happens, this creates a snowball effect, potentially damaging chances of success at other stages. Again, these coping behaviors translate into adult behaviors in our lives.

The chart that follows shows the eight stages of development:

THE EIGHT STAGES OF DEVELOPMENT*

STAGES	TASK/CRISIS	SUCCESSFUL OUTCOME	UNSUCCESSFUL OUTCOME
1st Year Up to 18 months	Trust vs. Mistrust	Hope. Trust others in the world.	Fears future. Struggles to trust in relationships.
2nd year Up to 24 months	Autonomy vs. Shame and Doubt	Control of self. Will. Secure. Independent.	Self-doubt and shame. Loss of self-control.
3rd – 5th Year Up to Preschool	Initiative vs. Guilt	Sense of purpose. Ability to self-start.	Lacks self-initiation.
6th -11th Year Puberty	Industry vs. Inferiority	Competence in skills. Understands how things work.	Inferiority. Gives up easily.
12th -19th Year Adolescence	Identity vs. Confusion	Strong sense of self, values and ideals	Confusion over roles. Non-committal.
20s–30s Early Adulthood	Intimacy vs. Isolation	Ability to commit to self and others. Love.	Avoids closeness. Distant with others.
40s–50s Maturity to Midlife	Generativity vs. Stagnation	Concern for family. Care for one's legacy and society.	Selfish. Unconcerned and self-indulgent.
60s + Old Age–Death	Integrity vs. Despair	Fulfillment. Gains wisdom, sense of integrity is high.	Regret. Disgust with life, grieving loss of loved ones.

* Based on **Erickson, Erik.** (1963). *Childhood and Society*

Attachment Theory

Relationships involve people, and people – all people – you, me, everyone – we all have certain responses, tendencies and patterns, and more importantly, relationships themselves follow certain patterns. I want to talk about those patterns, and how you can use the Tarot to help your client work through their relationship issues, understand how the bonds they formed in the past have affected their choices, and, ultimately – the most important thing – help them make better relationship choices.

Dr. John Bowlby, one of the most noted theorists on attachment stated, "The initial relationship between self and others serves as blueprints for all future relationships." (Bowlby, 1975). This became important to my approach to relationship readings.

Attachment is the close emotional bond between two people. It is referenced as the relationship between caregiver and child, but encompasses our intimate relationships well into the mature years.

The study of attachments has illuminated which variables interact in the development of attachments, and which behaviors should be expected, considering these interactions.

Research by others in the field of psychology, such as Mary Ainsworth (1967) propelled the history of attachment to include nonverbal cues and relation of the self to experience. Attachment theory extended to adult romantic relationships in the late 1980s. (Hazan & Shaver, 1987; Main et. al., 1985.)[7]

Mary Ainsworth, who collaborated with Bowlby, is noted for her *Strange Situation* (Ainsworth, 1973, 1979, 1991), an experiment that demonstrated how infants responded to their mother's absence and return. From this demonstration, Ainsworth found that the children responded in three main ways termed, ambivalent/anxious-ambivalent, avoidant, or secure. Further research resulted in a fourth style called disorganized.[7a]

There are four primary attachment styles, just as there are four suits in the Minor Arcana. Six total styles have been identified, including casual and uninterested, but these types don't need relationship readings. So we don't need to focus on those.

The four are: secure, anxious-preoccupied, dismissive-avoidant, and fearful-avoidant. We will discuss these more in a bit.

Research suggests that the goal of the attachment system is so that we feel a sense of security. In other words, it is patterns that help us feel secure in a relationship with another person.

We have all developed ways to use our attachment relationships as a platform to significantly reduce the hurt we want to avoid.

Conclusions drawn from this research are that feeling both safe and secure are important factors in long-term, intense romantic relationships.

According to the article, "What's Your Attachment Style?" Sheila Robinson-Kiss writes that:

> Many adults breathe a sigh of relief when they identify their predominant attachment style because so many questions are answered.[8]

The desire for closeness, physically or psychologically, with another person is a part of our basic human need. It is beyond the scope of this book to go into all the research regarding attachment theory, but I feel knowing the basics of these processes, although presented here in general, will give you resources and background to keep in mind for your Tarot sessions. This will also give you a foundation to explore and access some unconscious experiences that may be unexpressed that hinder healthy relationships.

The goal for you as a reader is to provide transformative sessions whenever you lay out the cards, whether for yourself or someone else. The goal also includes helping the questioner become more attuned to their emotional predicaments and thus be able to collaborate on the effort to transform their lives.

What causes insecure feelings?

Feeling too close to another individual makes certain people feel insecure and too much intimacy creates uneasiness for them. These types are independent and value their alone time.

On the flipside, for some partners, being alone brings about unsure feelings, especially when feeling scared, threatened, or stressed. For those who have a strong dependency on others or fear being separated from loved ones, there is a tendency to experience insecurity or separation anxiety.

These degrees of insecurity can be measured. Let's take a look at how they are labeled and paired with Tarot.

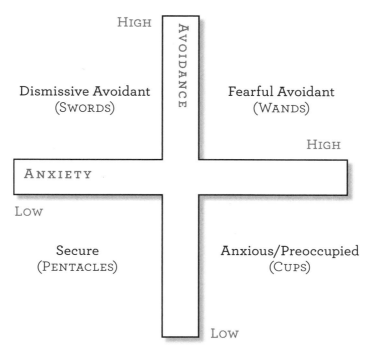

HIGH

AVOIDANCE

Dismissive Avoidant
(SWORDS)

Fearful Avoidant
(WANDS)

HIGH

ANXIETY

LOW

Secure
(PENTACLES)

Anxious/Preoccupied
(CUPS)

LOW

Attachment Chart Showing
Spectrums of Style

PENTACLES (DISKS) ARE:

Secure
Easily exchanges feelings
Will bounce back easier after breakup

CUPS ARE:

Anxious-Preoccupied
Overly sensitive/concerned with feelings/clingy

WANDS ARE:

Fearful Avoidant
Fickle
Feels Rebuffed Easily

SWORDS ARE:

Dismissive Avoidant
Skittish/Independent

The first part of the spectrum that corresponds to a preference of those who avoid being alone during hectic times, is called attachment anxiety, which is shown horizontally. (See diagram.)

The aspect that represents secure feelings when keeping others at bay (emotional distance) is called attachment avoidance, shown vertically.

On this diagram, you can see the four common attachment styles and the extremes to which they are experienced by a partner or individual. You can also see where I have corresponded the four suits of Tarot to each attachment dimension.

Down in the left corner where both kinds of attachments are at the low end of the spectrum, are individuals who are easily secure. This is the secure attachment style and would correspond to the suit of pentacles.

These secure types do better in close relationships, and they get back in the game faster than their counterparts in time of stress, such as a break up.

Out of the opposite extreme corner, in the upper right, you'll find certain individuals who feel insecure, no matter the circumstance.

People who experience greater attachment anxiety find they experience security when they are emotionally or physically close to their partner.

They express feelings of loneliness and depression fairly easily, and partners may find them to be needy or clingy, which adds to their anxiousness about separating from a partner. They fall into the style called preoccupied which is corresponded to the suit of cups.

The people who want to deal with things more independently avoid attachment, which makes them feel secure. This style is called dismissing and is related to the suit of swords. They dismiss the importance of close attachments. Partners often see them as cold or dull when it comes to closeness.

Lastly, there are the people who seriously are scared to be alone and are hesitant about approaching others. They constantly suffer from conflicting feelings. This style is called fearful-avoidant and would be corresponded to the suit of wands. They tend to have more issues in relationships.

Four Attachment Styles and Four Suits

SECURE (PENTACLES)
- *Have lasting, trusting relationships*
- *Tend to have healthy self-esteem*
- *Comfortable sharing feeling with friends and partners.*
- *Seek out social support*

Anxious-preoccupied (Cups)
- *Very charming*
- *Reluctant to become close to others*
- *Worry that their partner does not love them*
- *Anxious about being abandoned*
- *Become very distraught when relationships end*

Dismissive-avoidant (Swords)
- *May have intimacy problems*
- *Invest little in social and romantic relationships*
- *Unwilling and unable to share thoughts and feelings with others*

Fearful-avoidant (Wands)
- *Tend to be explosive*
- *Often experience jealousy*
- *Desire passionate closeness with partner*
- *Sometimes seek less closeness – chaotic*
- *Crave security but untrusting*
- *Intense and enthusiastic with ability to distance emotionally*

Developmental Injuries/Challenges

From the socialization, developmental, and psychological perspective, challenges are negative outcomes from inadequacies in nurturing rather than wrongful acts. Mistakes happen in even the most stable environments, according to Harville Hendrix in *Keeping The Love You Find*. Hendrix explains that "things that go wrong have more impact on our development than those that go right... it's the degree and type of failure that constitute the idiosyncratic details of our wound."[9]

The responses to these failings basically become defenses that turn into adult behaviors. In our adult romantic relationships, we can trace such behaviors to our early development years. This offers at least some clues to some of the reactions to our partners. Hendrix notes that:

As long as we remain unaware of our defense mechanisms and their causes, our frustrations will continue. Only when we can trace our childhood wounds to their source, and see the effect they have produced in the present, can we effect change in the future.[9a]

Much has been researched and written about the influence of our parents (caretakers) on our adolescent and adult partner choices. One in particular discovered that fathers have more influence on their daughter's lives than their mothers, especially in areas of body image and sexuality.[9b]

This is interesting when one considers that we all have a subconscious mate or internal model that is in place and activated when we are searching for a relationship partner. In some individuals, in spite of idealizing a partner, there may be a choice to remain single or uninterested in finding a mate. Some relationships are purely physical or sexual. In that case, you would most likely not read for those individuals.

Tarot is an extremely effective way to reflect on possible "failings" that have contributed to challenges, and after familiarizing yourself with the concepts I am presenting, hopefully you may be able to recognize certain influences that cause limitations in your romantic life.

Although I do not intend to infer that you should fault your parents or any caretaker for the past. It should be kept in mind that many factors contribute to relationship woes. The concept here is to consider these factors in conjunction with Tarot as a reflective journey to find your authentic self.

Maybe your parents gave you everything that you wanted and when you didn't get something you wanted, you threw a fit, became angry, and cried your heart out. Your parents responded by telling you how silly you were for being such a baby and they made you go to your room for the rest of the evening. As a child you may have felt inadequate and abandoned, and now when your partner does not meet your demands, you may get angry and distance yourself from your partner ,or they may tell you they need a break from the relationship. You in turn may feel abandoned, even questioning the maturity of your reaction or that of your partner.

INJURIES/IMPAIRMENTS
- *Is not necessarily about abuse or other psychological damage*
- *The focus is on negative programming or dysfunctional development, rather than tragic events*
- *Grows to become a blockage in the way we relate in intimate relationships*

CAUSE AND EFFECT
- *Adult behaviors*
- *Temperament*
- *Beliefs about partners, relationships and even ourselves.*

Example: Alice and Paul

In order to better understand what I have presented up to this point, let's take a look at Alice and Paul as an example.

Note: Rx indicates ill-dignified (reversed) cards.

ALICE'S CARDS	PAUL'S CARDS
1. 3 of Swords	Hierophant
2. The Empress	Queen of Cups – Rx
3. 7 of Cups	King of Pentacles
4. Ace of Wands – Rx	The Devil
5. 8 of Cups	4 of Pentacles
6. 5 of Cups	Knight of Swords
7. 6 of Swords	Strength –Rx
8. King of Cups	Page of Cups
9. 3 of Wands	The Hermit

ALICE	PAUL
Parents – divorced	Parents – married
Mother – overprotective	Mother – unavailable emotionally
Fantasy world – often alone	Father – workaholic
Hindered sexuality	Lives in fear; loss of parent
Distances herself from control	Needs not met; others unreliable
Loves mother; fears smothering	Seeks attention often
Never approaches	Internal anger and panic
Partner: Too dependent; needy	Tries to please but resentful
Relationship: Limits on togetherness, distances self	Partner has no needs; aloof

Alice's mother, a survivor of a traumatized childhood, lacked consistency in parenting operating as distant or sometimes overbearing. Alice, escaping this over-protectiveness, found solace by isolating herself from friends and family.

With a tendency towards magical thinking, Alice adopted the persona of a mystic shaman, occupying herself with the study of aboriginal spiritual practices. Alice's mother viewed her as the innocent child she lost in her youth and fiercely protecting Alice's virginity, became less than enthusiastic as Alice explored her own sexuality maturing into a young adult. With such restrictions, Alice, now promiscuous, began to sneak out of the house to meet with her friends.

Alice meets Paul, who felt his parents were never present. His father worked all the time and his mother was often ill. He suffered emotional neglect, often placing the needs of his ill mother ahead of his own.

Alice, on one hand, met her mother's needs, and Paul could not get his needs met. This became evident in the course of the their relationship. Alice feared losing control, and Paul's emotional ambivalence morphed into dependence, because he subconsciously did not want to lose Alice's attentiveness.

Paul thus became demanding of Alice's attention whenever he sensed distance; although he was happy to accommodate Alice's need for space, Paul sought constant reassurance of her love.

From this we see that Paul's dominant need for closeness is recessive in Alice, and vice versa.

Alice feared becoming smothered by his demands. Tension is created in the relationship when one or both engage in behaviors that trigger old patterns of coping. ◎◎

CHAPTER 7

TAROT AND THE FACES OF PERSONALITY

The meeting of two personalities is like the contact of two chemical substances:
if there is any reaction, both are transformed.

~C.G. Jung

Personality Functions

The secret to a happy relationship starts with finding the right person. Tarot is often put to the task of match making for the love seeker. Shortly after being assured that a questioner will find love in the future, curiosity about physical features and personality were sure to follow in my practice.

Like it or not, people will ask these types of questions, in spite of knowing readings are not an exact science. Dating website eHarmony.com, promotes commitment to helping singles find a love match based on science and "29 Dimensions® of Compatibility" unique to their approach.[1]

Jung's theory of psychological types says each person has "inclinations" with different attitudes and tendencies. His theory includes four functions (feeling, thinking, intuition, and sensing) and the two attitudes (extraversion and introversion). Jung gives a thorough description of each in his work, *Psychological Types*.[2]

The chart in this chapter takes a look at the functions of these personality types and how they correspond to the elements and suits in Tarot.

In his work, Jung concluded that everyone has typical differences that he placed into groups or types. The two basic psychological types are introverted and extraverted. One of these mechanisms was found to be more habitual or a primary preference.

Within this grouping described by Jung were also the four psychological functions (feeling, thinking, intuition, and sensing).

Introversion is defined in Jung's *Psychological Types* as an "inward turning of libido" and extroversion as an "outward-turning of libido."[2a] To simplify it would be to think of the introvert as withdrawing or going within and the extravert as externally interested.

Defining the four functions is a complicated task. Jung explained that none of the functions could be completely explained in terms by another.[2b] The feeling function is explained as processing something in terms of personal worth or personal values ("like" or "dislike") whereas it is judged or as a "mood."[2c]

The thinking type tries to makes sense or logically conceptualize ideas or data. The sensing type considers internal and external stimuli, while perceiving through the body or five senses. Intuition is defined as unconscious knowing or instinctual perception. The combination of any four "preferences" defines our basic personality type.

This system has been used to test individuals in order to find the best fitting personality types suited for duties in certain industries, such as the military or as career guidance.[2d] It has also been shown that personality types operate within our love relationships and by knowing the personality of each type could potentially benefit partner choices. One such discovery is a dating program called *LoveTypes*, invented by Dr. Alexander Avila, and is based on the research from the fields of psychology and relationship compatibility. This system is explained in Dr. Avila's book, *LoveTypes: Discover Your Romantic Style and Find Your Soul Mate*.[3] Today, there is ongoing research on love style identification and relationship compatibility based on personality types.

The four functions of thinking, feeling, sensing, and intuition, along with introversion and extraversion, are combined with perceiving and judging, producing sixteen distinct personalities identified by Katharine Briggs and Isabel Briggs Myers.

Let's briefly review Jung's personality functions with the four Qabalistic worlds and the four Tarot suits, along with an overview of the Myers-Briggs theory.

ELEMENTS	FUNCTIONS (JUNG)	TAROT SUIT	4 WORLDS OF QABALAH
FIRE	Intuition Type *(Emotional Thought)*	WANDS	Energy/Will Atziluth *(Emanation)*
WATER	Feeling Type	CUPS	Shape/Heart Briah *(Creation)*
AIR	Thinking Type *(Logical)*	SWORDS	Measure/Mind Yetzirah *(Formation)*
EARTH	Sensing Type *(Organize Data)*	PENTACLES	Reality/Sensation Assiah *(Manifestation)*

PRIMARY MODE OF OPERATION	POSSIBLE DOMINATE FUNCTION
Likes external activities or comfortable with own thoughts/inside own head	Extraverted or Introverted
Prefers to experience world with 5 senses or enjoys thinking about what's next, or possibilities	Sensing or Intuitive
Decisions are based on confirmed facts or emotional connections	Thinking or Feeling
Structure/finalized/closed or Flexible/unfinalized/open	Judging or Perceiving

INTROVERTED (I)

Introverted types have a preference to focus on the inner reflective world.

EXTROVERTED (E)

These types have a motivating "energy" about them. They pull in energy seemingly from their exterior surroundings and others.

SENSING (S)

Sensing refers to how people process information from their physical surroundings. Sensing people focus on the present and what's in real time. They process information through all physical senses.

INTUITION (N)

Intuitive people focus on possibilities. They process data patterns and symbolic language.

Thinking (T)

Thinking types analyze all sorts of data to make decisions. Thinking people are objective and tend to make decisions based on actual facts. They rule by their head and not their emotions. They are the logical decision makers.

Feeling (F)

Feeling types make decisions based on emotional impressions or personal connections. They are concerned with a harmonious outcome for all involved.

Judging (J)

Judging does not mean "judgmental." Judging people like end results. They want finalization and closure.

Perceiving (P)

Perceiving people are flexible; they like to keep their options open and they operate on whims. They are extremely adaptable.

What is MBTI®?

- *16 personality types – certain types are attracted/compatible*
- *Not age or gender based*
- *Type testing will give the best match for significations*
- *MBTI® has been corresponded to court card personalities*

Myers-Brigg Type Indicator®[4]

Whenever personality types are mentioned, the name of Carl G. Jung comes up as the originator of the theory of preferences. Isabel Myers and Katherine Briggs, a mother/daughter team, furthered Jung's ideas and developed the theory of the fourth preference, which is concerned with how we prefer to deal with the external data from our world on a day-to-day basis. In the 1940s, the mother/daughter team invented a test and called it the Myers-Briggs Type Indicator® (MBTI®).

In addition to the four types, judging and perceiving was included. Because of two possibilities of the four types, the MBTI® instrument concludes sixteen combinations. These combinations have been a comparable fit to sixteen court cards.

A comparison to the sixteen MBTI® types and the card's royal court members has been a hot topic in online forums and many have suggested pairings.

Have you ever been *a day late and a dollar short*? That is how I felt when I discovered the similarity between the Myers Briggs types and the sixteen court cards and that this was practically "old hat"' in Tarot study. I stumbled on the connection by happenstance on my own, after the fact, so to speak.

The drawback to the correspondence between the court personalities and MBTI® types is that the matches are as varied as card meanings. There is no agreed-upon conclusion. Linda Gail Walters, Jana Riley, and Mary K. Greer have their findings that have been compiled on a chart in *Understanding the Tarot Court,* written by Mary K. Greer and Tom Little (Woodbury, Minnesota Llewellyn Publications, 2004).[5]

I'll present here my own findings without prior knowledge or research of any other correspondences.

This chart shows my correspondence of the sixteen personality types and the Tarot court and those of Walters, Riley, and Greer. Your own further research of the characteristics associated with these types will help you to determine what matches work best for your desired use of MBTI®.

	WANDS	CUPS	SWORDS	PENTACLES
KING	ENTP (Riley, Greer)	ENFJ (Walters)	ENTJ	ESTP (Riley, Greer)
QUEEN	INTJ (Walters, Riley, Greer)	INFP	INTP (Greer)	ISTJ (Riley, Greer)
KNIGHTS	ENFP (Riley, Greer)	ESFJ	ESTJ	ESFP (Walters, Riley)
PAGES	INFJ (Riley, Greer)	ISFP	ISTP (Walters, Greer)	ISFJ (Riley, Greer)

**Note: There are many personality type tests available online.

All human types are expressed by the court cards. Humans grow and age; these changes can be personified in the images of the court.

The Hermetic tradition teaches that court card types are not permanently fixed, but are prone to changes. In considering who is who in a reading, you may want to keep this in mind. Defining someone as king, queen, knight, and page has nothing to do with sexual orientation. (See Chapter 12 on Court Cards.)

Personality Functions/Characteristics

EXTRAVERT CHARACTERISTICS

- *Gregarious*
- *Assertive*
- *Talkative Social/outgoing*
- *Likes groups, parties, etc.*
- *Energized by interaction*
- *Expressive & enthusiastic*
- *Talks about personal information*

SENSING CHARACTERISTICS

- *Concrete*
- *Realistic*
- *Lives in the present*
- *Aware of surroundings*
- *Notices details*
- *Factual*

THINKING CHARACTERISTICS

- *Logical*
- *Objective*
- *Decides with head*
- *Wants truth*
- *Rational*
- *Impersonal*
- *Critical*
- *Thick-skinned*

INTROVERT CHARACTERISTICS

- *Energized by time alone*
- *Private; keeps to self*
- *Quiet*
- *Deliberate*
- *Internally aware*
- *Fewer friends*
- *Prefer smaller groups*
- *Intuitive Characteristics*
- *Future-focused*
- *Sees possibilities*
- *Inventive*
- *Deep*
- *Abstract*
- *Idealistic*
- *Complicated*
- *Theoretical*

FEELING CHARACTERISTICS

- *Decides with heart*
- *Dislikes conflict*
- *Passionate*
- *Driven by emotion*
- *Gentle*
- *Easily hurt*
- *Empathic*
- *Caring of others*

JUDGING CHARACTERISTICS

- *Decisive*
- *Controlled*
- *Good at finishing*
- *Organized*
- *Structured*
- *Scheduled*
- *Quick at tasks*
- *Responsible*
- *Likes closure*
- *Makes plans*

PERCEIVING CHARACTERISTICS

- *Adaptable*
- *Relaxed*
- *Disorganized*
- *Care-free*
- *Spontaneous*
- *Changes tracks midway*
- *Keeps options open*
- *Procrastinates*
- *Dislikes routine*
- *Flexible*

INTUITION CHARACTERISTICS

- *Pensive*
- *Sees possibilities*
- *Independent*
- *Internally conscious*
- *Private*

Let's depart briefly from the Court cards and return to them in Chapter 12 as we explore the Minor Arcana. I would like to talk about interpreting the cards and the therapeutic reading structure followed by chapters on the meanings of the cards. ◎◎

The diagram below compares the sixteen Court Cards and my correspondence to the sixteen Myer-Briggs types along with potential partner matches based on Dr. Alexander Avila's system in *LoveTypes* as an example of how you can use Tarot and personality typing to find your best match in a relationship partner.

There are variances depending on the researcher in terms of what types makes the best partners. If you do not know your type, there are several assessments available for free online. I recommend taking at least two different assessments to establish your most consistent type.

The types indicated in italics are the best match for a female or dominant feminine type/role in a partnership. The shaded areas indicate the best matches for a male or dominant masculine type/role. Remember the sixteen personality types apply to either gender and with the Court members think in terms of personality rather than gender.

COURT CARDS WITH PERSONALITY TYPES AND LOVE PARTNER MATCHES

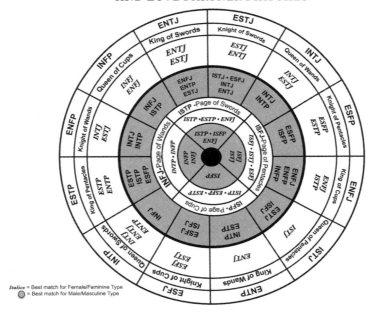

Italics = Best match for Female/Feminine Type
◐ = Best match for Male/Masculine Type

CHAPTER 8

RELATIONSHIP COACHING AND TAROT

An idea is just an idea until it becomes part of your experience.

~Harville Hendrix, Ph.D. and **Helen LaKelly Hunt**, Ph.D.
Receiving Love[1]

Deciphering Information

Reading the Tarot means locating the significance that allows you to draw conclusions about your personal strengths, childhood wounds and lacking qualities in order to bring into your life the love you desire.

Deciphering the information from the cards can be used to bring you to a place of consciousness in your relationship.

Even seasoned readers like to revisit accumulated meanings for cards. In examining each individual card, pay attention to every detail. Some of you may feel the urge to learn the card meanings quickly. It is possible to familiarize yourself with the cards within a short time to weave together intuitive meanings. I encourage you take more time to familiarize yourself with the material presented here.

Once you know it will be more than making predictions, it will be invaluable information for both you and those you are trying to counsel about relationship connections.

Integrating new information is a gradual process. I recommend reviewing a card several times over a period of up to three months or more.

The energy of the card can manifest itself in surprising ways. If you trust that you can be a channel of the wisdom of Tarot, then you must trust that you can in turn channel its significance from your own higher source.

From doing this type of in-depth study, you will experience the cards through your own feelings; you may discover meanings that assist you better than any book will give you.

This may seem a Herculean effort to obtain card meanings, but there are other aspects that are helpful in determining a card's significance. They are:

- *Patterns*
- *Elements*
- *Contemplation*
- *Iconology*
- *Numbers*
- *Astrology*
- *Mythology*

Any of these aspects can be used independently or in combination to gain insight into the cards meaning.

PATTERNS

The first pattern that catches your attention within a card may be items that repeat themselves or form a particular model. This can include the number of people on the card, similar shaped objects, or and repetitive use of color.

ELEMENTS

The magical tool of each suit is not only elemental; so are the astrological signs that correspond to each card. For instance, a Watery Piscean aspect. Items also have elemental significance, such as butterflies or birds being symbols of air.

CONTEMPLATION

Contemplation on the images draws away the chatter of the numerous meanings you'll have floating around in your subconscious and allows new insight to emerge that may not have occurred previously.

ICONOLOGY AND ICONOGRAPHY

In Studies of Iconology: Humanistic Themes in the Art of the Renaissance, *Erwin Panofsky tells us that "iconography is that branch of the history of art which concerns itself with the subject matter or meaning of works of art, as opposed to their form", and further distinguishes meaning and form.[2] Iconology would entail more of an analysis of the art work, and as explained by Biddingtons.com, a website offering art history information, "iconology finds meaning by reconciling it with its historical context and with the artist's body of work."[2a]*

NUMBERS

"The Greek philosopher Pythagoras thought odd and even numbers as workings of a dualistic universe of opposites," author Jack Tresidder explains in his work, The Watkins Dictionary of Symbols.[2b] Odd numbers carry one type of force and even numbers carry another. Correlating the card's central symbolism with the energies of its number fosters an immediate understanding of the cards meaning.

Astrology and mythology are referenced in other books. Please see the references in the Bibliography of this book.

PHYSICAL CUES

The body has its own language. Attention to the subtle cues of the questioner physically present for a reading are good sources of information. Even in readings by phone, the sound of an individual's voice tells you a lot.

In addition to the solid facts of flesh, blood, muscle, and bones, the human body provides symbolic messages to us through observation.

We create meanings for our bodies as part of the way we experience the world surrounding us. Unlike lower order animals, humans have the ability to "see" their bodies, which then become objects of a meaningful experience. We use our body's gestures and positions to communicate in a non-verbal way.

These non-verbal symbolic gestures, shown in the cards, can be used to illicit meaning. Telemarketers or phone salespeople are trained to smile while speaking, as this is conveyed through their voice.

Observe these non-verbal cues and gestures when you are reading your clients and consider their variety of messages: smiles, thrust of jaw, sitting stiffly, crossing arms, clenching fists, tapping fingers, twisted torso, slouching, standing, kneeling, sighing, twisting mouth, biting fingernails, and rolling eyes.

Epistemology: Accessing How We Know

As mentioned in earlier in this book, Tarot's most promising use is to explore hidden or unconscious knowledge. Many times during a reading, my clients say, "I knew that" or will totally ignore what is said, only to repeat it to me towards the end of the session.

My observation is that by focusing on words or information, they are disconnected and perhaps viewing outside of themselves the issues of the reading or they are inside their head analyzing every detail.

Each word is scrutinized and/or sometimes they utterly disagree with the reading (or at least at the time). They are separated in "knowing" until they can reach a logical conclusion.

I have a client who is very involved and connects very easily in her understanding of the reading. She is very perceptive and empathic towards others. She often says she has an intuitive "sense" of things.

She has a nonjudgmental understanding of my views. She uses adjectives and words filled with emotional descriptions. She becomes enmeshed in her surrounding environment and has to work hard to uphold boundaries.

I became interested in human cognition and how data is received, which not only lead me to personality typing as described earlier, but also to epistemology, which concerns knowledge.

It is the philosophical study of how we acquire knowledge and understand it to be true. It is what we come to believe or what makes us skeptical. Ultimately, justifications are made about information that we acquire.[1a]

Theories concerning knowledge have been around since the early great philosophers. Many theories about epistemology have been further developed and researched.

I encourage you to do some further reading outside of this book. I think it is important in the context of advising others, that we understand this aspect of knowledge acquisition and how that applies to your questioner's responses and disagreements, and honors their intuitive insights.

I often hear that practitioners are frustrated because they feel their clients do not hear the message. You may have shared this experience.

Realize that you shouldn't take it personally. It could be simply that they are processing the insight given to them. Do not be surprised by resistance.

What Needs Healing?

At the onset of a reading, even if the questioner does not have a question, there should be a focus.

In many cases, people in crisis may not be able to articulate or identify what they need resolved or what they are trying to heal.

If a person is not truly conscious of their faults and needs, it is more complicated to express what needs to be worked on.

For instance, my questioner, Alissa, inquired about finding the right partner. Suddenly, she had a change of heart. She was uncertain about whether she should look at her love life or just a general reading.

She informed me of her desires for someone who drives a certain car, earns a particular salary, in a half-joking manner, but brushed it off, as if it were a silly thing to get a reading on.

She minimized the fact that she was lonely and expressed this in a way that made her appear externally tough.

I suggested opting for the general reading, despite the impasse, a breakthrough in the reading was possible.

I began the process and drew three cards: the 10 of Pentacles, 6 of Cups, and The Empress. I placed them in that order in a row.

Alissa immediately exclaimed, "I pulled The Empress when I was reading for myself!"

"Oh wow!" I replied.

"Perhaps we should start the reading with that card?" Alissa agreed. "That's the card that is the mother card, isn't it?" she asked.

I said, "Yes. Mother issues can be represented by this card."

Alissa replied, "I don't have issues with my mom, but she has been on my mind lately. Guess I need to call her."

I continued, "This card suggests that female influences are strongly represented here for you, and you see yourself as a strong female. Perhaps, too strong to be dependent on a male."

Alissa responded, "I like my independence for sure!"

I went on, "The Empress looks comfortably supported by pillows, and she exists in a beautiful, serene environment. Bottom line, she is very well cared for, and although she could be considered wealthy, she has the wealth of natural surroundings, where she feels supported and everything flourishes."

I moved to the first card, the 10 of Pentacles. I said, "The importance of status and material wealth is suggested by the 10 of Pentacles. Interesting how this reads. If we take in account the 6 of Cups, this indicates great responsibility; perhaps you have the pressures of responsibility or had them placed on you as a child."

Alissa responded with, "uh hum." She said, "I've worked really hard to take care of myself. I have dated a few guys, but they always seem to be underemployed."

Alissa, a very successful real estate agent had never been married. At age 29, she was one of the highest producers in the office where she worked. She was an attractive female who has no difficulty attracting lovers.

"When will I meet someone who is at least gainfully employed?"

I responded, "I honestly don't think meeting anyone is the issue; the surroundings in the cards indicate that you are surrounded by attractive men and go to all the right places."

I added, "I would say that, based on these cards, your lack of finding a suitable partner relates to security and feeling supported by the person in the relationship."

Alissa blurted out, "Or by my family – most of all my mother!"

The keyword in this reading was support. Alissa mentioned that no guy was ever good enough. When she had a chance to introduce someone she felt serious about to her family, if he did not reflect her family's criteria on the outside, her dates were scrutinized and then dismissed by them. Alissa endured years of ambivalence from her mother towards anyone she dated. As a result, she never felt any support around dating or her partner choices.

Alissa needed a realization that not only was the lack of support an issue, but criticism was one as well.

I pointed out that by ignoring these deep issues, she was at risk and it was amplified and perhaps contributing to her bad choices. It was all validating the negativity. Alissa made a decision to express to her mother how the criticism made her feel and what could be done to enhance the mother-daughter relationship she wanted.

New Awareness

Many believe that relationships are a spiritual path, rather than just *a part* of the spiritual path as a whole. Some propose the notion that everything experienced in a love relationship – the good times and not so good – should be viewed from a higher perspective.

In order to love, you must first learn to love yourself. But as demonstrated through earlier chapters, there are developmental reasons making that much harder than just relaying the notion of "love thyself."

You may have heard this as "love thy neighbor as thyself." It has been said many times that how we feel inside filters to our treatment of others. It's also cause for what we attract to our lives. Instead of being truly open to love and success in relationships, many are closed, defensive, scared, frustrated, and sometimes traumatized.

Let's face it: rarely will someone seek advice on conditions that are going well in their lives. For instance, you are not going to be asked, "My boyfriend and I have been dating for two years and are totally in love; I have everything I want. What could make us happier?"

Of course readings are not always about shadowy circumstances. As a practitioner, should you find your readings too negative for one reason or another, it may be time for a vacation from readings. Although, we have to be aware of "the shadow." Shadows are created by obstruction of light; this obstruction creates shade from the heat of the sun, so shadow has purpose.

I use this metaphorically, of course. It's ironic, if not funny, that peoples' reluctance around getting a reading is a fear of bad news. They also avoid therapy out of fear that it won't make a difference or that they may be labeled, or discredited in some manner.

This brings to mind Tony Soprano in the hit HBO® series *The Sopranos* who went to such great lengths to keep his own visits with a psychiatrist secret.

Your clients have good reasons for a discreet approach. My point is that in society there is a tendency to disassociate from events that are unpleasant because it overwhelms our sense of normalcy.

Shedding light on the shadow aspects help propel us to better behavior in relationships and in society. I recall watching the reports about the mass shooting at a theatre in Aurora, Colorado, that took place in July of 2012. The perpetrator of the heinous act was apprehended after killing twelve people and injuring fifty-eight others, innocently out to enjoy the film *Batman: The Dark Knight Rises* (2012).

The tragedy did not only affect the victims, but had a ripple effect throughout the nation and beyond. Interviews were given to survivors and family of victims who made requests that the media not mention the name of the person who brought such darkness that fateful day. Instead of placing attention on the man who took their loved ones, they asked to only to honor the victims and allow people to learn and focus on their loves. Many felt that people who commit these acts do such things for attention or martyrdom.

They, in essence, proposed to deny this criminal the satisfaction of notoriety of any sort, without intention to hide the truth, perhaps a lesson for the media to avoid frenzy if not elevating notorious villains to fame, or glamorizing serial madmen.

It happens in more intimate family matters, too. For decades, hundreds upon hundreds of incidents of child sexual abuse and domestic violence go unreported. These atrocious acts are swept under the rug because, in addition to these things being crimes, they disrupt normalcy and activate denial.

Collectively, our attempts at denying or refusal to look at such things are mute, because the denial seemingly has proven to be fertile ground. Instead, they haunt us, each time seeming larger and more sinister than ever: case and point, Jerry Sandusky and Penn State.

Discussed earlier, infidelity, also one of those matters best dealt with in the privacy of homes and therapy offices, becomes intensely focused upon when it involves celebrities or other figures on the worldwide stage. It's not happening to us, it's those people out *there* with a problem.

These issues in the macrocosmic sense are abstract and easier to deny when not experienced directly. Indeed, our values are high; we are deeply spiritual, living souls taking care of our families and living life to the fullest. I wonder, with all the advances in technology, psychology, and medicine, why we are suffering further decline in society? One could argue that the world is no worse now than it has been at other times in human existence.

Traumatic experiences are a double-edged sword, on one hand allowing contrast so we recognize misdeeds, and on the other, leaving behind distortions to overcome maladaptive behaviors or mental disorders.

What's my point with all of this you may wonder? My point is simple: we must still inspire to a healthy and prosperous life. Individuals whose lives are interrupted by trauma need support and information.

The shadow for some is a source of distrust in oneself. It is doubly complicated to read the symbols of the unconscious where the shadow lurks. As conscious rationality escapes this, it is the time that the Tarot can help bring insight about patterns that have formed since entry into this life and will continue to impact us negatively.

The good news is that if you are willing to go deep into yourself, you will come out armed with the capacity to increase your chances of better relationships.

Ambition to obtain the perfect relationship partner is the goal for some, while others desire to return to a previous state of passion that once existed in the relationship. Many have advocated intuition's valuable role in accessing your relationship.

How could you know that the insight you get from your reading is wishful thinking versus genuine intuition; and better yet, is the information correct? One long-standing issue is whether to read for yourself or not. My personal opinion on self-reading is that it is important to learn your spiritual tool and how you plan to use it. Also, always read for yourself, with the exception of issues which you are emotionally biased and that include the people with whom you are attached.

At this point, I want to introduce some basics of my use of relationship coaching; in another section, I will show you how to conduct a relationship reading.

Coaching relationships differ from readings in that you are not so much beating yourself up about failures; rather, it is more focused on setting specific goals, working on your hesitations or fears, adjusting your attitude, learning self-value, and motivation.

Life is progressive; what worked for you at one time may not work for you at this point in your life, and what works now may not in three months.

About four years ago, when I worked for a major department store as an HR assistant, my home life was structured much differently than it is now. Life operated by the tune of how much time was allotted to the hours at work and duties of home and building my own business. Structures worked relatively well, but as I left to pursue a different path, time structures were different, erratic even.

For some people, being in a good relationship adds, or at least they hope to add, solid structure to their lives. This is also where coaching works well. Tarot is not the coach itself, but the tool you'll use to spark ideas, make resolution, and gain inspiration – and as a compass.

Personal Relationship Coaching

You may want to have a special notebook or journal (computer or iPad® works, too!) used separately from your Tarot journal. You can also divide your journal into two sections, one for exploring Tarot, and the other for your relationship journey.

EXERCISE: LIFE OVERVIEW

Some of you are exactly where you want to be in your life. But let's examine your life. A review of the following sections may give you some insight about the particular area you life needs attention that may surprisingly place relationships at the bottom of your priorities.

On a page, in separate columns, list each area of your life where you feel necessary or most chaotic at this point in time. For instance, career, relationship, spirituality, life path, finances, education, etc.

Thinking about each area you've listed, under each separate column, jot down one or two things that are troubling in each listed area. For instance:

CAREER: dislike office politics
FINANCES: need a budget and pay off credit cards
HEALTH: need to exercise and lose extra 20 pounds

Take your time with the process. When you are done, look over what you've listed and notice which area of your life begs for an overhaul – even though relationships may be your intended focus.

What you find may surprise you. It is possible that one of these areas affects positively or negatively where you are in terms of your love life, and in cases, may prove to be where you should place your goal setting focus first. ◎◉

CHAPTER 9

RELATIONSHIP READINGS USING THE TAROT COUPLING METHOD

"No matter what your laundry list of requirements in choosing a mate, there has to be an element of good luck and good fortune and good timing."

~Patty Duke

Tarot Coupling Relationship Spread

In this chapter, we will discuss the necessary components of conducting a relationship reading. Keep in mind: our focus here is on love connections between two consenting adults.

In other chapters, we have discussed factors relating to attraction, interpersonal relating, and personalities that potentially contribute overall to the whole relationship.

The reading allows the querent an awareness of interactions so that they have a basis to work from as a beginning towards positive changes.

The cards provide the questioner a figural observation of their relationship and the reader acts as conduit. This can be accomplished in conjunction with the reader's own methods and interpretations of the cards.

A thorough relationship reading takes into consideration the behavioral patterns emerging in the cards of each partner or the characteristics of the significator, designated by a court card representing each partner.

For instance, I get a sense of the whole background and elemental temperature of the relationship when there are a majority of wands, indicating a level of passion in the connection.

This passion is hot and heavy to begin, but potentially moves fast and wanes just like a fire. To keep this connection going, something has to sustain it before the flames of passion die out. If the right supply is not sufficient to wands connections, in my experience they burn out and are over quickly.

For each card, there are six categories that make up *Tarot Coupling* keywords. (See the beginning of the chapter on the Major and Minor Arcana for a detailed explanation of each category.) These help you to quickly understand the potential plus or minuses in certain relationships. As an example, we will do a relationship reading on Rita and Ricardo.

We will use the *Tarot Coupling* Relationship Spread for the reading (see Chapter 13 on spreads). The spread is divided so that the left side would be for Rita (Partner 1) and the right side for Ricardo (Partner 2).

POSITION 1 AND 2 – POSITIVE QUALITIES

The cards in these positions indicate the qualities/positive characteristics of each partner or are exhibited as a mask to the world.

POSITION 3 AND 4 – WOUNDS/FEAR

The cards placed here are representative of what negativity impacts each partner or the negativity that is at the heart of the relationship from each partner's viewpoint.

POSITION 5 AND 6 – PERCEPTION OF PARTNER

These cards indicate how each partner views the other. It is not necessarily how the partner actually behaves, but is strictly what is perceived or projected from the partner.

POSITION 7 AND 8 – HOW PARTNER RELATES

The cards placed here show how each partner interacts or behaves in the relationship. These behaviors may not be apparent in a newly formed connections.

POSITION 9 AND 10 – CHALLENGES/COMPLAINTS

These cards show what each partner will potentially desire of the other, but may be challenged to express or to exhibit in the relationship.

POSITION 11 AND 12 – EXPECTATIONS

These cards indicate strengths or desires of the partner from the view of each person it represents.

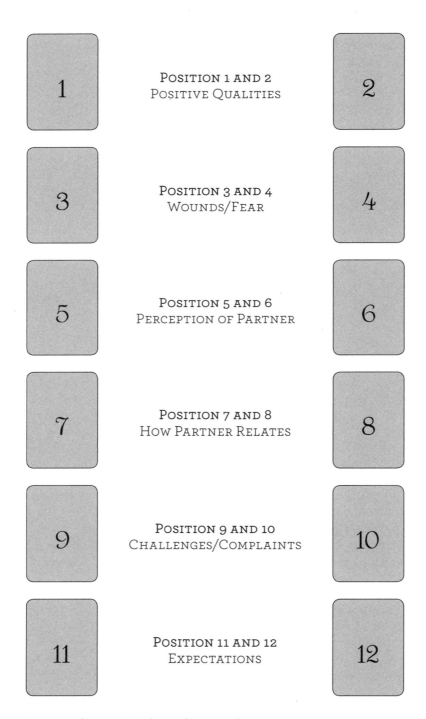

POSITION 1 AND 2
POSITIVE QUALITIES

POSITION 3 AND 4
WOUNDS/FEAR

POSITION 5 AND 6
PERCEPTION OF PARTNER

POSITION 7 AND 8
HOW PARTNER RELATES

POSITION 9 AND 10
CHALLENGES/COMPLAINTS

POSITION 11 AND 12
EXPECTATIONS

Tarot Coupling 12-Up Relationship Spread

After, you have assessed each partner, you will look at what each of them feels about the relationship. These feelings are relative to either side of the last six months of the couple's dating tenure.

Next, look at each partner's spiritual potential and purpose in context of the relationship. This examines the type of connection they have to each, such as teacher of important life lessons.

The next step is to look at which cards represent their compatibility.

It's important to look carefully at each partner concerned in the relationship you are reading. Also, I recommend studying their Birth Cards. Several people teach methods to find your Birth Cards with variances. Birth cards represent the interplay of energy in two pairs of Major Arcana cards that are calculated based on your date of birth.

Note: *I use the method taught by The Tarot School (see their website, listed in the Appendix for more information). This step is optional and only mentioned here for informational purposes.*

Recently, practitioners have become aware of the impact of seekers' relationships and the effect in society and assumptions about the intuitive arts. What becomes evident is that therapeutic readers need to recognize several facets of how perspectives from psychology play out in the reading encounter.

1. Practitioners should educate themselves with information about what is valued by the seeker and incorporate this into the therapeutic reading discourse.

2. You could supplement what you intend to read in the cards with background knowledge on such areas as gender, ethnicity, sexual orientation, and mid-life adult development.

3. Practitioners need to recognize that when a seeker opens up to new awareness, it may be difficult for them to adopt or integrate.

4. People won't always like or agree with the discourse of the reading. You are often going against the grain of established values and personal philosophies.

While arming yourself with information, spiritual "health and wellness" should not be dismissed.

Therapeutic Reading Structure

Therapeutic Reading Structure, or TRS, is another system of checks and balances I came up with to maximize my client's reading experience. Tarot readings could be, and often are, regarded as insight-oriented therapy. Readings should also:

- *Draw in the questioner and actively place responsibility and accountability on them*
- *Provide additional resources when needed*

Here is how you can make TRS work for you:

1. Explain your reading style to the questioner. Set a positive environment.
2. Clarify and pay attention to the question. Questions help vague problems become more concrete. Find out what questions are easier to address, then why.
3. Familiarize yourself with your questioner's thinking or communication style. This proposes better communication and will assist in relaying solutions in language they can process. You can determine this by having them select from a king or queen of the four suits.
4. Set the intention for the reading by paraphrasing the agenda and proceed to your way of laying out the cards.
5. Explain what you see positively. Make the reading a two-way conversation. One of the goals here is to help the client own their own behaviors and issues in the relationship.
6. Notice the questioner's body language.
7. Plans, advice, or solutions should be tailored to the needs of the client.

TRS endeavors to shed light on the unconscious, repressed issues that are the potential source of resistance in life. Along with Tarot, it helps move the questioner away from the traumas of inner childhood and put them on a path of developing outer adult. ◎◎

CHAPTER 10

THE MAJOR ARCANA

The Fool through The World

Symbols are not lies; symbols contain truth. Allegories and parables are not falsehoods; they convey information: moreover, they can be understood by those who are not as yet prepared to receive the plain truth.[1]

~Paul Carus
History of the Devil

How to Use Tarot Coupling Card Keywords

To be clear, please know that there are no rigid rules in interpreting Tarot cards. Use these as suggestions or to expand your own concepts of what the card means in context to the situation you are reading.

General interpretations and symbolic meanings are given for each card along with its application in relationship scenarios.

The significance for each category is as follows:

CATEGORIES:
1. Positive Qualities of one or both partners are recognized in this section.
2. The second category reflects the basic fears or unconscious challenges of the questioner or the person they are concerned about. For instance, Jane is the questioner and her partner, Jennifer, is whom she is concerned about.
3. The third category indicates viewpoints of either partner: how they see each other or how the questioner views the person they are concerned about in the reading.

4. The fourth category represents how the questioner relates to their partner or vice versa.
5. The fifth category represents challenges that are issues, where one or the other partner struggles or wants to improve.
6. The sixth category indicates complaints that frustrate the questioner's partner or irritates the questioner about their partner.
7. The seventh category represents desires that one or both partners feel, such as the desires or hopes they would like to receive from the relationship.

The interpretations supplied are also uniquely arranged according to relationship stages called N-E-E-Ds. The letters indicate:

(N) **new** relationships or those who are seeking a relationship
(E) for recently **established** relationships or for situations of individuals invested long-term
(Ex) means **expanded** meanings and spiritual or relationship advice
(D) suggests **deteriorating** issues that could potentially challenge the relationship. This can also be used as reversed meanings and/or for cards that are in unfavorable positions.

The Most and Least Compatible categories in the Trump cards (Major Arcana only) give representations of astrologically based flow in the relationship, potentially demonstrating how well the connection works overall.

Each card will also have a section that contains suggestions for romantic movies, date nights, and gifts for special occasions.

0. THE FOOL

GOLDEN DAWN/ESOTERIC TITLE: The Spirit of Aether
HEBREW LETTER: Aleph
MEANING: Ox
QABALISTIC ATTRIBUTION: Eleventh – Scintillating or Fiery Intelligence
ELEMENT: Air
PLANET: Uranus

By innocence I swear, and by my youth,
I have one heart, one bosom, and one truth...

~William Shakespeare
Twelfth Night

GENERAL COMMENTARY

Key 0 – The Fool is traditionally depicted as a wandering buffoon and described by Amber Jayanti in *Living the Qabalistic Tarot* as "a symbol of the soul just prior to its next cycle" of manifesting in the material realm.[1a] It describes the incipient stage of existence.

In most decks, The Fool is commonly depicted as seemingly close to stepping off a high cliff without regard for what is below, or following his own bliss amidst a scenic countryside.

The Fool is ever moving on a path without a certain destination. The journey is the lesson. It benefits The Fool with an accumulation of wisdom from varied life experiences, which is symbolized by the purse tied to the wanderer's staff and carried over his shoulder.

Purses or bags are commonly used to hold personal valuables or items of sentimental value. Although women are typically purse carriers, "historically purses are gender neutral,"[2] much like the figure on the card. The purse is representative of The Fool's spiritual achievements as well as his "bag of tricks," for a "fool" could also be experienced in magic, composing verse, and /or playing musical instruments.

While on its face this card implies that one may not take life too seriously, it has a profoundness that attempts to relay this meaning of an ancient archetype.

The Fool's attire was very much a uniform for the Court Jester, a role integral among court life in medieval times.

The Fool was immensely trusted and also one of the only ones who dared to speak his mind to his employer, if only in jest. Jesters were periodically eradicated because of their candid views and thus many fools/jesters took to the road in order to speak more freely to a wider audience; their first duty being an entertainer under the guise of bubbling idiot.

The Fool may have started from an inferior status (No-thing), but ends up as something very important, such as a hero. In order to be of continued use, the court jester had to be witty, intelligent, and creative.

The word "fool" originates from the Latin word *follis*, which translates as "bellows" or "bag full of wind," referring to the element of Air.[3]

Two distinct archetypes can be seen in The Fool, that of the child and the trickster/beggar. In some decks, the figure is a child or depicted as youthful. Most decks show a figure dressed in a colorful costume, some the trousers or tights being ripped by an animal; usually a dog accompanies him on the journey.

Canines have been tied to humanity as companions for over 10,000 years acting as guides and protectors. The dog symbolizes our natural instincts. Dogs have been credited as having the capacity to see beyond our realm, often seeing spirits or other supernatural beings that are invisible to the human eye.[4] It accompanies the Fool in its aspect as soul/spirit on the spiritual path reflecting the lower of the three worlds – animal, human, and divine symbolically represented by the dog, the human figure ,and the sun.

The Fool has played an important role universally in folk traditions and mythology.[4a] Fools have been integral to society, rather than just a comic relief that often pushed their luck and took great risks if their employers lacked a sense of humor. This card has collectively represented the notion of wild abandonment, haste, stupidity, and malicious jokes. On the surface, the meaning of The Fool can be foolishness or carelessness, but it also paradoxically indicates a higher wisdom.[4b]

Occultists assigned Aleph, the very first letter of the Hebrew alphabet, to this path, indicating the start or new beginning of things. Aleph means "ox" or "castrated bull" referencing The Fool's androgyny.[5]

The ox is a symbol frequently used in Tarot, representing St. Luke, one of the four evangelists. In its hermaphroditic motif, The Fool, therefore, could be seen as a mythological "child god" who were often destined to be saviors to humanity.

In Waite's version, The Fool wears a wreathed headdress, a red feather emerging from it indicating that he/she imparts the truth from the experiences of a long journey. The white sun in the corner shines down on The Fool, Divine blessings allow a worry-free adventure.

The white rose represents duality in this card, a delicate, "pure essence"[5a] and uncomfortable prickliness of its thorns.

In Waite's version, The Fool's tunic features ten yellow spheres divided by eight red spokes, which Paul Foster Case explained are the "Wheels of Spirit." [5b] These represent the ten sephiroth on the Tree of Life. The Fool personifies ten levels of consciousness represented by the ten sephiroth on the Tree of Life. These circles are Kether's decent into the world of form via the Fool.[6]

The twelve signs of the zodiac are represented by the orbs featured on the Fool's belt.

There is some confusion, adding to this card's many paradoxes, one being the letter Aleph (corresponding to the number 1 in Hebrew) and the card's assignment to the number 0.

Some place The Fool at the end of the Major Arcana after The World, while others place it before Key 1 – The Magician. Historically, the zero seems to be a later addition to the card. As an unnumbered card, The Fool could be seen as a cipher containing both everything and nothing.[7]

TAROT COUPLING KEYWORDS

Positive Qualities: Lovable, non-judgmental, trusting, and egoless
Impairments/Fear: Trust issues and abandonment

Perception of Partner: Childlike, impulsive, immature, and naïve

Dyadic Interaction: Changeable, lacks understanding, fears commitment

Challenges: Jumps to conclusions, takes gambles, fearlessness, and sexual identity issues

Complaints of Partner: Thoughtless, nonconformist, promiscuous, lacks discernment, and careless

Desires: Stability, freedom, and ordinary life

GENERAL INTERPRETATION

The Fool is the archetypal Child who is pure, hopeful, and trusts in his surroundings. The Fool desires to be free of emotions that are taxing or require great emotional responsibility.

Here is an encounter with someone driven to experience and potentially lacks interest in serious relationship, for they are a thrill seeker. This thrill seeking activity may bring out some parts of the person that they do not normally allow others to see.

Sexual identity crises, exploring bisexuality, or bi-curiosity are represented here with openness to a variety of sexual exploration that feeds a potentially high sex drive.

The Fool's mind is always churning. The red feather featured on some cards, indicates an active mind and therefore shows that The Fool is not a bumbling idiot, but does not readily expose his wits. Over analyzing as one strives for perfection causes procrastination.

The Fool teaches to pay close attention to the inner child. The little white dog suggests influence by natural survival skills. Pleasure seeking becomes more important to happiness, rather than being tied to anything or anyone.

This also indicates those who are full of energy and motivated by risks. There is NO-thing, no mood, nor person that can keep you feeling down for long. The Fool usually bounces back quickly from any setback. Lucky fellow!

NEW

Your approach to finding love is outworn and you need a new approach to love relationships. You are unsure where a relationship will lead, but you are willing to take the risk to find out.

You are encouraged by the possibilities of a new encounter that fills you with a sense of excitement. You could find it difficult to define the impact of a new encounter because it feels different than anything you've experienced prior to now. To love is to take risks and The Fool is no stranger to taking leaps of faith. Is it wise to make a move? The Fool has a tendency to find bliss only in the moment as he embraces spontaneity.

This represents chasing the new shiny thing, fling, or the "bigger," better deal.

Established

This card indicates that trust is a major issue for one or both partners. There is no motivation to change anything about the relationship. Your attitude is if it's not broken, it doesn't need to be fixed.

You or your partner may consider starting a family out of the blue or could be surprised by news of pregnancy.

There could be uncertainty or hesitation regarding plans or decisions.

Expanded Awareness

The Fool is the only one who doesn't think he is a fool because he is just going with the only flow he has ever known. Perhaps there is dysfunction at the root of the foolishness occurring in the relationship.

Openness and honesty will strengthen your connection. The feather is an emblem of right order and truth, and associated with Maat, the Egyptian goddess. Truth is valued and important in your relationships. You may have a partner who is proud and values independence. If you exhibit helplessness, it could frustrate your partner.

Deterioration

Good intentions may not go as expected. Advice is not heeded. The situation appears absurd and you are not able to determine the object of your affection's true intentions.

As much as attachment plays a role here, so does detachment. Detach from overwhelming emotional situations. After enduring a long-term connection, such as an unsuccessful marriage, the desire to suddenly commit is not a priority.

Romantic Suggestions

Movie: *The Court Jester* (1956)

Starring: Danny Kaye, Glynis Johns, and Angela Lansbury

Date/Outing: Hire a babysitter (if needed) and randomly surprise your lover with an evening out that is unplanned and spontaneous

Gift Ideas: Travel accessories, handbags, luggage, fan, and peppermint candies, or adopt a new pet

Most Compatible Cards: The Lovers, Justice, and Temperance

Least Compatible Cards: The Hierophant, The Chariot, and Death

I. THE MAGICIAN

GOLDEN DAWN/ESOTERIC TITLE: The Magus of Power
HEBREW LETTER: Beth
MEANING: House
DOUBLE LETTER: Life-Death
QABALISTIC ATTRIBUTION: Twelfth –Intelligence of Transparency
ELEMENT: Air/Earth
PLANET: Mercury

> *This rough magic I here abjure and when I have required some heavenly music,*
> *which even now I do, to work mine end upon their senses that this airy charm is for,*
> *I'll break my staff, bury it certain fathoms in the earth, and deeper than did ever*
> *plummet sound, I'll drown my book.*

~William Shakespeare
The Tempest

GENERAL COMMENTARY

Key 1 – The Magician is the next archetype encountered on the path of enlightenment and in some decks, the first numbered card of the Trumps or Major Arcana. The Fool enters the trickster archetypal cycle in this card. While entertaining and playful, The Magician is a professional that understands when to abandon trumpery for the more important task of soul development. The Magician shows an acquired maturity in the awareness of self and helps us reflect on the foolishness of our past. At this stage, one gains familiarity with strengths and the shadows that dominate your life, giving you the capacity to "transform your weakness in order to shift the state or shape of your life," explains Jayanti in Living The Qabalistic Tarot.

The Magician was called il Bagatella, i Bagatto, le Bateleur, and le Mage in earlier decks and is generally portrayed as a sleight of hand street performer or mountebank, but Decker, Depaulis, and Dummett add in the description of The Magician in *A Wicked Pack of Cards* is "definitely not a Magus or Magician...in the sense of an adept in high magic."[7a]

The Magician is associated with the alchemical figure Mercurius, the planet Mercury, and the Greek Hermes. Like Mercurius, The Magician is endowed with the "power of shape-shifting."[7b] As Hermes, the Greek patron of thieves, The Magician can be guileful and deceptive. These qualities along with the curious talent of pranking, are a common trickster motif of the shaman or medicine man, which is how the Magus in this card can be defined[7c] – and as such, is the "walker-between-worlds."

Waite's Magician card depicts a figure dressed in ceremonial garb of a red robe, white gown, white headband and a snake as a sash around his waist. The headband shows The Magician can readily access alternative levels of consciousness. A figure eight-shaped infinity symbol appears above the figure or is incorporated in the design of the hat worn on some cards. He welds power through the double-headed wand in his right hand, harnessing the power of the Divine and directing its energy to the earthly realm. The figure is positioned behind a table, which is the field of focus and is the area where the four magical tools on the table will be used for discord or harmony as The Magician wills it. The other important tool used by the performer is his hands. Hands are symbolic of one's creative talent at work and are the instrument through which healing and psychic energies flow.

The garden of red roses and white lilies surround the upper and lower borders. The delicate red rose is endeared to Venus, the goddess of love,[7d] and the white lily the chaste qualities of the Virgin Mary.[7e] The garden represents the presence of the Divine on the earthly plane. It represents a world without disharmony and defines sacred sanctuary in which all magic is performed.

Tarot Coupling Keywords

Positive Qualities: Great communicator, talented, initiator and charming
Wounds/Fear: Self-doubt and fear of change.
Perception of Partner: Demanding, controlling, powerful, and egotistical.
Dyadic Interaction: Difficult, narcissist, omnipotent, and discouraging.
Challenges: Selfish, guilt trips, manipulation, and confidence.
Complaints of Partner: Competitive, over-achiever, doesn't communicate, lack of concentration, loss of magic.
Desires: Strong dedication, deep purpose for being together, powerful connection.

General Interpretation

The Magician is The Fool at a higher octave. He is like a child playing dress up. Think about the first steps you would take to find someone to love. The Magician is the true master of all elements. In order to gain respect in a relationship, it may be good to start with self-respect.

The tools on the table suggests that other options for resolving issues and exploring each others needs are available to you and your partner. The sword is a symbol of understanding, the cup emotional feedback, the wand for sexual needs and the Pentacles for investing quality time together.

The association with Mercury means that words are integral to your partnership. The Magician is the agent of transmission that uses Divine energy individually. The Magician functions in your relationship as a catalyst for change.

NEW

In a new relationship, The Magician suggests a new phase of transmitting energy in the connection. This could be in the form of thoughts that flow through the day about your beloved, the small smile upon your face when you spot their arrival for a date, or other ways you spend time together.

You are excellent at communicating your needs and wish to transform your connection into something magical and extraordinary. This is a connection where individuality is respected and you both allow the other to do things without the complications of jealousy. Creating a romantic environment with wine, flowers, and candles will demonstrate your affection and impress you partner.

ESTABLISHED

In essence, lots of energy is generated to ensure the connection is solid and lasting. Your relationship has endured many trials that, in due time, strengthens your love for one another. Participate in tasks that make you proud of yourself or your partner. Strong communication skills are the hallmark of a conscious partnership.

EXPANDED AWARENESS

Co-dependency issues complicate the relationship. Take off the blinders and see past illusions. Is there too much of an overwhelming ego issue in your relationship? Gifted with the communicative power of Mercury, this represents the power to express and reveal aspects of your individuality without compromising the partnership.

All relationship experts agree communication is the key to success in a solid commitment. True love comes through keeping both your will and ego in balance. It involves work that requires you to be present. Success comes through using your intentions for the highest good.

DETERIORATING

Elusive behavior leads to suspiciousness. Negative energy adds to inadequacy and low self-confidence.

The archetypal trickster represented by this card is a notorious talker. Too much chatter can bring confusion and miscommunication, much like The Fool in his nonsense stage.

Are you attempting to Will something into being? Something to bear in mind is that the ego wants to be satisfied and drives behavior to do just so.

This suggests a control–freak, an egomaniac, an opportunist, and a charlatan.

Sometimes, this is also one who causes friction with all their activity. You may see this when your partner tries to get a rise out of you through nagging and pushing your buttons. As much as this card is about action, it also cautions you to pause and think before you react.

You may have heard "it takes two to tango," but it takes one to actively repair what's not working. You may feel victimized and defensive, therefore, unable to use your own resources to effectively navigate your circumstance. The longer you are involved with someone, the more difficult you will find it is to manage your ego at times.

Lastly, The Magician encourages you to react from a place of self-intent. You don't want to exhaust yourself trying to please the Will of others.

Romantic Suggestions

Movie: *Harry Potter and The Sorcerer's Stone* (2001, Warner Bros. Pictures, 1492 Pictures, Heyday Films)

Starring: Daniel Radcliffe, Rupert Grint, and Richard Harris

Date/Outing: Visit or plant a rose garden; go shopping together for items that bring magic to your sex life

Gift Ideas: Cooking lessons, power tools, gardening tools, roses, snakeskin belt, robe, or wand

Most Compatible Cards: The Emperor and The Star

Least Compatible Cards: The Hermit

II. THE HIGH PRIESTESS

GOLDEN DAWN/ESOTERIC TITLE: The Princess of the Silver Star
MEANING: Camel
HEBREW LETTER: Gimel
DOUBLE LETTER: Peace-War
QABALISTIC ATTRIBUTION: Thirteenth – Uniting Intelligence
ELEMENT: Water
PLANET: Moon

> *The secret things belong unto the Lord our God:*
> *but those things which are revealed belong unto us and to our children for ever,*
> *that we may do all the words of this law.*
>
> *~Deuteronomy*
> *ch. XXIX, v. 29*

GENERAL COMMENTARY

Key 2 – An expressionless woman is seated with stillness in the seclusion of a sacred temple. The High Priestess is seated on a cubed throne. She is positioned between two pillars of polarized energy.

Pillars are especially noticeable for the symbolism of the ceremonial chamber. The pillars on the Waite's version are a representation of the pillars that adorned the eastern gate of the Temple of Solomon.

In their collaboration, *The Hiram Key*, authors Christopher Knight and Robert Lomas tell us that the black pillar on the left marked with the initial "B" "was named after Boaz, the great-grandfather of David, king of Israel", the great ancestor of Jesus Christ and the white pillar on the right with the initial "J" was named after Jachin (sometimes spelled Joachim), "the first high priest who assisted at the dedication of the porchway section of the Temple of Jerusalem."[7f] Duncan Moore explains in his work, *A Guide to Masonic Symbolism* that the columns and pillars featured in lodges are to be distinguished as they hold different meanings. He also points out in contrast to Knight and Lomas that:

> Jachin, by the way, was not the Assistant High Priest who officiated at the dedication of the Temple, as ritual tells us. The Dedication was performed by King Solomon and by him alone… The word simply means "to establish" as the ritual points out and is conjoined with Boaz (meaning "'in strength") to give the joint meaning stated in ritual.[7g]

Pillars are decorative yet add significant strength to any structure. Has anyone ever wondered what a female priestess is doing between the columns of the Temple of Solomon?

The answer lies in perhaps the mystery of the goddess aspect of divine. The pillars also represent opposing dynamic interaction that permeates our existence. We find masculine and feminine symbolism on the veil hung between the two lotus-topped pillars which is decorated with date palm plants and pomegranates. Pomegranates have long symbolized fecundity and particularly female power. Many designs feature water or a large river representing The High Priestess as the container from which all life flows.

The robe she wears in Waite's version morphs into waves of watery blue, which is life giving and purifying. The blue in which this powerful figure is garbed, represents Divine "beauty and perfection."[7h]

It is also the silver-bluish color of moon that is shown in triple phases representative of lunar goddesses who are associated with cycles of birth, flourishing and death. Blue is the color of contemplation, faith chastity, and the spiritual life.[7i] Because of their noble dedication to divinity, priestesses were often "married" to the temple. The moon is the symbol of the subconscious mind, governing intuition, insights, and instincts.

The cross on the High Priestess is symbolic of the four directions and equidistance and implies a sacred power of the station she holds. She is veiled which signifies that the knowledge she holds in the TARO scrolls contain spiritual secrets that only an initiate can comprehend.

Tarot Coupling Keywords

Positive Qualities: Pleasant, agreeable, pure, powerful, and sensitive
Wounds/Fear: Isolation, oversensitive, inferiority complex, and toxic shame
Perception of Partner: Aloof, mysterious, neutral, and impressionable
Dyadic Interaction: Hides feelings, ridicules, hides knowledge, and secrets
Challenges: Awareness, being cognizant, confusion, vision, and discretion.
Complaints of Partner: Shortsighted, one-track mind, unrealistic, and moody
Desires: Respect, closeness, and equality

General Interpretation

In *The Tarot of the Magicians*, Oswald Wirth explains that "The High Priestess is Isis, the goddess of deep night," and "without her assistance, the human spirit could not penetrate the darkness."

This darkness is surrounding you at this time and you are possibly trying to keep someone in the dark, or alternatively, you are not able to penetrate someone else's "darkness."

In a reading, it suggests that you may sense something is not quite right but you don't have all the pieces to the whole puzzle. A significant feminine energy has a powerful role in your connection.

The High Priestess has energy that is very intriguing, especially when there are strong feminine vibrations that pull at you. You can flirt with The High Priestess (or she with you) but you cannot corrupt her. Ultimately, she acts as a vessel of balance and uncovers the mysteries of the Self.

Secrets withheld from your partner can create peace or cause a war. A secret, as defined in the context of relationships, is that which is concealed or helps in confidence between two people or withheld from a partner. Here it defines knowledge that only one person in the relationship has.

In practical terms, this card suggests information that is both alluring and dangerous. Secrets are kept for negative as well as positive reasons, potentially destroying or saving a relationship. In a reading, this points to making the right decision around disclosure; in due time the secret will be revealed.

NEW

The relationship is both mysterious and alluring, but you may not be able to articulate the reasons why. Your relationship feels as if you both have known each other prior to this lifetime.

Issues regarding virginity and abstinence may come up in discussion. One or both partners could be practicing abstinence. This suggests how well the relationship fits, but the partners are unaware of what makes it so.

ESTABLISHED

You may know each other very well and are both intuitive. Partners are connected more than just through compatibility and physical attraction, but have unconscious attractions that are not consciously apparent.

You see slivers of unacceptable parts of yourself in your partner and part of the attraction is that these parts are experienced vicariously in your relationship. This suggests quietly contemplating taking your relationship to the next level.

EXPANDED AWARENESS

Respect the sacredness of your union. This relationship is powered by deep connection; and similarly to the moon's influence to our planet, you feel this amazing, mysterious pull that draws you in.

Your partner's irresistibility is like an intoxicating potion or drug. This suggests a psychic bond in which partners often correctly perceive and identify what the other is feeling.

The High Priestess suggests an interesting intrapsychic process occurring as part of partner unconscious communication called projective identification by psychoanalyst Melanie Klein (1946).

This intricate process happens when one partner (A) has good or bad stressors, and projects them into partner (B), who experiences these unexplained feelings, and partner (A) falsely attributes these to partner (B) and thus controls partner (B).

DETERIORATING

Both partners have habits that affect the other, which they may not have full awareness. As mentioned above, projection identification causes certain feelings of inadequacy to damage (or enhance) the relationship. Fantasies are also a part of this unconscious process.

Hypersensitivity may be working for or against you.

Do not ignore your intuitions or gut feelings concerning your partner. The answer to your questions cannot be known at this time, but will require patience.

The High Priestess could mean what is called the "silent treatment." This passive-aggressive behavior is classic in emotionally unhealthy relationships.

ROMANTIC SUGGESTIONS

Movie: *The Mistress of Spices* (2005)

Starring: Aishwarya Rai Bachchan, Dylan McDermott, and Nitin Ganatra

Date/Outing: A quiet candlelight dinner, visit to a local bookstore or library, an early evening stroll, share a bottle of red wine in your backyard or patio under the moonlight

Gift Ideas: Books, monthly subscription to a favorite magazine, Tarot decks, a new dress, scarves, handkerchiefs, satin underwear, or sheets

Most Compatible Cards: The Chariot, Death, and The Devil

Least Compatible Cards: The Lovers, Temperance, and Justice

III. THE EMPRESS

GOLDEN DAWN/ESOTERIC TITLE: The Daughter of The Mighty Ones
HEBREW LETTER: Daleth
MEANING: Door
DOUBLE LETTER: Wisdom - Folly
QABALISTIC ATTRIBUTION: Fourteenth – Illuminating Intelligence
ELEMENT: Earth
PLANET: Venus

> *Venus salutes him with this fair good-morrow;*
> *"O thou clear god, and patron of all light,*
> *From whom each lamp and shining star doth borrow*
> *The beauteous influence that makes him bright,*
> *There lives a son that suck'd an earthly mother,*
> *May lend thee light, as thou dost lend to other.*

> ~William Shakespeare

GENERAL COMMENTARY

Key 3 – The Empress is the Great Mother of All combining aspects of all that is feminine, maternal, and warm. In contrast to the restriction of the temple, The Empress is depicted in Waite's deck reclining among the greens of the land with an ever-flowing waterfall of life-giving water, symbolic of her earthly connection. The womb of the Empress brings forth all life into existence.

The Empress is associated with Venus or Aphrodite, the great goddess of love. She is linked with all maternal deities and shares similar characteristics of The High Priestess.[7j] The Empress, like other great goddesses, is also the bearer of the gods. Because she is the giver of life, she is often depicted as pregnant.

She appears beautifully crowned with twelve stars, which gives a luminous light to her. The golden globe she welds gives her a regal authority. The Empress in Waite's deck is dressed in a robe covered with pomegranates, the fruit of sexual lure. In some decks, a shield is among the décor that surrounds her throne, with either an eagle or the symbol of Venus, the Goddess of Love. The Empress is filled with transformative lessons of love and desire, but the capacity to create or destroy also lies in her grasp.

Tarot Coupling Keywords

Positive Relational Qualities: Nurturing, caring, and peaceful
Wounds/Fear: Impoverished
Perception of Partner: Overbearing, smothering, and altruistic
Dyadic Interaction: Smothers, overprotective, less affectionate, impatient, sees togetherness as suffocating
Challenges: Creating sense of family, ideating, and being solutions-oriented
Complaints of Partner: Over-parents, controlling, creativity, too relaxed, and selfish
Desires: Motherhood, good provider, luxury items, and fine living

General Interpretation

The Empress is the great comfort that only a mother's affection and careful nurturing brings. You want so much to love and be loved in return.

The Empress is an archetypal anima image appearing in dreams as a goddess or other primitive female maternal image. What is projected on your partner has deep significance to the relationship with your own primary maternal caretaker. There is a desire to be pampered or spoiled, or showered with affection. You may find that you and your lover are flowing together harmoniously at this time.

Motherhood issues may be at the forefront of your concerns. Advice from your mother about love and life may reverberate in your thoughts or motherly advice could be useful right now.

The notion of Universal Love is central to this card. As the saying goes, "You must learn to love yourself before you can love anyone else," this is one way to understand how relationships are created from within the self. Therefore, you are able to create the type of relationship you desire by being aware of how to love.

New

What really matters in your relationship above all is to be loved and wanted. You could invest much creative energy into transitioning your relationship into something that flows and operates smoothly. You are recreating your image to become more sexually attractive.

Established

You are thinking about special moments or memories that were created in an outdoor setting. Since The Empress is correlated with Venus, the implication here (or caution) concerns sexual objectification. This occurs when an individual sees you as only being worthy in terms of physical attractiveness and their own sexual gratification.[7k]

The lighter aspects of The Empress suggest a relationship where both partner's love and care for one another and each partner contributes 100% while remaining true to their individuality.

Expanded Awareness

Closeness and intimacy comes when you create an atmosphere of beauty and nurturing perhaps in your physical surroundings. You may want to create spark in your connection by increased attention to your diet and weight. Physical attraction is important to you. You build your self-confidence by working out and exercising more.

Deteriorating

An extreme show of affection may be perceived as being too overbearing. Motherhood issues may be at the root of your problems.

The role you play in your marriage is one that you are only seen as Mom. You become self-sacrificing and may have lost your own personality to play the role of perfect partner.

The Empress is aware that what she creates may not be able to sustain life or thrive. Just as the natural cycles in nature, some things grow, some are harvested for nourishment, and some things just wither and die.

Three is a symbolically harmonious number of gregariousness, group energy, loyalty, and charm. It can feel extremely flattering to be the object of someone's desire and a boost to your confidence. On the other hand, this card in its negative aspect means that same attention can turn into humiliation, such as that seen in sexual abuse or assault.

Romantic Suggestions

Movie: *The Scarlett Empress* (1934, Paramount Pictures)
Starring: Marlene Dietrich, John Lodge, and Sam Jaffe
Date/Outing: Shop together for healthy food items, plan a relaxing day of pampering at a spa, have a romantic picnic near a river or waterfall
Gift Ideas: Linens, jewelry, plants, lacy lingerie, sandalwood scented incense, candles or oils, pillows, picture frames, art, or home décor
Most Compatible Cards: The Devil and The Moon
Least Compatible Cards: The Star and Justice

IV. THE EMPEROR

GOLDEN DAWN/ESOTERIC TITLE: Sun of The Morning, Chief Among The Mighty
HEBREW LETTER: Heh
MEANING: Window
SIMPLE LETTER: Sight
QABALISTIC ATTRIBUTION: Fifteenth – Constituting Intelligence
ELEMENT: Fire
SIGN: Aries

To you, your father should be as a god;
One that compos'd your beauties, yea, and one
To whom you are but as a form in wax
By him imprinted, and within his power
To leave the figure or disfigure it."

~William Shakespeare
A Midsummer Night's Dream
(1.1.50-4)

GENERAL COMMENTARY

Key 4 – This high-ruling chief is capable of just as much as The Empress, but on a somewhat different level, that being the masculine. The Emperor and Empress represent parenting. While The Empress is sensitive and feeling, The Emperor is rational and methodical in his reasoning. He typically bears the symbols of the zodiacal Aries, the Ram in most versions.

The Emperor is a powerful masculine energy. He is capable of classification and systematizes like no other card in the deck. In *Living the Qabalistic Tarot,* Jayanti, in her commentary on the BOTA version of The Emperor, explains that the twelve triangles featured on The Emperor's helmet shows he is a "thoughtful and compassionate" overseer of all that is "birthed into being" through The Empress. Jayanti further relays how The Emperor stands as the "father" aspect of all deities as the masculine creator reminiscent in the tales of Zeus, Osiris, among other powerful gods, in other traditional creation myths. (Amber Jayanti, *Living The Qabalistic Tarot: Applying An Ancient Oracle To The Challenges of Modern Life.* York Beach: Weiser Books, 2000, 2004, 68.)

He is a considerate overseer of all that is brought forward through The Empress. He is the paternal aspect of all deities as the masculine creator reminiscent in the tales of Zeus, Osiris, among other powerful gods, in other traditional creation myths.

The Emperor in most decks is shown to rule over his domain from a cubed throne. Sometimes his legs are crossed forming a triangle and he sits posed with his head in profile.

The Emperor's reign is granted by Divine right and he believes in the principles of universal laws. He is fair and just, loving, and feels just as deeply as The Empress does.

The Emperor's white beard shows his great age and wisdom. He is suited in armor as the defender and protector of his realm. His red cloak, that wraps over his shoulder, is linked to the element of fire and corresponds to the sign of Aries. He sits among the rugged, rigid mountains of golden hues.

The Emperor carries a staff topped with an Egyptian ankh symbolizing life and male potency. He also holds in his other hand a gleaming sphere common to most portrayals, often referred to as the "Orb of Dominion." (Robert Wang, *The Qabalistic Tarot.* York Beach, Maine Samuel Weiser, Inc., 1987, 229.)

Tarot Coupling Keywords

Positive Qualities: Leadership, imperial, and authoritative

Perception of Partner: Disciplinarian, rigid, and distant.

Dyadic Interaction: Cautious, domineering, and inflexible

Challenges: Taking orders, great organizer, sticking to standards and concern for self or others

Complaints of Partner: Disrespects authority, demands obedience, but doesn't respect

Desires: Fatherhood, to protect, creates structure, and foundations

General Interpretation

Who is the best authority in your life? The Emperor speaks to responsibility and the creative male energy. Your values regarding love are high and it will be hard for you to accept anything less. You impart wisdom as if from the mind of a great sage. You are ambitious and value innovation and ingenuity.

Ultimately, you are the head of the household and are seen in the role of Great Organizer and patriarch. However, there is a saying that "behind every great man is a woman." From this saying you can derive that men are shaped by a strong female figure, such as a grandmother or mother. The Emperor seeks some counsel from his Empress, but will always make decisions that he concludes from his own wisdom.

The color red dominates this card, especially in the Waite deck. Red symbolically represents life, libido, and sexual arousal. (Ami Ronnberg and Kathleen Martin, eds., *The Book of Symbols: Reflection on Archetypal Images*, ARAS. Cologne, Germany, Taschen, 2010, 638.)

As The Emperor is seen as an aged, bearded man, it doesn't mean he is incapable of performing sexually.

What makes a man a man, and a woman a woman, are so very different. In many cases, this comes down to socialized roles in which The Emperor suggests are related to masculine tendencies and roles regardless of sexual orientation.

In addition to referencing paternal power, political power is also seen in this card. Possible negotiations are ongoing in efforts to prevent a war in the relationship.

The energy of The Emperor card is very focused and goal-oriented. It also means viewing things from a logical and mature perspective.

It speaks to coming from a place of authority in knowing what is best for you and your family. No one should have any more control over your life than you. The Emperor has appeared to enrich and enhance your life through active and Constituting Intelligence.

NEW

Your ideal partner will be able to exhibit strength combined with tenderness. Productivity and a commitment to seeing things through could be your goal at this time. The Emperor calls for you to see the truth of any matter so that you may become conscious in your relationship and bring about a level of organization.

ESTABLISHED

You are passionate and protective of the one you love. There is a need to protect or be protected. Issues related to fathers or fatherhood may need to be resolved.

EXPANDED AWARENESS

The way to progress may be through removing "armor."

Defense mechanisms are in place that drives your behaviors. There may be a need for bravery on your behalf to address sexual dysfunction.

There is great necessity in maintaining stability for the good of everyone involved, especially in cases where there are considerations of a separation or divorce.

In self-development, setting obtainable goals is important. These goals should be clearly defined and redefined as often as needed until they are reached.

It requires reasonable assessment of your situation and to have compassion for yourself as well as your partner.

DETERIORATING

You may not be playing by the rules, and the expectation of what a relationship entails may not match or conform to your partners. Are you behaving the way a father or masculine caretaker influenced you in childhood?

Aggressively pursuing control, power, and domination, partners are cruel to one another or plot against each other, turning their backs on all that was so cherished in the beginning of the love affair.

You may feel like you are being dominated or bossed around by your partner. There is also a certain amount of stubbornness and loss of cooperation with your partner.

If you are red with anger, you will not think rationally. You should become aware that when people are angry, they say mean things to each other that they often later regret.

Be aware of where your mind and reactions to the nuances of anger will lead you.

ROMANTIC SUGGESTIONS

Movie: *The Emperor's Club* (2002, Sidney Kimmel Entertainment, Live Planet, Fine Line Features)

Starring: Kevin Kline, Emile Hirsch, and Joel Gretsch

Date/Outing: Bowling for two or with friends, build an outdoor fireplace, organize your schedules to spend more time with kids, and then each other

Gift Ideas: Wool coat or sweater, golf clubs, cigars, incense, lambskin wallet, decorative horns, and Dragon's Blood oil or incense

Most Compatible Cards: Strength, Temperance, and The Star

Least Compatible Cards: The Chariot and The Devil

V. THE HIEROPHANT

GOLDEN DAWN/ESOTERIC TITLE: The Magus of The Eternal
HEBREW LETTER: Vau
MEANING: Hook or Nail
SIMPLE LETTER: Hearing
QABALISTIC ATTRIBUTION: Sixteenth – Triumphal or Eternal Intelligence
ELEMENT: Earth
SIGN: Taurus

The love of heaven makes one heavenly.

~William Shakespeare

GENERAL COMMENTARY

Key 5 – The Magus of The Eternal is the spiritual elder of the Tarot. The Hierophant has spent many years studying the principles and laws of the universe.

In most religious traditions, there is a high office in which there is a dedicated person who acts as mediator with the Divine. The Pope or Hierophant – a derivative from the Greek word *hiero+phantes* – represents this in Tarot.

The Hierophant is pictured with a triple jeweled crown known as a *triregnum* and is dressed in the traditional papal vestments of the Roman Catholic Church. (Holy See Press Office, "Tiara", http://www.vatican.va/news_services/press/documentazione/documents/sp_ss_scv/insigne/triregno_en.html.) He is seated on a high-back throne between two large and finely ornamented pillars.

As far back as ancient Egyptian times, the High Priest was regarded as having the power to guide those seeking the wisdom of the gods. This royal office was responsible for the religious rites of society as delegated by the Pharaoh. In the temple, they acted as dream interpreter and teacher to the average seeker as pontificator of the religion of the gods through a variety of ceremonies.

In addition to religious functions, the High Priest was also delegated as a royal administrator and substitute for the king in title only.[7L] In Europe, the Pope was referred to as "king maker," thus anyone wanting to become king would seek the blessings and cooperation of the papal office.

The simple letter meaning of Key 5 is associated with hearing. The two figures kneeling below the Pope are listening to him deliver the Divine word. The Hierophant is the authorized bridge between God and the people. The Hierophant is the "nail" that connects inner spirit with the outer world.

The Hierophant holds the papal or triple cross in his left hand. This is a symbol of a shepherd-king and signifies ultimate temporal powers. The triple cross also represents the Holy Trinity.

Sacred vestments, the triple-crowned miter and the white shoes with crosses are all part of the elaborate attire worn during ceremonial rites. The kneeling figures on either side attending the pontiff are dressed in dalmatics, one featuring lilies and the other roses. These are symbolic of the joy and happiness that are the fruit of the priestly dedication to God. They are also decorated with yellow palliums. The Hierophant wears a white pallium decorated with three crosses. This item is usually made of white wool when worn by the pope.

Tarot Coupling Keywords

Positive Qualities: Fair, moral, involved, and determined

Wounds/Fear: Unworthiness and loss of integrity

Perception of Partner: Righteous, traditionalist, zealous, and charismatic

Dyadic Interaction: Authoritative, self-possessed, demands obedience

Challenges: Stubborn, sense of integrity, clarity, strong beliefs and traditions

Complaints of Partners: Rigid, initiates arguments, changes mind and has no clear direction, traditions are worn out, acts as enforcer

Desires: Truthfulness, humbleness, chaste, and spiritual connection

General Interpretation

The Hierophant is the spiritual leader. This card symbolizes a teacher and someone who holds the highest spiritual position. The Hierophant is the voice of reason and a source of comfort.

You, or the person you are involved with, may focus much of your attention on information that confirms your beliefs without regard to those who disconfirm them.

In psychology, this phenomenon is known as confirmation bias. Confirmation bias is selective assignment of data that supports your own beliefs. (Gary Walters et al. "Confirmation Bias," http://outofthefog.net/CommonBehaviors/ConfirmationBias.html.) Similarly to The Hierophant, you may feel that the only true path is *your* path and ignore all other viewpoints.

New

When confronted with brand new information, you may have a tendency to view it through the mindset of The Hierophant and only trust your own authority.

Established

In a relationship, you share the same values and traditions. Belief systems play an important role in decision-making. Spirituality plays an important role in your life and should be at the center of your relationship.

Expanded Awareness

Advice from a counselor or therapist may benefit you at this time. You will find a deeper significance to your connection as you focus and stay connected to Source or God in whatever form that works for you.

Deteriorating

Respect and integrity issues are at the forefront of your relationship problems. One or both partners are audaciously righteous and uncompromising.

It is important to be heard in a relationship. You may spend much time talking and never really listening. This does not only apply to your partner or spouse but to your own intuition.

Before you seek outside advice about your situation, you may want to listen to your own inner voice about the situation, just as God speaks directly to the High Priest.

Romantic Suggestions

Movie: *We Have a Pope* (2011)
Starring: Michel Piccoli, Nanni Moretti, and Jerzy Stuhr
Date/Outing: Tour local historical cathedrals or basilicas, go out for Sunday brunch
Gift Ideas: Bedroom slippers, symbolic jewelry, religious items, or a five-course dinner
Most Compatible Cards: The Moon, The Hermit, and The Chariot
Least Compatible Cards: The Lovers, Death, and The Star

VI. THE LOVERS

GOLDEN DAWN/ESOTERIC TITLE: The Children of the Voice; The Oracle of Mighty Gods
HEBREW LETTER: Zain
MEANING: Sword/Armor
SIMPLE LETTER: Smell
QABALISTIC ATTRIBUTION: Seventeenth – Disposing Intelligence
ELEMENT: Air
SIGN: Gemini

> *You and I are essentially infinite choice-makers. In every moment of our existence,*
> *we are in that field of all possibilities where we have access to an infinity of choices.*

> ~Deepak Chopra

GENERAL COMMENTARY

Key 6 – What we see on The Lovers card is an all too familiar scene depicting the Garden of Eden in the biblical creation story in Genesis. On the Waite card, we have a male and female who are presumably Adam and Eve with an angel that hovers above.

The astrological significance of Key 6 is associated with Gemini, The Twins, Castor, and Pollux. The interesting thing about this particular set of twins from mythology is that one of the twins, Castor, was said to be mortal, and the other twin, Pollux, was an immortal. Some decks will have two or three figures, depending on the tradition it follows.

A choice was given to the pair living in the garden in the story of creation. Two trees were there as seen on the Waite card. We know them as the tree of life and the tree of the knowledge of good and evil. With the ability to choose apparent, it is less mentioned that desire plays a role in the human psyche.

The tree on the left side of the card containing the fruit is the tree of knowledge. A serpent coils itself around its trunk as it looks over the shoulder of the female. On the right side of the card is the tree of life with twelve flame-tipped leaves behind the male figure.

The pair is significant in that they represent the principles of polarity in everything. Both figures are naked and the angel with flaming hair wears a purple flowing robe and is floating out of the mists of clouds. Traditionally, this angel is Raphael, the angel of those who seek love. Earlier cards depict Cupid, the God of Love, with an arrow ready to hit an unsuspecting victim.

The large hill that rises between the two figures represents the union of male and female energies. This form is interesting in that it resembles an omphalos (from the Greek word *navel*), a large stone that is rounded at its head. This sort of stone was found at the cult of Apollo at Delphi in ancient Greece and was believed to mark the center point of the entire world.

The Egyptian tradition says that the first physical matter in the newly created universe, manifested itself as a mound or island resembling a pointed cone, similar to what is shown on the Waite card.

In the Egyptian mythology, this mound represented the island of first creation called the Duat.[8] As the navel is the place from where a fetus is nourished; thus, the beginning of physical matter in creation was due to a link to a heavenly source.

It symbolizes the prima material of alchemy, which reveals itself when it sweeps up out of the abyss as we explore our human potential. This puts perspective on what Robert Wang wrote in *Qabalistic Tarot* when he states that the Lovers "connect the pure consciousness from which form emerged with the central point of all manifestation."[9]

It is also interesting to note that this card is called "the Oracle of the Mighty Gods" sharing resemblance to the title Oracle of Delphi, whose story also involves a great serpent.

Tarot Coupling Keywords

Positive Qualities: Neighborly, civil, and affectionate

Wounds/Fear: Rejection and Separateness

Perception of Partner: Closed, emotionally unavailable

Dyadic Interaction: Inconsistent, detached

Challenges: Consistent and balanced availability

Complaints of Partners: Indecisive, non-commitment, frigid

Desires: Commitment, companionship and compatibility, and attachment

General Interpretation

When The Lovers card appears in a reading, there are interactions involving two or more people. Influenced by Mercurial Gemini, The Lovers suggests that communication is essential to honesty and integrity in any relationship. One could choose to use an intellectual approach in emotionally charged matters.

Modern interpretations of this card include love, engagements, and marriage. It can be a bit naïve to think these as the only options of interpretations for this card. The more profound meaning has nothing to do with ordinary love shared between two people.

It represents separation, a split from that completeness, which is shown by the male and female figures. We long to get back to that state of oneness and seek to do this in love partnerships.

NEW

This suggests an understanding of commitment and true love. An ideal relationship is one where mutual views and temperaments enhance the lives of each partner. One or both partners want to impress the other.

This card also appears when there is a search for a spiritual love partner also known as the "twin soul," or searching for a partner with the intent of building a committed life together.

It also suggests taking time to learn what a partner likes and dislikes prior to entering a physical union,

ESTABLISHED

In spite of this deep connection, this suggests a need to maintain a sense of Self and independence. One or both partners enjoy the steadiness of a committed partnership, but want the freedom on occasion, to appear desirable to those other than their partner.

Under many circumstances, this card can indicate an important union. This could be in the form of a marriage, wedding, or other legal commitment. Choice between a current partner and another love interest is also suggested.

EXPANDED AWARENESS

An innocent attraction turns into a love affair, often taking its participants by surprise. We should keep in mind the story in Genesis did not end well for Adam and Eve. It is thus always described as humanity's fall. With this in mind, The Lovers card suggests endings, separations, or "death" in relationships when one partner breaks commitment rules.

The card also suggests the nature of dualism. The Lovers could, figuratively represent Jungian archetypal "anima and animus" of the unconscious mind.

Psychologically, the anima, describes the woman within a man, and the animus, the man within a woman. These dormant archetypal images from our unconscious are personified in dreams.

In relationships, when a "fall" occurs, evaluating the emotional investment required to continue the relationship takes a fair amount of trust and willingness to be vulnerable in order to repair the connection.

The angel in The Lovers suggests a willingness to place faith in another to assist in maintaining a healthy relationship, mediated through couples counseling.

DETERIORATING

Partners alienate each other, feel unattached, or are unwilling to engage in the union. At the root, these issues may be due to a lack of secure attachment that causes complications with closeness.

One partner brings into the dispute an outsider in order to gain support for their position. This suggests that a partner, not wanting to directly blame the other for their problems, become convinced the source of evil is interference from an outside source. An overwhelming amount of anger and hurt has potentially damaged the relationship. You will have to move mountains to resolve the issue.

ROMANTIC SUGGESTIONS

Movie: *Vicky Christina Barcelona* **(2008)**
Starring: Rebecca Hall, Scarlett Johansson, and Javier Bardem
Date/Outing: Visit your local farmers market or county/state fair to look for fresh fruits and vegetables to include in a romantic meal; engage in physical activities, such as mountain climbing, or hiking
Gift Ideas: Unisex spa packages, garden tools, or orchid plants
Most Compatible Cards: The Emperor, Justice, and The Star
Least Compatible Cards: The Hermit and The Moon

VII. THE CHARIOT

GOLDEN DAWN/ESOTERIC TITLE: The Child of the Powers of the Waters; the Lord of The Triumph of Light
HEBREW LETTER: Cheth
MEANING: Fence, Enclosure
SIMPLE LETTER: Speech
QABALISTIC ATTRIBUTION: Eighteenth – House of Influx
ELEMENT: Cardinal Water
SIGN: Cancer

Live daringly, boldly, fearlessly.
Taste the relish to be found in competition – in having put forth the best within you.

~Henry J. Kaiser

GENERAL COMMENTARY

Key 7 – A successful leader stands erect in a canopied chariot being drawn by two beasts, one black and the other white. Two opposing forces that are working together, only guided by the charioteer's mind. The figure is proudly masculine, macho even as he stands confidently in his victory.

In many of the older Tarot decks, The Chariot's horses appear in full gallop. Waite's design shows two sphinxes appearing stationary and relaxed. Crowley's design of this card has four creatures that stand idle before the vehicle. This effect is a concluded agreement by the designers that the numerical significance of Key 7 is rest. The black and white colors represent two distinct light forces that support the title of the card The Lord of The Triumph of Light. Sphinxes are enigmatic creatures often depicted with combined features of different species.

We tend to look at this card in parts, one being the chariot, then the charioteer, and finally the sphinxes. They all work together to symbolize something very profound.

In Egyptian mythology, the sun god Ra (charioteer) created Shu (represented by an ostrich feather) and Tefnut (represented as a lion or woman with a lion's head). In lion form, these two guarded the eastern and western horizons. The two lions could also be the god Aker,/Akeru, guardian of the traveling sun.

Ancient Egyptian texts describe Shu and Tefnut as parent of Geb and Nut. Shu is the god who holds up his two children Nut, the sky goddess (canopy), and Geb, the god of earth (cube). Shu was also represented as the four pillars that stood at the four corners of the earth (four canopy posts and square). The charioteer and chariot are symbols for the protected soul (ba) passing through the underworld to be born again as the Sun God. The sun god in Egypt was represented by the winged disc as seen on the front of the chariot.

The red roofed buildings in the background are pyramid shaped and could be said to resemble the sunlight kissing the tops of the pyramid as the sun god passes overhead. He heralds as the Lord of the Triumph of Light.

Tarot Coupling Keywords

Positive Qualities: Productive, passionate, influential, and enlightened

Wounds/Fear: Disapproval and powerlessness

Perception of Partner: Opinionated, calculating, and productive

Dyadic Interaction: Critical, competitive, and bossy

Challenges: Accepting partner's capacity to achieve

Complaints of Partner: Never satisfied, impulse and control issues

Desires: Embraced, active in community, and organized

General Interpretation

Do you feel as if your partner is playing mind games with you? Do you feel like you are being mentally manipulated in some way? This card is here to tell you that you are not crazy and your partner may try to make you feel that only they are right and your opinion is not needed, heeded, or otherwise wanted.

An outsider may be vying for the attention for your love mate, giving you some competition for your relationship.

You have outside support that is routing for you to succeed. Support from other family member or community is needed at this time. If they offer support, you should take them up on this generous offer.

In a general sense, this card is about success and accomplishing anything you set out to do. You win! It is time for you to take your victory lap.

New

In a new relationship, you may need to take some risks or make a move on someone who you once considered out of your league. The charioteer controls the beasts – not with reins, but with his extraordinary mental power. This intellectual strength is part of the attraction for both partners.

You share your principles, beliefs, and visions with the person you love. There is a sense of a spiritual connection.

This suggests dating someone a few years older with a motivating, powerful spirit that inspires you to work hard and create a positive existence and worthwhile life.

Established

Discussions about moving, traveling, or rearranging your home may come up when The Chariot appears. The nurturing aspect of Cancer places a focus on home and protection of your loved ones. Partners make each other feel safe and secure. Partners aim to create order and contentment in their relationships.

As an executive, one or both partners, run their home life as extensions of their business. This leaves no doubt about who controls or wears the pants in the union.

Expanded Awareness

The Chariot has captured two opposing elements, which he now is able to command. This interestingly shows unifying dualistic sexual elements within oneself.

You may want your partner to champion your cause or situation. This suggests a circumstance has placed you in a position where you could really use a hero and your partner would be just the one.

Mastery of regulating emotions and self-discipline are goals pursued by the charioteer. This also suggests a conscious partner in successful relationship.

Deteriorating

You or your partner behaves in a competitive or dictatorial fashion. The struggle for one of you to have the upper hand in the relationship leads to a no-win endless competition. The desires of the partner are under consideration, you fear they are usurping your control. Do you need to dominate the relationship in a tyrannical manner? It is possible that you want control because of fears.

You are vulnerable and move to protect your emotional interest at all costs. The Chariot wears armor as an indication that you need to protect and shield yourself from attacks, such as verbal or physical attacks.

Romantic Suggestions

Movie: *Ben Hur* (1959, Warner Bros, US)
Starring: Charlton Heston, Jack Hawkins, and Stephen Boyd
Date/Outing: Spend the day at a track for horse, greyhound, or car racing; go for an after-dinner walk under the starry night sky
Gift Ideas: Briefcase, car cover, a new set of car tires, a riding lawnmower, riding boots, or leather belt
Most Compatible Cards: The Hierophant, Death, and The Moon
Least Compatible Cards: The Emperor, Justice, and The Star

VIII. STRENGTH

GOLDEN DAWN/ESOTERIC TITLE: The Daughter of the Flaming Sword
HEBREW LETTER: Teth
MEANING: Snake
SIMPLE LETTER: Taste
QABALISTIC ATTRIBUTION: Nineteenth – Intelligence of All Activities and Spiritual Beings
ELEMENT: Fixed Fire
SIGN: Leo

Thou shalt tread upon the lion and adder:
the young lion and the dragon shalt thou trample under feet.

~Psalm 91:13

GENERAL COMMENTARY

Key 8 – On most decks, a dainty yet refined female engages a fierce lion in an ambiguous embrace. Her effort shows great courage in her proximity to the burly beast. Many traditional cards show a lovely queen seemingly prying apart the lion's jaws. In others, she is sometimes riding or standing alongside the "King of The Jungle.".

This card represents discipline and mastery over instinctual forces in efforts to become responsible for one's actions. This is not just an indication of brute muscle, but power in creative intelligence and motivational instincts. It shows the feminine principle of our nature in contrast to a primal urge.

In some decks, Strength exchanges with Justice becoming Key 11, rather than Key 8. It does not necessarily change the interpretation of the card except in astrological correspondences.

The lion, symbolically a representation of zodiacal Leo, is thought to be the most powerful creature witnessed by man. Interestingly, another powerful animal, the serpent is also an important symbol to this path by the Hebrew letter Teth, assigned to this card which means snake.[9]

Because of its dominance as a top predator in nature, it is easy to see how the lion evolved into a popular emblem that reflects noble authority and dignity. It is often connected to fire and sun worship. The beaming rays of the sun are identified with the tawny-colored radiance of the male lion's mane.

Both the symbol of the lion and the snake are combined in an image representing the time god AION, a monstrous figure with the head of a lion and the body of a human entwined by a large serpent.

An interesting connection to mention is that Aion, a god of eternity, was also associated with time or the zodiac wheel and depicted with an orb or *ouroboros*, a snake with its tail in its mouth. Eternity is symbolized by the lemniscate appearing above the woman's head on most cards.

In some cases, this was a god of good, and in others considered a god of evil. Aion is connected to the Sun god Mithras.[9a] Tarot expert Robert Wang in *The Qabalistic Tarot* mentions that "the lion is occasionally related to Saturn' another time god. (Robert Wang, The Qabalistic Tarot. York Beach, Maine, Samuel Weiser, Inc., 206.)

Although "brute force" is the implied meaning of this card, in most decks the force seems applied with pliant yet steady grace that Dr. Wang notes could be used "constructively or destructively."[9b]

We are motivated by our desires. The lion and the woman dressed in pure white garments are enmeshed in a garland of flowers in Waite's version. It shows the delicate nuances intertwined between our human and animal natures.

Although the lion is a dangerous predator, in Waite's card he appears docile or tamed. The two figures meet with a mutual respect, if not love for one another. This represents the love humans have for nature and also animal lovers. Biological and emotional urges can overwhelm us if they are not kept in balance.

According to some, Strength suggests a take on the legend of Hercules. The woman on this card represents a heroine who has taken her power back and is no longer afraid to take on challenges.

Tarot Coupling Keywords

Positive Qualities: Graceful, stable, and sympathizing

Wounds/Fear: Mistrust, overly controlled

Perception of Partner: Rebellious, methodical, and persistent

Dyadic Interaction: Wants conformity and tries to control

Challenges: Learning to be less suspicious and giving freedom

Complaints of Partner: Unable to hold things together; uncooperative

Desires: Consistency, leadership, and loyalty

General Interpretation

This card shows a maiden who has decided to confront her fears. As the name of the card implies, now is the time to progress and become stronger. Endurance and strong wills are a must in times of struggle. You are learning that you can use sensitivity and love to conquer challenges.

Potentially, one partner is a bully or one or both partners try to manipulate a way out of a situation instead of using diplomacy and tact to achieve peace. Sometimes, it may be necessary to restrain yourself in order to keep the peace.

It is crucial to guard what is valuable in the relationship and subdue energies that uncontrollably well up causing negative reactions. Now is the time for your shame to become your glory.

NEW

You muster up the courage to ask out a love interest you've admired from afar. You may agree to go on a blind date set up by an acquaintance. You may feel it silly to live by a certain set of rules and allow yourself to be flexible around partnership choices.

ESTABLISHED

You may confront issues that welled up from the past with new insight. Through maturing and healing you have learned to be less angry and more forgiving toward your partner.

EXPANDED AWARENESS

Avoidance of a problem delays putting it behind you. It is time to take responsibility for your actions and perhaps notice how you have contributed to past mistakes. It is important to consider underlying forces, such as parental influence or sociocultural factors that blocks your path to relationship harmony.

One of the strengths of this connection is the partner's ability to influence each other in positive ways. The lion would be an inspiring totem for the relationship used a positive reminder to remain diligent in the face of obstacles.

DETERIORATING

One or both partners attack through criticism and finding fault. You are not acting in the most loving way towards yourself or your partner. After much rationalizing and soul searching, a decision is reached to end a relationship.

ROMANTIC SUGGESTIONS

Movie: *The Chronicles of Narnia: The Lion, the Witch and the Wardrobe* (2005 Walt Disney Pictures)

Starring: Tilda Swinton, Georgie Henley, and William Moseley

Date/Outing: Plan a visit to a local zoo

Gift Ideas: Furry slippers, animal print fabrics or clothing, a membership to a gym or strength conditioning class, or make a donation to your favorite animal cause

Most Compatible Cards: The Emperor, The Lovers, and Temperance

Least Compatible Cards: Death, The Hierophant, and The Moon

IX. THE HERMIT

GOLDEN DAWN/ESOTERIC TITLE: Prophet of the Eternal, Magus of the Voice of Power
HEBREW LETTER: Yod
MEANING: Hand
SIMPLE LETTER: Sexual Love
QABALISTIC ATTRIBUTION: Twentieth – Intelligence of Will
ELEMENT: Mutable Earth
SIGN: Virgo

*And an highway shall be there, and a way, and it shall be called The way of
holiness; the unclean shall not pass over it; but it shall be for those: the wayfaring
men, though fools, shall not err therein.*

*~Isaiah 35:8
King James Bible
(Cambridge Ed.)*

GENERAL COMMENTARY

Key 9 – The Hermit is one of several cards in the deck whose appearance in
a reading evokes ambivalence to the questioner. This could be due to the fact
that not many people identify with isolation, which is associated with monks
and spiritual aesthetics.

The Hermit, traditionally portrayed as the archetypical wise old man, sits or
travels alone in search of some higher truth. Separating oneself from society is not
something we find easy as social creatures. It is a very extraordinary commitment
to ascetics to be able to withdraw from all that is familiar and dedicate one's life
to spiritual pursuits.

Alternate titles have been given to this card, such as the "Hunchback" and
the "Old Man."[9c]

A typical card will show an aged, bearded man wearing the cloak of a simple
monk. The cloak's hood is often shaped to resemble the Hebrew letter Yod.

In some versions of this card, the elderly wanderer appears with an animal,
usually a snake that may be coiled around the tall staff carried by the hermit.
The serpent coiled around a branch or staff is a symbol for Asclepius, the ancient
god of healing and medicine. The snake is a symbol of wisdom known to possess
healing properties in its venom.

This monastic figure also carries a lantern lighting his path as he crosses
arid deserts and a frozen mountain landscape. The lantern replaced an hourglass,

an emblem of Time, another original title and most probable meaning for this card. It was only later that The Hermit was then accepted as a wise man of age living in solitude.

The mountains are a place of ascent a "symbol of transcendence."[9d] It is where the Hermit goes to connect with Spirit and the Higher Self. The mountains have long been known as the place where the gods resided, such as Mount Olympus.

In contrast, the desert is a place of exclusion, despair, and spiritual darkness. Hermits went to the desert, withdrawn from society to feed his urging of high spiritual transcendence and in order to gain the highest spiritual opulence and perfection.

This urging, Thomas Moore tells us in *Soul Mates: Honoring the Mysteries of Love and Relationships*, was The Wise Old Man as an archetype that Jung from time to time thought was the equivalent of humankind's love of meaning. The Hermit also makes his way on the path to find the meaning of the things he wishes to understand.

Tarot Coupling Keywords

Positive Qualities: Self-reliant, pure, wise and oracular

Wounds/Fear: Ostracism, restricted and rejected

Perception of Partner: Lacks ability, calculating nosey, intrusive and inclusive

Dyadic Interaction: Independent and excludes from life

Challenges: Sharing and joining in partner's activities

Complaints of Partner: Bothered by others. Partner seems to demand much of your time

Desires: A healing relationship and freedom to grow

General Interpretation

You are concerned with life as a single when this card appears in a reading – whether truly single and seeking love or preferring to have some space in your current relationship, The Hermit indicates that your own introspection and getting in touch with a deeper part of your inner wisdom is needed.

The Hermit's lantern represents a bright spark of consciousness. You may grow more conscious about what you desire from a partner through keen spiritual awareness.

Maturity and experience are keys in dealing with certain behaviors in human relationships. Many times giving a person space is a necessity for the survival of the connection.

Do you feel that your partner is isolating you from friends or family? Closeness is nice; however, if they are doing this out of their own insecurity, it is not such a good thing. There is a sense of detachment or ostracism.

Fear of being alone is causing you stress at this point in your life. You cling to your partner because you may have a hard time with the possibility of not being with someone. You could find yourself on a search for your true love. You desire something serious and no longer want short-term, fun relationships.

New

You may be newly single or have been living the single life for sometime. If you are single by choice, then know that there is nothing wrong with your choice and you should celebrate your singleness. After a long period of celibacy, it's time to get it on!

Established

While you are in a relationship you may find yourself plagued by loneliness. This may be something that you are not able to articulate to your partner. It may be time to do some soul searching around why you are experiencing such a lonely state.

Expanded Awareness

Give your partner a chance to support you when you feel alone. The time has to see the bigger picture or look at things from a higher perspective. Time spent apart may be a blessing in disguise. Nine is the number of completeness. Many people feel that a relationship adds wholeness to their life, but The Hermit teaches the importance of retaining individuality regardless of your attachment to your partner.

Deteriorating

This card suggests that one or both of you are not suited to settle down in a committed long-term partnership. Hermits are not necessarily willing to give up their freedom. Their sense of adventure matches their need to explore and search for the meaning of life. They are often not the best relationship partners.

Romantic Suggestions

Movie: *Extreme Pilgrim* – TV Series (2008)
Starring: Peter Owen-Jones
Date/Outing: Take a break from one another for the evening by doing something you want to do all by yourself
Gift Ideas: Candles, a new robe, or a winter cloak
Most Compatible Cards: The Devil and The Magician
Least Compatible Cards: The Emperor, The Sun

X. THE WHEEL OF FORTUNE

GOLDEN DAWN/ESOTERIC TITLE: The Lord of the Forces of Life
HEBREW LETTER: Caph
MEANING: Fist
DOUBLE LETTER: Richness – Poverty
QABALISTIC ATTRIBUTION: Twenty-First – Intelligence of Conciliation
ELEMENT: Fire/Water
PLANET: Jupiter

From sullen earth, sings hymns at heaven's gate;
For thy sweet love remembered such wealth brings
That then I scorn to change my state with kings.

~William Shakespeare
Sonnet 19

GENERAL COMMENTARY

Key 10 – The wheel is one of those ever-present symbols in human existence. It represents constant change, motion, and the Law of Cycles. The depiction of the card has many variations and has just as many interpretations. Most associate this card with its name, The Wheel of Fortune, meaning fortune or luck.

The wheel, a symbol of the goddess Fortuna, represents the ancient concept of fate and the future. It's turning indicative of time, karma, life, death, and rebirth.

Fortuna, often pictured as a blindfolded woman, was referred to as an insane and fickle goddess. She operated the wheel by turning its hub, moving the figures riding it in alternating forward and backward motion, creating unsteadiness, which was beyond their control. Figures on the wheel were symbolic of the fours stages of life: childhood, adulthood, maturity, and death.

Our ancestors saw a cyclic pattern in the seasons and thus used the wheel to symbolize the Universe. The Wheel of Fortune places emphasis on other cyclic patterns found in the natural world.

In alchemy, the wheel represents spiritual highs and lows, a cyclic process of circulation and change. In addition to the change of seasons, the wheel is used to show the zodiacal signs fixed in the starry night sky.

Found in every corner of the globe, man's creations of circular patterns of wheel configurations exist in stone. Seemingly mysterious, the ancients made a natural connection between the wheel and the sun. Many cultures declared the sun sacred and dedicated circular altars, mounds, and temples for worship of the sun as the most Supreme Being.

Waite's Wheel of Fortune shows in each corner one of four Cherubim or Holy Living Creatures that appeared in Ezekiel's vision. The bull, lion, man, and eagle are powerful symbols in astrology. Most notably, they are the Christian representation of the four evangelists, Matthew, Mark, Luke, and John.

Each creature holds a book possibly signifying different levels of knowing or pieces of higher knowledge. The four creatures also correspond to the four elements and the signs of Taurus, Leo, Scorpio, and Aquarius. A sphinx is often pictured on decks along with a serpent and a jackal-headed creature known as Hermanubis.[9e]

TAROT COUPLING KEYWORDS
Positive Qualities: Productive, efficient, docile
Wounds/Fear: Feels undeserving, unaccomplished, and loss of approval
Perception of Partner: Needs to win, values success over emotions
Dyadic Interaction: Sabotage and patronizing
Challenges: Accepting ups and downs
Complaints of Partner: Never gets credit for effort
Desires: Luck in love, increase, whirlwind romance

GENERAL INTERPRETATION
You are adored by your love ones and they feel blessed to have you in their life. Your relationship flows well despite fluctuations of good and bad times.

Jupiter brings increase and expansion to you when this card appears in a reading. This is a card of generosity, destiny, and good fortune.

Generally, when this card is drawn, it speaks to a very good omen. When bad times occur, you can be assured that good times will soon follow as part of Fortune's spin of the Wheel.

Positive changes and improvement are highlights of your relationship. You may feel quite lucky about your chances at love.

There could be a repeating pattern of attracting the same type of partner and those typically turn out the same way. It may serve you well to educate yourself on love and relationships especially if you have not had great success in love in the past.

The Wheel of Fortune appears to remind you that life is about success and misfortune. The only things you can control are your actions. These actions in turn have consequences. Make sure to live with honor and you will see things manifest in positive ways.

New

A chance meeting provides opportunity for a new love. You are feeling hopeful about a new love interest. There is a belief that you are destined to meet a soul mate. Your new relationship is on the brink of a new phase and perhaps after resolving a minor setback it will progress to the next serious phase and you decide to date exclusively.

Established

Love is being tested by life's ups and downs. Although your relationship is generally harmonious, issues at work or other life stresses, like a vehicle that needs to be repaired, may not put you in the most romantic mood.

Expanded Awareness

Disagreements are a natural part of any relationship's cycle. Notice the patterns when you and your partner have differences. Pay attention and become attuned to the fluctuations of your relationship. By doing so, you may move more quickly through the times that don't flow so well.

Deteriorating

An unfortunate incident may be the cause of a relationship dilemma when this card appears in an ill-dignified position. You may desperately be trying to return to happier times, but are quickly losing hope. One or both partners are continuing to act in a manner that does not benefit the relationship.

Romantic Suggestions

Movie: *The Five-Year Engagement* (2012)
Starring: Jason Segel, Emily Blunt, and Chris Pratt
Date/Outing: A Ferris wheel ride, skating, or a Sunday drive to the countryside
Gift Ideas: Hershey's® Peanut Butter Cups, a watch, or a clock
Most Compatible Cards: Justice, Strength, and The Moon
Least Compatible Cards: Judgment and The World

XI. JUSTICE

GOLDEN DAWN/ESOTERIC TITLE: The Daughter of The Lords of Truth; the Ruler of the Balance
HEBREW LETTER: Lamed
MEANING: Ox Goad
SIMPLE LETTER: Work
QABALISTIC ATTRIBUTION: Twenty Second – Faithful Intelligence
ELEMENT: Air
SIGN: Libra

Power at its best is love implementing the demands of justice, and justice at its best is power correcting everything that stands against love.

~Martin Luther King, Jr.

GENERAL COMMENTARY

Key 11 – Justice is a classic virtue of fairness and equality. This card is commonly associated with justice, balance, moral law, and regulation of opposing forces.

Often depicted as a seated woman, Justice is usually holding scales, referred to as the scales of justice, and wielding a large sword, sometimes referred to as the sword of justice. Justice has been associated with the Egyptian concept of the weighing of souls in the afterlife. The Egyptians believed the soul has to be weighed and measured against the feather of Maat, the goddess of universal order and truth.[9f]

Similar to Cupid, Justice is often depicted wearing a blindfold as a symbol of her impartiality. Blindness is also a metaphor for objective viewing. Symbolizing inner vision or clairvoyance, "second sight" is considered the source of spiritual illumination.

As the Faithful Intelligence, Justice guides balance of mind and body. Lady Justice sits upon a throne between two columns with the cloth of honor draped behind.[9g] In Waite's design, the figure wears a red robe, which signifies the Hermetic connection to Mars, and a green stole and cloak, the color of Venus, which rules Libra, the astrological attribute assigned to this path long symbolized by scales. Libra falls during the calendar cycle where day and night are in equal balance.[10]

Scales measure items of value and substance. Eventually, the idea of human principles and actions were "measured" as a summary of how one lived. A verdict is rendered at the end of an individual's life in death. This principle was crucial to the Egyptian preoccupation with the afterlife.

In most decks, the figure is female and wears a jeweled crown or other elaborated headpiece. Waite's figure wears a square-shaped cloak pin that also represents equilibrium and balance.

Although balance is more commonly the theme of this card, reincarnation, karma, and truth are also key aspects here. This is a path where, in the pursuit of justice, the process is not necessarily pleasant. Sometimes the scales tip in a seemingly unfair direction. In Justice, the notions of right or wrong and bad or good are nonexistent. The belief of reaping and sowing are ways by which justice is served.

Tarot Coupling Keywords

Positive Qualities: Merciful, faithful, and trustworthy

Impairment/Fear: Fear of punishment

Perception of Partner: Unfair and rigid

Dyadic Interaction: Scrutinizing and judgmental

Challenges: Impartiality, non-judgment of partner's talents

Complaints of Partners: Needs to be heard, unjust treatment, criticism

Desires: Fairness, stability, peace, make love, not war

General Interpretation

"All is fair in love and war," so the saying goes. You may want your partner to play by some unspoken rules. You and your partner may equally contribute to the success of your relationship. Sometimes one finds they give more than a fair share. Hold no resentment towards your partner, for they may feel the exact same way.

Truth and honesty are top priority for this coupling.

Libra is the sign of partnerships and relatedness. You feel best when you have a partner and seek to share your life with someone at any cost. Rules and boundaries are at the foundation of your relationship perimeters. If ideals or expectations for the relationship have not been communicated, now is the perfect time.

An inherited sense of entitlement (spoiled rotten) makes it seem that one of you owes the other in some way. It may be a sense of entitlement. You may want to give this relationship a second chance in order to improve on things that did not go well previously.

New

Truth and trust are the foundation of your relationship. You may see a few flaws in your new partner, but are willing to let go certain prejudices that may stem from your own insecurities. Pros and cons are weighed before getting romantically attached.

Established

The beauty of your connection is due to mutual trustworthiness and acceptance. Healthy boundaries are established and respected in your relationship. You and your partner may want to have a deeper connection and commit legally to one another through a civil ceremony or other contracts.

Expanded Awareness

It may be time to look at all sides of a matter and reach a balanced, well-considered solution. Stand up for your rights. Making things official may entail dealings with lawyers or lawmakers. Be mindful of harsh self-judgment.

Deteriorating

Reason has gone out the window. Neither partner can live within the strict boundaries set by the other. Mistakes are scrutinized and feelings of unfairness and misjudgment surface.

Romantic Suggestions

Movie: *The Pelican Brief* (1993)
Starring: Julia Roberts and Denzel Washington
Date/Outing: Art galleries, lectures, theatre, and fine dining; spend time organizing all of your official documents; create a will
Gift Ideas: Office furniture, a decorative sword, kitchen or hunting knives
Most Compatible Cards: The Lovers and The Star
Least Compatible Cards: The Moon and Judgment

XII. THE HANGED MAN

GOLDEN DAWN/ESOTERIC TITLE: The Spirit of The Mighty Waters
HEBREW LETTER: Mem
MEANING: Water
MATERNAL LETTER: Water
QABALISTIC ATTRIBUTION: Twenty-Third – Stable of Intelligence
ELEMENT: Water
PLANET: Neptune

> *He lost his Self a thousand times and for days on end he dwelt in nonbeing.*
> ~*Siddhartha* by **Hermann Hesse**
> (New Directions edition translated by Hilda Rosner)

GENERAL COMMENTARY

Key 12 – It is curious how The Hanged Man caused such an impressive stir over the centuries. The complication here is that the card conflicts being called the Stable Intelligence. A stable intelligence in psychological terms is indicative of healthy psychic symmetry.

What could be considered a very unfortunate position appears tolerable by the figure's expression in some decks. The upsidedown figure hangs in an unfortunate position with a noose around his ankle from the gallows, a T-shaped tree, or in Crowley's version, a reversed ankh. It is difficult to conclude whether the figure's demise is the result of punishment of others or is self-imposed.

Being surrounded by so much wood, it's hard to make the connection to water that is so significant to the Qabalistic association.

To get a better understanding of this card, one needs to delve into historical references for perspective.

The Hanged Man would have been well recognized and common in most of Northern Renaissance Italy.

Renaissance artists were regularly commissioned to paint *pittura infamanti*, meaning "defamation portraits," as a way of ridicule or shaming targeted individuals.[11]

Portraying an offender in this manner was done so that the victim's reputation was beyond repair. The pittura infamanit, of which there were many on the walls of the Bargello located in Florence, was an iconic portrait of "traitors" in the domain that made its way into the Tarot pack.

The figure brings to mind the myth of the demigod Achilles, who's mother held him by the foot baptizing him in the river Styx, or fire in some versions, to make him immortal.

Baptism and purification are the basis of all religious rites as a preparation that symbolized the washing away of sin, and it was also a rite centered on the mother's naming of a newborn child.[12]

Clues for possible origins in the symbolism of this card, point to Italian cathedral frescos in which artists would portray the gruesome horrors of hell.

In Bologna, Italy, inside the San Petronio Basilica, is a fresco by Giovanni da Modena. In this work, said to refer to King Ninus of Nineveh paying for his lustful sins, are two figures hung by the foot, one faces forward and the other backwards.[13]

The hanging pair resembles another story familiar to early Christian and Jewish scholars from approximately the second century B.C., in *The Book of Enoch*. It is the legend of two angels, Semjaya (Shemhazai) and Azazel along with 200 other angels who made a pact to go to earth and take human wives.[14]

In one version, both angels, bound hand and foot, were cast into the abyss with their followers and were unable to lift their eyes to heaven.

In another version, to pay for his grave sin Semjaya (Shemhazai), ashamed of facing God, suspended himself between heaven and earth head downward with rope for all eternity.

One possible place that Semjaya (Shemhazai) could have hung himself by a rope was from the "World Tree or Axis Mundi" believed to connect heaven, earth, and hell. (Philip Coppens, *The Stone Puzzle of Rosslyn Chapel*, 3rd Edition. Enkhuizen: Frontier Publishing, Adventures Unlimited Press, 2004.109.)

Enoch himself saw a great tree when he was taken through various parts of heaven and the earth by the archangels. Enoch's report of the places where sinners were punished seemed to contain a great many valleys, water, trees, and mountains; these places of the last judgment were depicted in church frescos.

This story tells of the Great Flood that was during the times of Noah. The flood was and still is of great significance to religion. Of course, one could find that God would have used the Spirit of The Mighty Waters to flood the earth; this of course is the esoteric title of this card.

Interestingly, a carving of a bound angelic figure hanging upside down can be found in Rosslyn Chapel of Scotland that is said to be of great importance to the Knights Templar and Freemasonry.[14]

The Qur'an also features a story of two angels, Harut and Marut, that came to earth and eventually succumbed to human lusts. They apparently suffered the same punishment of being hung upside down. Thus, this became the symbol of the shamed and penitent sinner.

Many references associated the figure as the betrayer to Christ, Judas Iscariot. Another name for the card from early decks is "The Traitor."

Ultimately, when one considers the story in both Genesis and *The Book of Enoch*, as well as other creation myths, it appears that the greatest error committed by any of God's creation were those of lust, pride, betrayal, revealing divine secrets, and misuse of power. These are the same offenses that would cause an enemy of Italy to have his likeness defamed.

By placing oneself in an altered or suspended state, one is allowed a different perspective and vision of most wondrous things and becomes like a shaman or "skywalker" that travels between heaven and earth.[16] (Ibid.)

Tarot Coupling Keywords

Positive Qualities: Consistent, passionate, intuitive, intelligent

Wounds/Fear: Betrayal and instability

Perception of Partner: Truth seeking, loyal, sometimes mistrustful; savior, difficulty with faults of others

Dyadic Interaction: Martyr, passive; hero worship

Challenges: Trusting self, escapism and others

Complaints of Partner: Uses guilt to obtain wishes; stalls; silent

Desires: Heroism, perfection, attuned to needs, eternal love.

General Interpretation

When The Hanged Man appears in a reading, it suggests that life has come to a phase that seems stagnant or at an impasse. Nothing seems right and it may require that you change your attitude or perspective. The key here is to not create chaos, but stability and consistency. It is the natural state we once existed in inside our mother's womb.

The Hanged Man also calls attention to anything we do not allow ourselves to think about. This is a coping mechanism in which disassociation occurs. Disassociation can be due to feeling betrayed or harmed in some way by someone you love. Those who are closest to us are the ones who usually hurt us. Forgiveness requires a willingness to sacrifice anger, shame, and guilt.

In a relationship, partners have different points of views. In order to keep the peace, there may be a shift or new way of reasoning by one or both partners.

New

A new love interest is perfect for you and you feel inspired. You are open to new ideas about finding a suitable mate. You feel hesitation about asking for a date with someone who seems out of your league. There is no interest in getting caught up in a serious relationship until your head and heart are in the right place.

Established

The relationship that quickly moved to exclusivity at the onset, has settled into monotonousness. Your partner means more to you now than ever. Unwarranted thoughts about betrayal or losing your partner dangle in your mind, but you cannot find out the cause.

Couples perceive each other's everyday needs because they are so highly attuned to one another. Being together helps you have a different outlook on life than previously.

Expanded Awareness

The relationship is viewed through rose-colored glasses. To you, the connection is a dream come true and you will probably do anything for him or her, including sacrificing your own needs at times. Use this time to compose yourself and plan for the next phase.

Deteriorating

Potentially, you are the only one making sacrifices in this relationship. Things are up in the air perhaps due to feelings of betrayal or procrastination and delayed decision-making from one or both partners. One or both partners have a difficult time working through problems because of thoughtfully analyzing the problems rather than having productive conversation to resolve the issue(s).

Indecisiveness could be the result due to the lack of trust in yourself and perhaps a low self-confidence. The very thing that you desire could also restrain you. You want a relationship but fear a loss of freedom.

Romantic Suggestions

Movie: *Hang 'Em High* (1968)
Starring: Clint Eastwood, Inger Stevens, and Pat Hingle
Date/Outing: Switch up your routine and duties
Gift Ideas: Resistance training class or exercise equipment, designer sunglasses
Most Compatible Cards: The Hierophant, Death, and The Moon
Least Compatible Cards: The Lovers and Justice

XIII. DEATH

Golden Dawn/Esoteric Title: Golden Dawn/Esoteric Title – The Child of the Great Transformers; the Lord of the Gates of Death

Hebrew Letter: Nun

Meaning: Fish

Simple Letter: Movement

Qabalistic Attribution: Twenty-Fourth – Imaginative Intelligence

Element: Water

Sign: Scorpio

Each night, when I go to sleep, I die. And the next morning, when I wake up, I am reborn.
~Mahatma Gandhi

General Commentary

Key 13 – Waite's depiction of Death, mostly recognized from the Book of Revelation, relays a vision of the prophet St. John the Divine. While on the island of Patmos, he envisions a figure on a pale horse and revealed that his name is Death. In different regions of the world, the ghastly figure is often found depicted as a skeleton or an old woman and sometimes even an innocent youth.

The mounted black armored skeleton of the Death card, was a common depiction in medieval art, which inspired the Waite/Smith version.[17]

In front of the white horse, appears a bishop dressed in ceremonial robes and a miter on his head.

Writer Judd Burton, in an article on the website About.com notes that miter headgear is purportedly an association to the fish-tailed god Dagon, that "figured prominently in the Philistine concepts of death and the afterlife."[17a]

The horse is the carrier of the soul to the land of the dead. Horses are often seen as an omen of death.[18]

The armored skeleton is a reminder that bones are all that is left when our flesh no longer exists. It demonstrates the vulnerabilities of mortality. It is the structure upon which a newly protected and transformed spirit will be constructed.

Three other figures shown on Waite's version, and along with the papal figure, symbolize the four Qabalistic worlds and the Tetragrammaton. They represent stages of life and movement. They also show that death has no boundaries; it subjects all living creatures to the universal laws of death and renewal.

Death is known esoterically as The Child of the Great Transformers and also the Lord of the Gates of Death. In life we refer to death as "passing on"[18a] or going to "Heaven's Gates" to pass into the eternal.

Today's Tarot interpreters comment that Death's appearance in a reading rarely refers to a physical death; although its earlier interpretation apparently suggested it was obvious. However, the most profound meaning behind Key 13 is transformation and renewed living. Tony Crisp writes that dreaming about death also "reflects attitudes about dying and loss."[18b] At times, when this card appears, it is not about what is dying out or leaving your life, but more about what you are attempting to keep from dying and the fight to stay alive.

TAROT COUPLING KEYWORDS

Positive Qualities: Giving and willing to face change, patient
Wounds/Fear: Loss, difficulty with endings, anger
Perception of Partner: Intimidating, motivating, controlling
Dyadic Interaction: Minimizes or alters moods, power struggles
Challenges: Supporting partner through transitions
Complaints of Partners: Too final, no compromising
Desires: Profound change for the better, to be uplifted when down

GENERAL INTERPRETATION

Death exposes that which no longer serves your relationship, as well as as people or circumstances to eliminate from your life. Old ideas and other possessions that are outdated can be dissolved. Examine your readiness to release and do so when it feels right.

Relax and release. Relationships follows a symbolic rebirth and death much like seasonal changes. It is not likely that this card's appearance indicates physical death. However, ideas and fears surrounding death may be at the root of your anxiety.

Changes that you cannot see are happening. These may not be visible to you at this time, and you may need to push through to achieve your goals. Change, welcome or not, is inevitable.

Consider consequences when making any decision at this time. Choose wisely and make sure you thoroughly contemplate important decisions.

New beginnings are just as important when it comes to death. This card indicates movement through one phase of life to another, such as puberty, early adulthood, menopause, or maturity.

Your partner is a bearer of transformation and acts as a great catalyst for major changes.

New

A new prospect for a relationship is on the horizon. After a period of grieving, a past break-up, or recent passing of a long-term partner, you feel regenerated and are ready to pursue a relationship once more. This new interest is both exciting and frightening.

Established

A sense of dread or gloom concerns you. You constantly worry about your partner's leaving you or focus on death. In spite of difficulties in your relationship, this is still progress. There are skeletons in the closet that you need to confront in order to move to the next level of commitment.

Expanded Awareness

It is important to allow healing to occur. No matter how long you have been emotionally attached to someone, when things are over, a period of mourning occurs. You should honor the process and know that all things are temporary.

Deteriorating

The end draws near. There is nothing fun about staying on a sinking boat. The relationship is over but you may not have quite let go for fear of being alone, which for some is even more fearful than death. You may have been out of the relationship emotionally for a long time, but your living situation makes it difficult to just leave.

Romantic Suggestions

Movie: *Meet Joe Black* (1998)
Starring: Brad Pitt, Anthony Hopkins, and Claire Forlani
Date/Outing: Yard work, rake up dead leaves, and plant a tree in memory of someone special
Gift Ideas: Any black or white, flags, violet-scented candles
Most Compatible Cards: The Hermit, The Tower, and The Devil
Least Compatible Cards: The Emperor, The Hierophant, and The Lovers

XIV. TEMPERANCE

GOLDEN DAWN/ESOTERIC TITLE: The Daughter of the Reconcilers, the Bringer Forth of Life
HEBREW LETTER: Samekh
MEANING: Prop
SIMPLE LETTER: Anger
QABALISTIC ATTRIBUTION: Twenty-Fifth – Intelligence of Probation
ELEMENT: Fire
SIGN: Sagittarius

> You can not hope to arrive at harmony in your life while stirring up disturbances in anothers...
>
> ~Rasheed Ogunlaru

GENERAL COMMENTARY

Key 14 – A beautiful winged figure pouring liquid from one amphora to another is the standard depiction of Temperance.

In the *Visconti-Sforza Tarot*, the figure that represents the cardinal virtue of moderation does not have wings, and according to Michael Dummett, the wings depicted on the *Tarot of Marseille* were due to an artist mistaking the high back of a chair for wings.

As one of the cardinal virtues, Temperance is often symbolized as an androgynous figure mixing water and wine, although the liquid depicted in the cards is not clearly defined. In the classical context, Temperance, like all the virtues, were depicted as wingless females.

Temperance is a derivative of the French word *temps* meaning time, another significance applied to this card. The figure of one illustrated on the edge of a cliff was reinterpreted to depict an angelic creature with one foot on solid ground and the other foot in water, symbolically indicating that this angelic being existed both in the physical and ethereal worlds simultaneously.

The figure is akin to a guide accompanying souls from life to the darkness of underworld in its role as psychopomp, a daunting task given its light and non-threatening setting.

The darkness on this journey symbolizes the progress of the soul through trials and tests that can best be demonstrated by stories such as the Exodus and the temptation of Jesus. This is a path of temptation, testing, and time. Temperance is called the Intelligence of Probation thus growth is progressed through character-building tasks.

Depending on the tradition, Temperance is sometimes presumed to be either Archangel Michael or Archangel Raphael. The connection to Raphael is the Hebrew letter *samekh* meaning "prop or crutch" that is also an emblem of Asclepius, the god of healing and Saturn, the Father of Time who was portrayed on crutches.

Archangel Raphael is the ruling angel of medicine, healing, surgeons, travel, overseer of the evening winds, chief of the order of virtues and regent of the Sun. Temperance is also attributed to the fiery Sagittarius, the Centaur and with Adnakiel, the ruling archangel of this zodiac sign and the month of November.

Three of the lowest paths of The Moon (Qoph), Judgment (Shin), and The World (Tau) spell the word "bow" or "rainbow" in Hebrew.[19] The yellow irises illustrated on Waite's version are a reference to the Greek goddess Iris who was the goddess of the rainbow and also a messenger of the gods.

In Greek mythology, Iris is often depicted carrying a vase in which she carries the waters of the river Styx, which was used by Zeus to test the other gods, verifying the truthfulness of their oath to him. If the offending god was found to be dishonest, he was placed on probation from Olympia.

Temperance references both the Sun and the Moon often depicted by gold and silver cups respectively.

This card leads the individual to the beginning of awareness of the Higher Self found in Tiphareth. The symbols on the card attempt to explain the experience of initiation on the path of spiritual evolution.

In the ancient art of transmutation, known as alchemy, temperance means "to mix" or "to bring together." Alchemy is often associated with the process of turning base metals into gold or silver. In its deeper sense, alchemy is a means of spiritual and personal perfection.

The important meanings of Temperance refer to its process of spiritual and physical path work and to build up a tolerance for the newly evolved "light body." This process needs constant surveillance and testing from the higher realms, hence the presence of the angel assigned at the inner gate for our protection.

Samekh is also translated as anger and lends to another interesting interpretation of Temperance. The idea of anger in this sense is that of a passion and rage that is divinely inspired. The word refers to a motion of vibrating or quivering with such force that it propels one into ecstasy – a spiritual orgasmic release.[20]

This card expresses the exchange of opposites, the interchange of Fire and Water, though all elements are present in this card.

TAROT COUPLING KEYWORDS

Positive Qualities: Creative, active, happy and optimistic

Wounds/Fear: Restriction, alienation

Perception of Partner: Mixed messages or moodiness

Dyadic Interaction: Influential, blunt, insists on information.
Challenges: Combining ideas and sharing physical space
Complaints of Partners: Disassociation and Unrealistic expectations
Desires: Humor and adventure

GENERAL INTERPRETATION

Self-restraint is the most basic and classic meaning of Temperance. Anger is one of those emotions that we have been conditioned to restrain early in life as a child. For example, parents are seemingly embarrassed when a child throws a temper tantrum in public and they are at loss as to how they should calm the child down.

In the meantime, you are in the midst of an episode of stress and your sense of peace has suddenly become included in the mix of chaotic expressions that are beyond your control, and you in turn have to restrain your own reactions.

Temperance implies blending of two opposites. It is true that relationships are most certainly the source of mixed emotions. It takes coordination of schedules or timing and perhaps an understanding of each other's worlds.

NEW

During the acquaintance phase of the relationship, couples are responding to chemical reactions that make up the feelings of falling in love. The heart flutters when your new love walks into the room, but sometimes it happens from simple thoughts throughout the day.

Due to the newness of the relationship, there is a tendency to control or modify old patterns of behavior. There is a sense and a chance that your partner is testing the depths of your feelings.

ESTABLISHED

Anyone in a long-term partnership can relate to the occasional compromise from time to time. There may be episodes of stress and strain on your relationship and one or both members are a bit snappy towards the other. On the other hand, a little romance may be in order to relieve pressures of stress.

EXPANDED AWARENESS

Things are changing and it's not your imagination. For both men and women this card suggests a potential chemical or biological reason for loss of the spark you once felt.

In the meantime, the right mix would make this relationship one where you both could create a very prosperous life. You both have the ability to generate wealth resulting in a blessed life.

Deteriorating

Like morning dew evaporates as the day progresses, you feel the chemistry is dissolving from your connection. You no longer see eye to eye, and you are reluctant to adjust your feelings for the sake of keeping peace. Heated arguments and clashing ideas happen more frequently.

Romantic Suggestions

Movie: *The Nutty Professor* (1996)
Starring: Eddie Murphy, Jada Pinkett Smith, and James Coburn
Date/Outing: An afternoon at a science or history museum
Gift Ideas: Wine decanter, goblets, or steins
Most Compatible Cards: Wheel of Fortune, Strength, and Justice
Least Compatible Cards: The Hierophant, The Moon, and The World

XV. THE DEVIL

GOLDEN DAWN/ESOTERIC TITLE: The Lord of The Gates of Matter; the Child of the Forces of Time
HEBREW LETTER: Ayin
MEANING: Eye
SIMPLE LETTER: Mirth
QABALISTIC ATTRIBUTION: Twenty-Sixth – Renovating Intelligence
ELEMENT: Earth
SIGN: Capricorn

GENERAL COMMENTARY

Key 15 – The Devil is first encountered by most Westerners in scriptural texts as a serpent, the tempter of Eve in the Garden of Eden. The Devil is the archetypal opposite of good. He is called by many names including Lucifer, the Prince of Darkness, and the Antichrist.

As far how the notability of the Devil came about, in *History of The Devil,* Paul Carus tells us:

of the accounts gleaned from Waitz, Lubbock, and Tylor, on the Primitive state of religion, the conviction impresses itself upon the student of demonology that Devil-worship naturally precedes the worship of a benign and morally good Deity.

An interesting twist in worship of deity was observed to originate from the exhalation of the lower stage of Devil worship to the heights of worship of God. Carus further explains:

this is the reason why the dark figure of the Devil, a powerful evil deity, looms up as the most important personage in the remotest past of almost every faith.

The Devil was a prominent figure in Jewish texts that highly influenced Christian ideas.

Humans have long feared things that they could not see nor control, especially sinister forces. Everything that was light and good was associated with God and everything negative and bad associated with the Prince of Darkness.

In one of the earliest depictions of the Last Judgment on a mosaic in Ravenna, Italy, about 500 A.D., there appears a portrayal of an angelic figure on Christ's left-hand side garbed in blue. Along with this angel are goats. On the right side is an angel in red shown with sheep. It is a portrayal of the Gospel of Matthew's referencing the separation of sheep and goats during the Second Coming.

Since there was no definitive description of the Devil's appearance, the goat was associated with Satan due to its unusually sinister look. Since Satan or Lucifer were known to be angels, albeit fallen, he was still illustrated as beautiful in appearance.

Starting in the medieval period, this diabolical figure became a frightening creature. It is not out of place to see that The Devil is found illustrated on medieval church walls. In a few of the early hand-painted decks, The Devil is missing or believed to be omitted for a reason.

Tarot Coupling Keywords

Positive Qualities: Seductive, fun-loving, clever, and ambitious

Impairment/Fear: Abuse, too weak, not powerful, intimacy

Perception of Partner: Cruel, impatient, shadowy, materialistic

Dyadic Interaction: Oppositional, cynical, provokes and creates chaos

Challenges: Overcoming addictions, sexual inadequacy, and facing fears

Complaints of Partners: Never satisfied, impulse and control issues.

Desires: Domination, indulgence, and sense of humor

General Interpretation

This card suggests the darker aspects and consequences of love. Relationships could suffer hardships and become unpleasant. Many scholars think that without evil, there is no purpose for good and vice versa. Blame, guilt, and shame are all represented in this card.

In a reading, it suggests dealing with your own "demons." With much negativity, things are not allowed nourishment and light. Natural goodness and innocent desires often become perversions.

In most cases, this card indicates a level of fear, selfishness, and narcissism. It also represents addiction, temptation, and other negative vices. Lust, magic, and sorcery are additional interpretations for this card.

New

You may try to discover the source of your attraction and find someone you'd never date, but find alluring. You wonder whether interest in a relationship is based on love or lust.

Established

Should you feel anger towards your partner, a heart-to-heart may be in order. You could suffer in silence due to guilt over a misdeed. Jealousy and envy are not necessarily negative signs for the relationship. While potentially bothersome, these are a manifestation of an individual's insecurity or self-consciousness.

Expanded Awareness

You may become increasingly aware of your or your partner's negativity that has manifested into a force to be reckoned with and you are considering a spiritual approach as a resolution. This could mean it is time for self-reliance.

Deteriorating

This indicates an obsessed personality in some cases. Perhaps your partner is keeping close tabs on you or doesn't respect personal boundaries. Are you with a "bunny-boiler"? Don't make excuses or ignore your intuition when something does not feel right. It is also a warning to protect your sexual health and practice safe sex.

Romantic Suggestions

Movie: *Bram Stoker's Dracula* (1992)

Starring: Anthony Hopkins, Gary Oldman, and Keanu Reeves

Date/Outing: Shopping for erotic toys, a masquerade party, spend the evening indulging in your passions

Gift Ideas: Lingerie, sex toys (him or hers), satin sheets, musk fragrances, or a kitchen spice rack

Most Compatible Cards: The Moon and Death

Least Compatible Cards: The Lovers and Justice

XVI. TOWER

GOLDEN DAWN/ESOTERIC TITLE: The Lord of the Hosts of the Mighty
HEBREW LETTER: Peh
MEANING: Mouth
DOUBLE LETTER: Grace-Indignation
QABALISTIC ATTRIBUTION: Twenty-Seventh – Exciting Intelligence
ELEMENT: Fire/Water
PLANET: Mars

GENERAL COMMENTARY

Key 16 – This card sometimes has a lightning bolt pulverizing the roof of a tower with two figures falling headfirst from a burning building, although on some decks, only the lightning bolt appears. In others, we see in place of a lightning bolt, a burst of flames shooting from a radiant sun above.

Many see this card as The Tower of Babel or the destructive period of The Last Judgment, both commonly portrayed on church walls.

The French term given to this card, *la Maison Dieu* (the House of God) adopted for the *Tarot de Marseille,* is thought to be a mistranslation. On the Italian side, this trump was call "Hell" or "House of the Damned"(Casa de Dannato).[20] Robert Wang in *The Qabalistic Tarot* explains that The Tower is a reference to explosive orgasmic virility of Martian energy. He explains that "the Mars energy is a universal sexual force of Microprosopus, and that the image of the Tower is some (though not all) ways the phallus."[22] Even though most would agree that the tower represents the phallus, Wang further writes: "the symbolism does not mean that the path is exclusive to those functioning in male incarnations. The Path of Peh exists prior to the point of differentiation of the sexes for incarnation, and is thus an amalgam of both masculine and feminine energies."[23]

The bolt of lighting also dominates the card, which is often relayed to the biblical tower of Babel account. In the story of "The Tower of Babel," the tower and ways of communication among the people were destroyed as punishment for their arrogance and boldness; however, lightening is not specifically mentioned as the cause of the tower's demise.

Lightening is often a precursor to powerful storms, and has long been associated with the Zeus and other powerful storm gods. Often the appearance of lightening was considered an expression of deity's displeasure with humankind. We now know that positive and negative electrical charges are the result of lightning. Lightning is quick and happens all of a sudden, which is one of the interpretations of this card. Lightning also represents clarity and a flash of genius. The Lightening Flash or Path of the Flaming Sword is an important concept in Qabalistic teachings and demonstrates a sequential flow of evolution.

Towers are often set in surroundings that isolate them from other parts of a building, city, or fort. While this separateness is an important element in the symbolism of this card as Wang notes, it does not relay any weakness; instead, towers were often distinguished as the last stronghold, or last to be conquered, in a seize, which shows it to be a symbol of strength as well as an impregnable defense.

The attribution to Mars, the god of war, is relayed in the card's powerfully destructive depiction.

A story that became popular among late medievalist was that of the 3rd century martyr, St. Barbara, who became the patron saint of those who worked with explosives and artillerymen. According to the legend, St. Barbara was the daughter of a wealthy pagan father who had her imprisoned in a tower, as a protective measure that possibly had to do with refusal of marriage.

During her imprisonment, St. Barbara learned of Christianity and converted. While her father was away, she had three windows installed in the tower as a symbol of the Holy Trinity. On his return, her father learned of Barbara's conversion and became infuriated.

Although spared through several miraculous events, Barbara was condemned to death by beheading and her father was given the responsibility of carrying out the sentence. He in turn was struck by lightning and his body consumed by fire. St. Barbara is often portrayed with the tower as one of her symbols.

The gloomy, darkness surrounding The Tower gives this card a very morbid and menacing quality, but the brightness of the bolt or in some decks a large beaming sun, is a symbol of a sun deity, in addition to lightning, is a sexual reference.

TAROT COUPLING KEYWORDS

Positive Qualities: Brave, quick-witted, and strong-willed

Impairment/Fear: Condemnation and malicious judgment

Perception of Partner: Unpleasant, intense charisma, strong-willed, and overly intense

Dyadic Interaction: Defensive, impatient, and sad

Challenges: Learning not to harshly judge

Complaints of Partners: Short-temper, thwarts or provokes arguments

Desires: To feel protected and not held prisoner, dynamite sex

General Interpretation

The lightning-struck Tower is commonly thought to represent destruction, calamity, and sudden changes. The crown falling from the top is a symbol of a toppled consciousness or falling from a state of grace.

Tower moments can include the sudden loss of anything. What was once so valued now lies in ruin and you most likely did not see it coming. You may feel that you are being punished for your actions, or, on the other hand, intend to leash your own wrath on someone who has caused harm.

In most readings, this card shows up as a warning sign that alerts you to something that doesn't play out as expected. Some plans may backfire or blow up in your face. The surprise you have in store may be spoiled.

On a lighter note, this card suggests release or pressures that are eased with the onset of new possibilities. Most often, concepts of pain, suffering, or shocking awakenings are familiar themes in The Tower.

The Hebrew letter *peh* meaning "mouth" is the source of words and spoken language, the use of which caused major upheaval in the Tower of Babel story. The mouth also references sexual or reproductive symbolism suggesting the female vagina.

This card could be taken as a spiritual metaphor, in the context that the powerful must fall in order to obtain salvation.

New

The news comes that your new love interest is no longer interested. This also suggests that you may discover your new lover is married or dating another. Boundaries are not respected or rules deemed old-fashioned may be dismissed for instance, never kissing or having sex on the first date.

Established

Sudden lifestyle changes are suggested here in a big way. Whatever the circumstance, there will be an element of surprise. One or both of you may decide to quit smoking or quit some other negative habit.

Now that you've found the perfect partner, don't disrupt your peaceful relationship by self-sabotage.

Expanded Awareness

Challenges in relationships are many and never easy. On top of dealing with challenges in the relationship, you or your partner could be in the midst of other family or work drama. You need simplicity. Simplicity in your life starts when you shed false beliefs that make things complicated and when you let go of the idea of always wanting to be in control of everything. If the Mars energy in the relationship is not constructively dispelled, you'll both bicker and nag each other.

Stay true to yourself, no matter what is crumbling around you.

One of the secrets of success in a Tower-dominated relationship is a constant refortifying of your bond.

DETERIORATING

Disinterest or boredom happens suddenly in the relationship. The relationship is filled with toxicity. You may feel the more you strive for accomplishments, the more you are isolated and unappreciated by your partner. In many cases, this card suggests violence or abuse. Aggressive behavior or hostility interferes with a promise of moving forward in the relationship.

ROMANTIC SUGGESTIONS

Movie: *World Trade Center* (2006)

Starring: Nicolas Cage, Michael Peña, and Maria Bello

Date/Outing: Lunch or dinner at your favorite restaurant that serves spicy foods, such as Thai or Mexican

Gift Ideas: Red lingerie, red pajamas, red boxers, or collection of hot sauces or peppers

Most Compatible Cards: The Chariot and The Devil

Least Compatible Cards: The Lovers and The Star

XVII. THE STAR

GOLDEN DAWN/ESOTERIC TITLE: The Daughter of the Firmament; the Dweller between the Waters
HEBREW LETTER: Tzaddi
MEANING: Fish Hook
SIMPLE LETTER: Imagination
QABALISTIC ATTRIBUTION: Twenty-Eighth – Natural Intelligence
ELEMENT: Air
SIGN: Aquarius

GENERAL COMMENTARY

Key 17 – A nude figure kneels next to a pond, intently pouring libation from two large vases under a star-filled sky. This kneeling figure acts in natural surroundings under the faint light of the stars. The star is frequently a hallmark of many important events, such as the birth of Jesus in Christianity. The biblical story of the celestial guide that brought three Magi to the place where Jesus was born has been told and retold with the basically similar components in various ways.

Many cultures have placed meaning on different members of the planetary cosmos, especially the stars, moon, and sun.

Stars are self-luminous balls created out of dust and gas that have guided stargazers, seamen, and seekers for thousands of years.[23a]

Not only were stars functional in orienting travelers, they were worshipped as deities and believed to be unborn souls in some traditions.

The muse of astrology held the star in earlier decks. Astrology was a favorite subject of illustrators. The Star sometimes included two or three different figures and was the symbol of the Virgin Mary called the Star of The Sea or Stella Maris.

Familiar to most designs is the large eight-pointed star surrounded by seven lesser eight-pointed stars. The large star, most often placed in the center, is considered to be the star of the great cosmic goddess, the "Morning Star," Venus. Venus is the personification of beauty and love.

The nude figure on the card in earlier decks was depicted as androgynous, although with long hair and female breasts. It is somewhat confusing that The Star is attributed to Aquarius, the Water Bearer, generally considered a masculine god.

One such deity is the Egyptian god Hapi who is associated with bearing water. Hapi was personified as a man with pensile breasts like those of a woman, holding two vases from which he poured out the divided Nile.

The letter *tzaddi* means "fishhook" and is suggested by the shape of beak of the ibis, who is known to hunt for fish using its beak, and appears in the background of some decks. Sacred to the Egyptians, the ibis was the emblem of the god Thoth, who was the god revered by the Egyptian scribes. The ibis perches on a tree that is related to the djed pillar – the backbone of the Egyptian god Osiris, who is the constellation of Orion. The larger star is also believed to be a representation of Sirius, the brightest star in the sky, whose heliacal rising was an important marker for the annual rising waters of the Nile.

In its most iconographic form, this card was most likely attributed to the study of astrology.

TAROT COUPLING KEYWORDS

Positive Qualities: Optimistic, accepting, and chaste

Impairment/Fear: Disapproval and powerlessness

Perception of Partner: Lacks ability, calculating, hopeful, yet naïve

Dyadic Interaction: Critical, competitive and bossy

Challenges: Accepting partner's capacity to achieve and spitefulness

Complaints of Partners: Never satisfied, impulse and control issues

Desires: Recognition, rewards, appreciation, and gratitude

GENERAL INTERPRETATION

The figure is similar to Eos the goddess who sprinkled dew upon the earth from twin vases. This is possibly one of the more delightful cards in a reading.

In a reading, it suggests a level a compassion that partners have for each other. It also indicates that each person is able to share his or her honest feelings as a constant source of refreshing fluidity to the relationship.

Stars are symbols of transcendence. Today we use "star" as a definition of those individuals who have achieved something beyond the norm.

When individuals excel to the heights of fame, we refer to them as "stars," implying that they have risen to a status to which only the lucky exist.

In a relationship, this indicates that there are issues regarding uniqueness or being treated as special. Sometimes our childhood experiences cause us to feel especially gifted or very wounded, and when we feel our partner doesn't cater to our "giftedness," an exaggerated self-importance leads to a feeling of frustration.

The Star tells us that healing and the state of well-being are available after the turmoil of The Tower. The Star can also suggests difficulty viewing the faults of others, because you choose to look past their wounds.

The Star shows us our importance in the cosmic scheme of things. You may feel that you and your partner are uniquely suited for each other or you may have hopes of finding the one who is uniquely suited to you.

NEW

Use your intuition to guide yourself to a suitable mate. You have a very high standard when it comes to finding a partner. You may be involved with someone who finally meets your idea of a suitable partner. You may have reached a point in your life where you want your dreams of a settled life with someone special to come true. You may find yourself daydreaming about the possibility of a new romantic interest becoming your future spouse.

ESTABLISHED

A keen awareness of the needs of others reflects in the attentiveness towards your partner. You may suspect that your relationship is not as stable as it appears. In some instances, this card indicates that the relationship has improved and you hope it continues in this direction.

EXPANDED AWARENESS

Individuality is very important, it may prove difficult to let someone close to you fearing being outshined or smothered by his or her affections. This indicates that you are embarking on a journey to access wisdom from a higher guide or you may look at aspects of your relationship through a composite chart in astrology.

DETERIORATING

It has become difficult to have hopes for a future relationship. The relationship is lacking in warmth and the light is slowly dimming on this connection. You want to continue with the relationship, but are less enthusiastic as time goes by.

Both partners may have full awareness that a relationship is close to ending, but neither wants to let go because of not wanting to fail. Deep down inside, you know a relationship will most likely not work out, but wishful thinking or denial suits you better than the loneliness.

ROMANTIC SUGGESTIONS

Movie: *Rock Star* (2001)
Starring: Mark Wahlberg, Jennifer Aniston, and Dominic West
Date/Outing: Visit a planetarium, a concert, or spend a romantic evening stargazing
Gift Ideas: Give a star a name for your sweetheart
Most Compatible Cards: The Fool and The World
Least Compatible Cards: The Hierophant, The Hermit, and Death

XVIII. THE MOON

Golden Dawn/Esoteric Title: The Ruler of Flux and Reflux; the Child of the Sons of the Mighty.

Hebrew Letter: Qoph

Meaning: Back of Head, Ear

Simple Letter: Sleep

Qabalistic Attribution: Twenty-Ninth – Corporeal Intelligence

Element: Water

Sign: Pisces

General Commentary

Key 18 – Like the proceeding card, The Moon also featured a female figure holding a celestial sphere in the early versions perhaps representing the Moon goddess, Diana.

The card in one of the earlier decks featured two astronomers who were at some point changed to two canines, usually considered a wolf and a dog, joined by a crayfish crawling from a pool of water. In some decks, the crayfish is exchanged for a crab, the symbol of sign of Cancer.

The moon has been the subject of many tales and legends. One legend was that of the Man on the Moon, which comes from the creative imagination of storytellers regarding the dark spots on the moon as the figure of a man sometimes accompanied with a canine companion.

From very early periods, the moon was recognized as an influence to earth's climate and weather. Many cultures, such as the Mesopotamian and Babylonian, knew that the moon had effects on tides of the sea. They associated the moon with a male lunar god. One moon god in particular, Sin, was often depicted standing upon the backs of two beasts. Interestingly, there are stelae discovered in parts in and around Syria, depicting what is called crescent-on-a-pole rising presumably from the back of a bull.[24]

Crowley's *Thoth* deck shows a dung beetle instead of a crustacean. Wang explains that The Golden Dawn manuscripts indicated that the dung beetle, typically associated with the Egyptian god Khepera, was the inspiration for the crayfish.

The dog-headed guardians of Anubis are also featured on Crowley's deck. Anubis was the Egyptian god associated with death and the Underworld that the two towers in the background of Waite's card alludes to as gateway to the unknown.

The Moon is the great illuminator of the night, the Ruler of Flux and Reflux, controlling the ebb and flow action of life that changes approximately every seven days, decreasing and increasing its size.

The moon has long been said to have mystical powers and to have biological and psychological effects on humans. The most well known include menstruation and childbirth.

Some decks show the waxing, waning, and full moon, which indicate three stages of human development of childhood, adulthood, and maturity or old age. The sign of Pisces associated with this card relates to dreams and psychic ability.

TAROT COUPLING KEYWORDS

Positive Qualities: Introspective, intuitive, and knowledgeable

Impairment/Fear: Disappointment and impaired instincts

Perception of Partner: Dreamy; unrealistic, yet sharp

Dyadic Interaction: Overly attentive and at times inattentive

Challenges: Living in the present

Complaints of Partners: Never satisfied, impulse and control issues

Desires: Easy going, understanding partner

GENERAL INTERPRETATION

When this card appears in reading, it indicates that something is up, but you may not be able to put your finger on it. Things that particularly happen at night are also suggested. The Moon is often described as a spooky card due to an old connection with werewolves and other creatures of the night. The Moon's energy can be described as that feeling that we have when fear of the dark is experienced. It points changing and fluctuation of emotional tides.

The Moon does tell us that we should not trust what we see in the dark. If we are not able to trust, this causes self-doubt and criticism of others and ourselves.

NEW

You and your new partner feel uncannily close and have a deep psychic bond. The two of you may have interest in the mystical or esoteric. You bond very quickly, as if you've been together in a previous lifetime. Part of the attraction is the air of mystery surrounding your partner. This suggests getting to know a person better before you reveal too much about yourself, not only to be emotionally protective, but in the interest of safety, too.

The Moon also shows up when a couple denies to outsiders that they are involved with each other, hiding their affections because they wish to keep the relationship hidden for a while.

ESTABLISHED

This suggests that some old fear has resurfaced that has prompted deep soul-searching. The Moon indicates that issues are deep in the subconscious, in which you are unaware that it effects you more than you think. You are trying to hide your true feelings from your partner or vice versa and those feelings are usually negative.

Expanded Awareness

Never avoid opportunities to grow and evolve. Many times these opportunities manifest as dealing with people or situations that we want desperately to ignore. Many of us are intimately familiar with deceptions and disappointments to the point where happy moments are only a facade.

We can't help but feel or expect the worst, especially when our relationships are running smoothly. Become aware of the cycles of joy and disappointment you experience. You can then put into place the practice of having fewer expectations from the way you feel things should be and how they really are. The Moon also suggests that you are on the road to recovery from old wounds. You may want to enlist the help of a trained psychotherapist or counselor.

Deteriorating

This card suggests deception and hidden aspects to the relationship, possibly because your partner feels if you knew the truth that you would leave. In some instances, you may deny and/or disassociate from the troubles in your partnership. This card typically represents situations that people commonly lie about in relationships, such as infidelity. Whatever the case, you may discover a dark side to your partner's personality.

Romantic Suggestions

Movie: *Moonstruck* (1987)
Starring: Cher, Nicolas Cage and Olympia Dukakis
Date/Outing: Create a special full moon ritual for your relationship; enjoy a bubble bath together
Gift Ideas: Moonstone jewelry, ambergris oils, or pet fish
Most Compatible Cards: Wheel of Fortune, The Hanged Man, Death
Least Compatible Cards: The Tower, The Lovers, and Justice

XIX. THE SUN

GOLDEN DAWN/ESOTERIC TITLE: The Lord of the Fire of the World
HEBREW LETTER: Resh
MEANING: Head
DOUBLE LETTER: Fertility; Barren
QABALISTIC ATTRIBUTION: Thirtieth – Collecting Intelligence
ELEMENT: Fire
PLANET: Sun

GENERAL COMMENTARY

Key 19 – Worshipped as a deity for millennia, the Sun in Tarot has been captured in various ways. Some decks have two youths frolicking in unity, others a single innocent youth on horseback carrying a banner. Still others display a couple basking in the light of daytime. The Waite design has a male youth riding a white horse while carrying a red pennant under prominent alternating rays emitted by the sun.

This is no ordinary child; he is Apollo, the Sun God. He, like many of the pagan deities, became inspiration for myths, art, and poetry since antiquity.

In the Golden Dawn tradition, these rays represent masculine and feminine natures, and in Sumerian lore, the sun god Utu or Shamash. One characteristic of the Sun God is that of righteousness and justice, as he has the power to light that which is hidden and is the enemy of the deeds of darkness.

In the myths of Apollo, it is told that at only four days old, Apollo wanted a bow and arrow in order to slay the Python that terrorized his mother. Apollo was depicted with curly golden hair and was the symbol of perfect maleness and eternal youth. On this path, we return to innocence and begin to remember our original state.

Unlike most gods in mythology, Apollo's function was less than clear. Instead of having a single domain, Apollo had many functions as a god of music, poetry, hunting, prophecy, healing and masculine beauty. It is no wonder that on this path the "Sun embraces the whole of creation in its rays."

In The Sun card, there are opposites and contrasts of light/dark, day/night, and masculine/feminine. The Sun can bring about great fertility or create barrenness and drought. Like the sun brings life to earth, we too are life givers in our reproductive capacity.

Tarot Coupling Keywords

Positive Qualities: Intellectual, harmonious, delightful
Impairment/Fear: Incapability, impotence, mediocrity
Perception of Partner: Brilliant, high visibility, performer, closed, grandiose
Dyadic Interaction: Encourages, instigates, warm.
Challenges: Melancholy, laziness, easily discouraged
Complaints of Partners: Hogger, unreachable, spiteful
Desires: Ecstatically in love, reawakened sexual desire

General Interpretation

In a reading, The Sun indicates a positive outcome in any undertaking. There is pleasure in life and joy in your relationship. The Sun shows you enjoy the company of your kids or grandkids. The news of an engagement, marriage, or birth can also be indicated by The Sun.

New

Your new love interest makes your day by surprising you with flowers or dropping by unexpectedly for a quick visit. You are beaming with joy.

Established

Both partners have a wonderful sense of play and humor that helps with any rough patch. The partners never take each other for granted and are uninhibited when it comes to showing their affection.

Expanded Awareness

Ablaze with creative ideas and a passion for learning, you and you partner have "the mind of a child" in that you want to learn new things. One or both of you may return to school or seek marriage counseling to improve on what you already know works.

Deteriorating

This indicates burnout. It could be from all the tension in the relationship or from eternal pressures. The couple may have a temporary lull in the relationship but it is only short-term.

Romantic Suggestions

Movie: *About A Boy* (2002)
Starring: Hugh Grant, Nicholas Hoult, and Toni Collette
Date/Outing: A day at the beach, or sunbathing by the pool (sunscreen, of course)
Gift Ideas: Sunstone jewelry or crystals
Most Compatible Cards: The Emperor, Strength, and Temperance
Least Compatible Cards: The Lovers, The Chariot, and The Devil

XX. JUDGMENT

GOLDEN DAWN/ESOTERIC TITLE: The Spirit of the Primal Fire
HEBREW LETTER: Shin
MEANING: Tooth
MATERNAL LETTER: Fire
QABALISTIC ATTRIBUTION: Thirty-First – Perpetual Intelligence
ELEMENT: Water (Fire)
PLANET: Pluto

GENERAL COMMENTARY

Key 20 – The Last Judgment was an all too common theme for medieval and renaissance art and religious iconography. The Last Judgment is a Christian theme of the resurrection of souls and the final judgment of humanity, bringing an end to time itself, marking Jesus' second coming. This card was called The Angel in the early versions and never Judgment.

Generally, Gabriel is the angel of announcements, and is assumed to be the angel on Key XX. Some occult traditions say that the angel here is Michael, because the path of Judgment on the Tree of Life is the path of elemental Fire. (Robert Wang, *The Qabalistic Tarot.* York Beach: Samuel Weiser, Inc., 1983.152.)

According to Richard Webster in *Communicating with Archangel Michael for Guidance and Protection,* (Llewellyn, 2004), Archangel Michael is rewarded with the duty of blowing the trumpet during the Last Judgment for defeating The Devil, expelling him from heaven.

This path's symbolism is primarily fiery and corresponds to mental and psychological evolution.

The Angel on this card is summoning the dead to spiritual reawakening. The trumpet sounds a call to rise to newer and higher levels of living. The trumpet is an important emblem of heavenly splendor, warnings, or announcements, often depicted as blown by angelic beings. This card can indicate a summoning out of a dormant state or renewed spiritual vigor. One may awaken from a mental slumber. Here, an examination of the meaning and purpose of life may occur. You may hear the call of a mission or life purpose.

TAROT COUPLING KEYWORDS

Positive Qualities: Visionary, reflective, and transcendent
Impairment/Fear: Dissatisfaction with life and feels despair
Perception of Partner: Ethical, cheerful, dull, whistleblower, activist

Dyadic Interaction: Jokes around, cheerful, short-tempered, or argumentative
Challenges: Trusting inner wisdom or positive self-image
Complaints of Partners: Harshly judges, attitude, lack or self-motivation
Desires: Vitality, renewed virility, and to overcome depression

GENERAL INTERPRETATION

The card suggests reawakening on the inner and outer self. You come out of the dread of your former casket and heed the call of The Angel.

In the relationship arena, you may change your whole dating game and make it your mission to find someone that is exactly fitting to your life needs at this time. Perhaps before you were focused on what a person could offer you in terms of a material life and now you want something deeper and more soulful.

NEW

You think twice, (if not thrice) about your dating life and review mistakes, realizing that you are older and wiser and no longer need to repeat them.

ESTABLISHED

As a couple, you have grown in many ways and could do so once more, this time with an addition to your family. You could be remodeling an older home to suit your growing family.

EXPANDED AWARENESS

As couples grow to learn and know each other, they learn to let go much of the anxiety of love and relationships. Accepting the confines of a committed relationship takes courage and selfless giving.

DETERIORATING

If you are dissolving your relationship, this suggests the next step may deal with the legal aspect. You may be going to an attorney or in front of a judge to finalize your ending.

ROMANTIC SUGGESTIONS

Movie: *Armageddon* (1998)
Starring: Bruce Willis, Billy Bob Thornton, and Ben Affleck
Date/Outing: Antique shops or historic tours
Gift Ideas: Ticket to jazz concert or symphony
Most Compatible Cards: The Chariot and Death
Least Compatible Cards: Strength and The Emperor

XXI. THE WORLD

GOLDEN DAWN/ESOTERIC TITLE: The Great One of the Night of Time
HEBREW LETTER: Tau
MEANING: Tau or Equal-armed cross
DOUBLE LETTER: Power-Servitude
QABALISTIC ATTRIBUTION: Thirty-Second – Administrative Intelligence
ELEMENT: Earth (Air)
PLANET: Saturn

GENERAL COMMENTARY

A centralized figure surrounded by mythical figures is common iconology that demonstrates the fascination with astrology and planetary organization.

What first appears as a man within a circle with astrological figures orbiting about found in early doctrines, became another prominent motif for Renaissance illustrators. (Jean Seznec, *The Survival of the Pagan Gods: The Mythological Tradition and Its Place in Renaissance Humanism and Art.* Translated by Barbara F. Sessions. Princeton: Princeton University Press/Bollingen, 1953, 1981.)

This pattern was the blueprint for what we have as The World card of modern decks, but a female replaced the male and the four beasts of the Evangelists are still representing the astrological signs Leo, Taurus, Aquarius, and Scorpio.

The male figure was that of Apollo the sun god thought to be surrounded by Muses. As Christian thought replaced pagan beliefs, this representation became Christianized.

TAROT COUPLING KEYWORDS

Positive Qualities: Successful, worldly, well-traveled, and strong communicator
Wounds/Fear: Despair over life, fears death
Perception of Partner: Competent, confident, well-rounded, slow to excite
Dyadic Interaction: Thoughtful, inclusive, offers advice but can be a know-it-all
Challenges: Incomplete projects and boredom
Complaints of Partners: Uninterested, no sense of adventure
Desires: Glory, connectedness and triumph

GENERAL INTERPRETATION

Relationships are in of themselves journeys, often very long ones. The journey often results in two principles conjoining their loves in the completeness of commitment with or without acceptance of those on the outside.

In The World we see the resignation of that which is too heavy to carry on this journey and have gained enough wisdom and security to expose who and what we've BECOME.

NEW

People say when you meet the right one you will know. You have the wonderful feeling of knowing that something special is happening with your partner, it's like a little dancer is twirling in your soul. You have found love, now go out and see if you can keep it.

ESTABLISHED

You are celebrating another year of being together, or perhaps celebrating a child/children finally leaving the nest. These milestones are significant and you may do something really special to commemorate it.

EXPANDED AWARENESS

Theoretically, if life came with a manual, there would certainly need to be a special section devoted to love, attractions, and partnerships. The World card shows us that love cannot be explained from one perspective, but all perspectives, including religious, scientific, and philosophy. To understand the whole of love and life, you must travel and search to draw your own conclusions.

DETERIORATING

On again and off again is the best way to describe what is going on here. It is possible that when problems arise, the sheer weight of the magnitude is too much to handle and you give up. The journey for the two of you may not be over; rather, you get sidetracked for one reason or another and possibly in the guise of returning former lover or something new and shiny.

ROMANTIC SUGGESTIONS

Movie: *Leap Year* (2010)
Starring: Amy Adams, Matthew Goode, and Adam Scott
Date/Outing: Renaissance fair, local festival
Gift Ideas: Globe, maps, compasses, GPS/navigation system
Most Compatible Cards: The Devil, The Hermit, and Death
Least Compatible Cards: The Lovers, Justice, and Strength

CHAPTER 11

THE MINOR ARCANA
Ace through Ten

The next section deals with the Aces – 10s of the four suits. The minor suits are corresponded to the four elements: Pentacles – earth, Cups – water, Swords – air, and Wands – fire, and makes up the larger of the two division of the deck.

The way to learn the meanings of each is by getting a sense of it through keywords that you'll find listed here. The most guaranteed way to learn the cards is by practice with and using them frequently. The divinatory meanings coupled with the other methods in this book take time to integrate.

One might say that the Minor Arcana, meaning "Lesser Mystery," seems to portray the more practical side of life. In the broadest terms, Cups were delegated to matters of the heart and what affects our emotions, Pentacles were related to commerce and finances, Wands concerned what we could do, actions, and creativity, and Swords related to intellect or learning.

Certainly anyone who has been reading the cards for a while could agree that you must remain flexible in assigning meanings to the cards, especially the Minor Arcana, or pips, another name for these cards.

What follows are suggestions of my own interpretations incorporating the four psychological types and the four NEED stages of relationships.

Suit of Wands

PSYCHOLOGICAL FUNCTION: Intuition
ELEMENT: Fire
ROMANTIC ATTACHMENT: Anxious-Preoccupied

TAROT COUPLING KEYWORDS FOR WANDS

Positive Qualities: Spontaneous, provokes growth, and idealistic

Impairment/Fear: Fears change, imbalance of masculine energy

Perception of Partner: Risk taker, somewhat needy and charismatic

Dyadic Interaction: All or nothing attitude, needs space, and shows enthusiasm about partner's ideas

Challenges: Spaces out, anxious, envy, and recklessness

Complaints of Partner: Impatient, exaggerates, playboy/girl antics

Desires: Connection that offers excitement, passion, and variety of experiences

ACE OF WANDS

GOLDEN DAWN/ESOTERIC TITLE: Root of the Powers of Fire

GENERAL INTERPRETATION

Ready, set action! The relationship is off to a hot start. You could also be renewing the passion in a once-stale connection. Partners communicate their needs effectively, rather than biting each other's heads off. On the other hand, one of you may initiate a much-needed heart-to-heart that you've been avoiding.

NEW

Passionate energy surrounds you right now and your feel as if you can tackle anything. Use a different approach in how you meet people. You should be careful of falling in love too fast.

ESTABLISHED

You could find yourself involved in activities with partner such as camping, but prior to that, you may want to discuss adding a member of the family. Thing happen fast and your partner may have trouble committing to something that will change them or require them to be the initiator.

EXPANDED AWARENESS

It takes a headstrong person to deal with a challenging partner. If you need something, you can take a chance on the answer being yes.

DETERIORATING

A decision must be made and you may not like the outcome. You need to talk with your partner to communicate some important idea or challenge and may be brushed off or in the midst of a huge argument.

2 OF WANDS

GOLDEN DAWN/ESOTERIC TITLE: Lord of Dominion
DECAN: 1° – 10°, Mars in Aries
YESOD OF ATZULITH: Influence over others, authority, power, dominion

GENERAL INTERPRETATION

On the outside, it may appear that you have everything you've ever wanted (and you may indeed have it), but you still want to progress or fill a void. Partners may not be on the same page as one is looking forward to the future, the other may be stuck in the present, or even the past.

NEW

This suggests a search for a partner, a fixed vision and determination. A desire for a very strong-willed partner who is unwavering at getting what they want. A relationship is possible with someone who you are unaware of – but they have had their eye on you from a distance.

ESTABLISHED

Partners enjoy spirited conversation and social gatherings. One or both partners are exceptionally savvy at business and may run a successful business. The consensus here is that partners are together to promote harmony in the world. They may dedicate a significant amount of personal time to charity or other causes.

EXPANDED AWARENESS

This relationship is based on courage of both partners to extend themselves wholly to themselves and to the world at large. Each partner is motivated by ambition to achieve material success, but often it conflicts with their spiritual views.

DETERIORATING

Bravado is the mask worn to cover up a partner's fear. They may act as if the effects of their negative behavior on their partner do not faze them. At the heart of the negative behavior, often disguised as courage, is fear of being alone. If this fear dominates, a partner is actually pushed away and a break up becomes a self-fulfilled prophecy.

3 OF WANDS

GOLDEN DAWN/ESOTERIC TITLE: Lord of Established Strength
DECAN: 10° – 20°, Sun in Aries
YESOD OF ATZULITH: Pride, arrogance, and self-assertion

GENERAL INTERPRETATION

The figure on Waite's card seems to be awaiting the arrival of someone or something from beyond the horizon. In some regards, he maybe considered a worrywart. This card suggests indecision around romantic partnerships. When it appears in a reading, the questioner could be searching for the perfect love, not satisfied in their current relationship or regrettably waiting for their love interest to leave another relationship.

NEW

A relationship seems to be a departure from the norm of your previous connections. This may be a good thing, depending on how this card is represented in your spread.

ESTABLISHED

Your partner meets your needs emotionally and physically. It could be exhausting trying to find ways to keep your partner interested in the relationship. This is a good connection for creative individuals.

EXPANDED AWARENESS

This relationship, like many others will not be void of ups and downs. The lesson for troubling times is for both partners to understand the restlessness and indecision that plaques one or the other partner.

There could also be reluctance or stubbornness to accept that your partner needs a lot more freedom than you are willing to tolerate.

DETERIORATING

This indicates that one member of this duo is ready to take off, possibly putting an end to the relationship. Partners talk past each other, instead of directly to one another. Sensing an imminent breakup, the one who wants in does not want to be honest about what they will face. A partner has communicated their desire to leave, but the other still has hopes for a future.

4 OF WANDS

GOLDEN DAWN/ESOTERIC TITLE: Lord of Perfected Work
DECAN: 20° – 30°, Venus in Aries
CHESED OF ATZULITH: Settlement, arrangement, completion

GENERAL INTERPRETATION

Hard work and diligence bring happiness to your relationship. Both partners value good relationship skills and are able to respect each other's personal space. This card suggests social and leisure activities that both partners enjoy. At this time, changes to living arrangements are discussed or a large home décor expense is made.

NEW

Mark the calendar! A chance meeting with serious romance potential happens at a wedding or other gatherings with family and friends.

ESTABLISHED

One partner may be a social butterfly and the other a homebody, preferring to go out for the occasional restaurant or special event. You both enjoy talking about your shared interests and have intense conversations. Partners feel secure and may not want to take too many risks once they have established a good foundation for their family.

EXPANDED AWARENESS

The desire to achieve total happiness is one of many goals. Extremely high ideals about love, romance, and commitment create a deep longing for the ideal partner. Home, family, financial security, and freedom to travel are your idea of a perfect life and that is what you and your partner want.

DETERIORATING

A fast paced relationship has lost its fuel. There is a sense of wasted time and effort because the relationship has become more trouble than it's worth. Resentments are due to a partner's unreliability and lack of devotion.

5 OF WANDS

GOLDEN DAWN/ESOTERIC TITLE: Lord of Strife
DECAN: 1° – 10°, Saturn in Leo
YESOD OF ATZULITH: Quarreling and fighting

GENERAL INTERPRETATION

Arguments erupt and are counterproductive when they are circular and no one is able to make a point. This card also shows that there may be too many things competing for attention at the moment and this could be frustrating for both partners.

NEW

Even though you like your new love interest, you have not agreed to a date. This is due to your fear of getting involved because you have your heart set on someone else. You are not interested in dating, only mating.

ESTABLISHED

Your partner thinks they are helping you by voicing their views, but sadly, they are not, and you secretly want to figure your situation out on your own. You are not able to express this because you don't want to hurt your partner's feelings. Perhaps after a heated disagreement, you need to take a walk or distract yourself to not think about your anger.

EXPANDED AWARENESS

Stand up for your rights and stick up for yourself! Going against others may seem the difficult choice; however, your integrity is at risk and you prefer to do what's right.

Interesting to note that one of the traditional meanings of this card is lust. Lust mentioned as one of the Seven Deadly Sins was long considered an urge of excess to be avoided; as it turns out, lust is one of those urges that causes great conflict in relationships because most people confuse lust with love.

DETERIORATING

There are displays of inappropriate behaviors, which are not only embarrassing to you, but have annoyed or angered others. Flared tempers and outbursts strain the relationship. You could demand that your partner enter counseling if the relationship is going to continue.

6 OF WANDS

GOLDEN DAWN/ESOTERIC TITLE: Lord of Victory
DECAN: 10° – 20°, Jupiter in Leo
TIPHARETH OF ATZULITH: Gain

GENERAL INTERPRETATION

Successful coupling with the right partner could be the last thing to accomplish; it may be important for the level of acceptance you want amongst peers and family.

NEW

You get a boost in your ego because several potential suitors may vie for your attention. If the question or concern is whether a person will call, the answer is yes!

ESTABLISHED

There is a good reason to celebrate. You can look forward to a promotion or new job; it could mean a boost to your income. This card is also a good omen for marriage or weddings. Yes, you'll get the ring!

EXPANDED AWARENESS

This connection's only rule is that both partners are loyal and support each other through thick and thin. The relationship acts as a model for success for others who struggle. You both actively listen and absorb each other's points of view about friends, family, or other important community issues.

DETERIORATING

An element of disrespect agitates one or both members of the couple. It may not be toward each other, but perhaps disrespect to a parent or other member of the immediate family.

7 OF WANDS

GOLDEN DAWN/ESOTERIC TITLE: Lord of Valor
DECAN: 20° – 30°, Mars in Leo
NETZACH OF ATZULITH: Opposition yet courage

GENERAL INTERPRETATION

Facing difficulties with others and taking a stand against unpopular choices. Battling inner demons. A person confronts one obstacle after the other before they are given proper credit.

NEW

A love interest's reputation precedes him/her.

ESTABLISHED

A rumor or gossip started by a person outside the relationship causes worry and stress. Ultimatums are used to control a partner's behavior.

EXPANDED AWARENESS

The relationship is riddled with many complicated issues such as threats of layoffs from a job; however, these issues bring both partners together and this suggests you go on offense instead of defense by planning ahead.

DETERIORATING

You are walking on eggs shells and never know what to expect from your partner. Constant nagging and prodding frustrates the relationship.

8 OF WANDS

Golden Dawn/Esoteric Title: Lord of Swiftness
Decan: 1° – 10°, Mercury in Sagittarius
Hod of Atzulith: Hasty Communication and messages; swiftness

General Interpretation

"Time flies when you're having fun" is an adage befitting to this card. There is doubt about hearing from someone, but another gives information regarding him or her, or you hear directly from him or her yourself. Exchanges of text, email or through social networking.

New

It's all about quantity. Interest is ludic at best; this suggests one or both partners are players. It additionally suggests falling head over heels in love without really knowing someone.

Established

The stakes are continually raised to keep partners interested, which is not necessarily a bad thing. You want your partner to be a little more sexually aggressive or maybe even a little less so. After being together for a while, you and your partner are psychically bonded and began finishing each other sentences, or when one of you says something, the other tells you they were just thinking about the same thing.

Expanded Awareness

Duration and longevity is not a priority for a connection; at least not at the beginning. What may have begun as a simple crush or lust has potential to expand and change a partner's outlook on settling down.

Deteriorating

Your connection has reached rock bottom, so there is nowhere to go but up and it will take the will of both to endure the climb. Things may be up in the air and one or both partners distances themselves further from the other.

9 OF WANDS

Golden Dawn/Esoteric Title: Lord of Great Strength
Decan: 10° – 20°, Moon in Sagittarius
Yesod of Atzulith: Strength, power, health; recovery from sickness

General Interpretation

"What doesn't kill you makes you stronger." How many times have you heard this saying? The Lord of Great Strength probably embraces this motto without doubt. This suggests that one had gone through experiences which are at best character building. There is no room for cowardice. This card suggests sharpening your intuitive and mental capacity.

New

Investigate potential through your gut instincts. You could be still beating yourself up because of a missed opportunity.

Established

The relationship has had its share of bumps. Understanding, in a deeper sense, could still be an issue. Potential drawbacks happen when your partner becomes stuck on the one thing that adds up to about 10 percent of negative impact on the relationship. The clue to resolution suggested here is reinforcing the positives, so that you can face the negatives.

Expanded Awareness

When the 9 of Wands shows up in a reading, there is a good chance that the querent has been through this situation before, or something similar. If this proves to be true, then it's time to figure out what was missed in the lesson of the last fiasco. Your friends or family wonders why you take so much *crap* from your partner.

If you've been single for a long time with out a long-term stable relationship, the issue isn't that all the good ones are taken. It may have to do with your anxiety around close intimacy, or better yet, commitment phobia.

Deteriorating

You knew from the very start of the relationship that it was probably not a good idea to get involved. You are stronger than you think, and if at first you don't succeed, try again! This also suggests that you may be involved in a tumultuous relationship and it is possible you partner will be the difficult one.

10 OF WANDS

GOLDEN DAWN/ESOTERIC TITLE: Lord of Oppression
DECAN: 20° – 30°, Saturn in Sagittarius
MALKUTH OF YOD: Cruelty, malice, revenge, and injustice.

GENERAL INTERPRETATION

Tens represent completion and the start of a new cycle. It is the combination of the masculine and feminine polarities that creates perfect wholeness. The 10 of Wands suggest bearing a cross or willingly taking up slack for your partner in the many responsibilities of domestic life.

NEW

Take care in over promising and not delivering on the promise. This indicates self-aggrandizing to impress someone new. You could negotiate sharing the cost of dating.

ESTABLISHED

Financial responsibilities may overwhelm the couple that may struggle to keep up the mortgage or other expenses. A partner or spouse may overwhelm you, be making more demands for time, money, etc., that you find impossible to satisfy. These of course are temporary setbacks.

EXPANDED AWARENESS

While the figure on this card is generally depicted as burdened by a load of sticks, it doesn't necessarily mean he is overwhelmed. This card suggests a certain strictness and discipline in training or education. You struggle with relationships in general and do not like opening yourself to emotional vulnerability.

DETERIORATING

The reality of a breakup comes crashing down upon you all at one time. You may have a range of emotions, and on top of everything, you still need to break the news to children or family.

Suit of Cups

PSYCHOLOGICAL FUNCTION: Feeling
ELEMENT: Water
ROMANTIC ATTACHMENT: Preoccupied

TAROT COUPLING KEYWORDS FOR CUPS

Positive Qualities: Sensitive, empathy, loyal
Wounds/Fear: Abandonment, change
Perception of Partner: Nice, caring, clingy, oversensitive
Dyadic Interaction: Doting, moody, irritable
Challenges: Boundaries, meanness, immature
Complaints of Partner: Smothers, dishonest, escapist
Desires: Emotional security, to be desired

ACE OF CUPS

GOLDEN DAWN/ESOTERIC TITLE: Root of the Powers of Water

GENERAL INTERPRETATION

The Ace of Cups could be considered a deep, soulful, spiritual love. When this card shows up in a reading, it sets an excellent tone for your emotional connection.

NEW

You love meeting new people and see the best in others. Above all else, you want a perfect love. Wherever life takes you, the search for this perfection is always at the forefront of your activities.

ESTABLISHED

The only way you could ever describe your sweetheart is to call him/her a soul mate. It also suggests a renewed interest in a former partner, possibly because of the deep emotional bond between the two of you.

EXPANDED AWARENESS

The highest achievements in life are those in which we can become self-realized. In taking care of others, you may find it hard to take care of yourself. You have the heart of a Good Samaritan and frequently open your home and your heart to those in need.

DETERIORATING

The bottom falls out and you find it hard to maintain the bond that kept you tied to your partner. Love goes out, but is not returned. You feel nothing for the one who loves you.

2 OF CUPS

Golden Dawn/Esoteric Title: Lord of Love
Decan: 1° – 10°, Venus in Cancer
Chokmah in Briah: Home life, pleasure, marriage, and commitment

General Interpretation

There is a yearning to be connected to someone who shares your idea of true romance and wants an equal partnership. This card suggests that you are not just into a frivolous romance; you do not want to waste time with someone who isn't serious about a commitment. Universally, this card also signals the announcement of an engagement or wedding news. If you haven't been getting along with your partner, it may be time to negotiate a fair agreement.

New

You've hit the love jackpot! You have met a new love interest and undoubtedly feel that you could fall deeply in love. This card suggests agreements, partnerships, and involvements of many kinds. You many feel a sense of harmony within and understand the meaning of self-love.

Established

In this relationship you have found the best of worlds, a friend and a lover. You are so deeply committed to each other that perhaps you may consider getting engaged, married, or renewing your vows.

Expanded Awareness

Closeness and separation are often balanced in relationships, yet they can change over time. You and your partner make attempts to maintain your relationship by symbiosis. When two people are symbiotic, they can't function on their own as an individual and still have a relationship.

Deteriorating

You will almost agree to anything in order to keep the peace. Romantic gestures are not reciprocated. This suggests a fear of exclusion and unrealistic beliefs about love and happiness. A partner may be keeping a secret in order to protect the other partner's feelings or to keep the relationship intact.

3 OF CUPS

Golden Dawn/Esoteric Title: Lord of Abundance
Decan: 10° – 20°, Mercury in Cancer
Binah in Briah: Hospitality, abundance, and merriment

General Interpretation

"Laissez les bons temps rouler" a saying often repeated in my birthplace, Louisiana. It's French for "Let the good times roll!" When you look at the 3 of Cups, enough said!

Like the traditional meanings indicate, this card concerns people, places, or events that serve emotional well-being.

New

You want your partner to know that you are more than just a lounge lizard that is only out for a good time. Change gears by showing your new partner your sensitive caring side and that you can be a supportive listener.

Established

A grand celebration is in order to commemorate the mutual love and respect between both partners and their interactions with close friends and family. One of the reasons that you fit so well together is because both partners are sensitive to the other, which is very healthy.

Expanded Awareness

Under the influence of this card in the spread, most situations are pleasant, especially if other people are in a supportive role. This suggests empathic feelings in which you are able to pick up on the nuances of what others feel. Upon entering, you are able to take the temperature of in a room filled with people.

Deteriorating

Instead of hanging with the crowd, you want to avoid them.

When a partner questions your avoidance, you evade answering them. Rather than being up front about your desires to end a relationship, you attempt to make your partner feel they are the crazy one, in hopes that they end the relationship, so you don't have to be the bad guy/gal.

4 OF CUPS

GOLDEN DAWN/ESOTERIC TITLE: Lord of Blended Pleasure
DECAN: 20° – 30°, Moon in Cancer
CHESED IN BRIAH: Pleasure with drawbacks

GENERAL INTERPRETATION

In spite of the figure on the Waite card, apparent disinterests, this card suggests a desire to involve oneself with others. There is apprehension to get involved, mostly related to the fear of being rejected.

NEW

In a new relationship, you want the romance, but not so much an attachment. You want commitment; however, this is not the right one, so you are settling for now.

ESTABLISHED

This well established relationship is one where both partners goes with the flow, passively allowing each other to do whatever they want to do. One or both partners stay in the relationship because they feel their obligations come first. There is always another option.

EXPANDED AWARENESS

While there is inclination to love your neighbors as you would love yourself, you hate to admit that others, including your immediate love ones, invade your space. This also suggests an overly sensitive character that has to appear tough. Never let them see you sweat!

DETERIORATING

One or both partners lack a sense of personal boundaries that are necessary for a good, functioning relationship. One partner may intentionally invade the other's privacy in order to intimidate. You could also be ostracized from your loved one because you expressed a different perspective (truth) on a serious matter.

5 OF CUPS

GOLDEN DAWN/ESOTERIC TITLE: Lord of Loss in Pleasure
DECAN: 1° – 10°, Mars in Scorpio
GEBURAH IN BRIAH: Breakups, disappointments, loss of companionship

GENERAL INTERPRETATION

Metaphorically speaking, The 5 of Cups suggests a strong power kept under wraps. When partners suppress their truest selves, the relationship is destined to be lifeless or lose its brilliance and flavor.

NEW

You are thoroughly infatuated with your new love partner – you know...the one you thought was all that and bag a chips? Well as it turns out, *nah*, not so much.

ESTABLISHED

The clichés attached to this card "don't cry over spilled milk" is "easier said then done." This suggests a relationship of necessity or obligation rather than true love.

EXPANDED AWARENESS

The card coveys the conflicting feelings you have about your partner or the relationship itself. Some things are great while others are not so great. While typical in every relationship, this card suggests the negative outweigh the positive.

DETERIORATING

What an icky feeling! The audacity of someone's betrayal fills you with disgust. Sorry may not be enough at this point. You have tried to work with your partner's shortcoming and now have given up.

6 OF CUPS

GOLDEN DAWN/ESOTERIC TITLE: Lord of Pleasure
DECAN: 10° – 20°, Sun in Scorpio
TIPHARETH IN BRIAH: Happiness, success beginning of wish

GENERAL INTERPRETATION

Very often, this card suggests memories of your prepubescent through adolescent years. These years fall into the stages of development called by Freud "phallic and latency." During these stages, we learn how to love and how to be loved. Because these are idyllic times of life, we often are reminiscent of our youth.

NEW

Even though you have found a new love partner, you still think about your former love. The old relationship had an intensity, which lingers. You are still not over them and there is a strong possibility of getting back together.

ESTABLISHED

You and your partner have created such a powerful existence that is quite different from what you've had in other partners. You feel that no one could possibly take your partner's place, and in a pragmatic reviewing of your past failure in relationships, you decide to make this arrangement permanent, if it is not already.

EXPANDED AWARENESS

Values, morals, and responsibility to self and others are qualities parents strive to instill in their young ones. You have carried these into your adult life and these are qualities that create a sense of peace within and in your surroundings.

DETERIORATING

Are you making a comparison between your former and current partners? Are you hammering your partner with details of your previous sexual conquests or vice versa? These are dating milestones that can irritate partners. If there is something to clarify in discussion that adds value to the relationship, that's fine. If not, you may only create distance between the two of you.

7 OF CUPS

GOLDEN DAWN/ESOTERIC TITLE: Lord of Illusory Success
DECAN: 20° – 30°, Venus in Scorpio
NETZACH IN BRIAH: Deception unfulfilled promises, illusion

GENERAL INTERPRETATION

The 7 of Cups conveys the internal process of a spiritual quest. There is plentitude in a variety of choices; unfortunately you can choose only one.

For some, romantic lifestyles are confusing and frustrating to family and some friends. You are disillusioned by the thoughts of loving only one person for the rest of your life and could resist settling down because commitment seems to be a daunting of choice.

NEW

Like a kid in a candy store, you are having trouble deciding on the best suitor. You need more time to make a decision because the jury is still out on this one.

ESTABLISHED

Both partners are accustomed to getting what they want and it doesn't matter what it is – collections of people, things, or money. Part of the reason is a sense of lack. When there is a sense of "not enough," partners compensate with more things to fill the void.

EXPANDED AWARENESS

The powers of the mind have been studied for centuries and yet uncharted territory still remains. Relationship issues are common themes in dreams. Many people dream of their former boyfriend/girlfriend or spouse. Repressed problems and desires are presented by the unconscious through the dream state in effort to safely work through these issues. An escape to fantasy is not such a terrible way to manage letdowns and lost opportunity.

DETERIORATING

Your partner no longer impresses you or on the other hand, you can no longer pull one over on them. The bubble of illusion has burst. This is an opportunity to come clean and address the problems truthfully and with clarity.

8 OF CUPS

Golden Dawn/Esoteric Title: Lord of Abandoned Success
Decan: 1° – 10°, Saturn in Pisces
Hod in Briah: Success abandoned; decline of interest in anything

General Interpretation

Interests that once meant something may not mean what they did when they were obtained or commenced. The commitment you wanted is unfulfilling and it could be a relationship that you took a lot of *crap* for or fought to remain in.

This card also suggests major life changes that some couples experience after many years of long-term commitment or marriages. In some cases, this is not so much a break up, but suggests a return to former lifestyles; for example, returning to a career after being a stay-at-home mom.

New

The dating scene has hammered down on you to the point where you are taking a break from it. You need to get a new "A" game or lower your standards.

Established

One or both partners, while committed, live apart because of professional obligations or perhaps because of taking care of another family member. It is also possible that a decision is made to relocate, leaving behind family or other important figures.

Expanded Awareness

The change of heart or life path is integral to your growth. Depression could be a concern. Turning away from painful emotional issues does not make them disappear. They are "de-pressed" in order to feel better. You may also turn to spiritual pursuits in order to address your spiritual health and wellness.

Deteriorating

As just mentioned depression could be at the root of some of your relationship problems. Instead of seeking professional help, you may self-medicate through one or more vices. This may add weight to an already unstable connection.

9 OF CUPS

GOLDEN DAWN/ESOTERIC TITLE: Lord of Material Happiness
DECAN: 10° – 20°, Jupiter in Pisces
YESOD IN BRIAH: Success abandoned; complete success, pleasure, happiness, wish fulfilled

GENERAL INTERPRETATION

This is a much-favored card when it appears in a spread because it potentially means that good wishes have come true. The love you work so hard to get is yours. The wedding you've always dreamed of planning happens to your satisfaction. One caveat to heed is to be careful what you wish for, because you just may get it!

NEW

The man or woman who fits your model of life partner is finally here! Everything will be perfect when you get past the smoking, alcoholic binges, or over-indulgent party life of this person.

ESTABLISHED

Both partners accept each other's shortcomings and make things work. For your relationship, that may be all that you've wished.

Expanded AWAreness

Strategies and proper planning are keys to success. You may look at the lives of others you feel are lucky and have it all, but you may not give thought to how hard they have worked to earn their accolades or achievements.

DETERIORATING

You justify your addictive behaviors and stubbornly refuse to get help or blatantly deny having a problem at all. The first step to recovery is taking responsibility for the resistance of any suggestion made by your partner.

10 OF CUPS

GOLDEN DAWN/ESOTERIC TITLE: Lord of Perfected Success
DECAN: 20° – 30°, Mars in Pisces
MALKUTH IN BRIAH: Matters definitely arranged as wished, complete good fortune

GENERAL INTERPRETATION

The 10 of Cups indicates you no longer chase rainbows; you are relieved that your life feels complete. The goal for the relationship when this card appears is living the good life and celebrating everyone in your family's success. Whatever dark times you've suffered through are over and you can give thanks and show appreciation to those who may have been the shoulder to cry on or showed other emotional support.

NEW

Similar to the Ace of Cups, this card suggests not only falling in love but saying it, too. You are looking for the right time and way to tell your partner how much you love him/her.

ESTABLISHED

You have committed yourself to someone who not only makes you happy, but your family loves this person, too. Your parents, sibling, uncles, etc., have welcomed your love into the fold.

EXPANDED AWARENESS

One thing to remember is that when you choose to merge your life with another human, you are also merging with family too. Although you are on your own (if not living in your parent's garage), family members will and do influence you and your life. It may sound old-fashioned, but it is best to lessen the anxiety of it all by making sure he/she is likeable.

DETERIORATING

Stress caused by raising a difficult child tries the patience of one or both partners. Disagreements that are small and large happen more frequently.

Suit of Swords

PSYCHOLOGICAL FUNCTION: Thinking
ELEMENT: Air
ROMANTIC ATTACHMENT: Avoidant

TAROT COUPLING KEYWORDS FOR SWORDS
Positive Qualities: Insightful, considerate, understanding
Impairment/Fear: Guilt, mental abuse
Perception of Partner: Courteous, wise, confidant, rigid
Dyadic Interaction: Respects, shows diplomacy, cold, indifferent
Challenges: Closeness, intimacy and showing affection
Complaints of Partner: Avoids being in the same space, distant, over analyzes
Desires: Mutual respect of input and intellect, learn from each other

ACE OF SWORDS

GOLDEN DAWN/ESOTERIC TITLE: Root of the Powers of Air

GENERAL INTERPRETATION

You are plagued by thoughts of love or something that someone said to you concerning your beloved. You may have been given an ultimatum and are considering all pros and cons, so that you have an advantage. You are mulling over which side to take in a matter. The sword is a dangerous weapon; it is also a peacemaker. You may have drawn the line in the sand and set new boundaries for yourself or your partner.

NEW

Up until now, you have had lots of challenges in relationships, but someone you met just recently may fit the model of your ideal partner. You set a new intention to triumph over any challenges in getting love you think you deserve.

ESTABLISHED

It is normal to have some disagreements in a relationship. There could be a battle of ideologies and there is stubbornness in one or both of you. You could be in the midst of a plan to get out of this relationship if the challenges don't improve.

EXPANDED AWARENESS

An honest listening of each other's idea without judgment would ease some tension. Avoid yelling and screaming matches, or arguments; one of you may suffer with migraines or have issues with allergies, perhaps from your sweetie's perfume or cologne.

DETERIORATING

You may have been taken advantage of in a negative way by your partner and want to go to war. Consider getting a mediator who will be able to help with your differences.

2 OF SWORDS

GOLDEN DAWN/ESOTERIC TITLE: Lord of Peace Restored

DECAN: 1° – 10°, Moon in Libra

CHOKMAH IN YETZIRAH: Quarrels made up, but still tense in relationships; actions sometimes selfish and sometimes unselfish

GENERAL INTERPRETATION

After being at a crossroads and giving it much thought, you have made up your mind on the next set of actions. This card suggests that partners need a "time-out;" however, who will be the one who has the courage to ask for the relationship hiatus? This card indicates that you are not getting direct answers or you find yourself vacillating between options.

NEW

There is some uncertainty about the next stage of your fairly new relationship. You may have trouble saying to your partner what's really bugging you.

ESTABLISHED

The two of you are going back and forth over an issue, but it's reached a stalemate. You experience psychic impressions, but are not sure of what you are feeling. If you are arguing with your partner, this card suggests backing down and formulating a way to communicate or share ideas.

EXPANDED AWARENESS

To be at peace is a desired state when you are in a committed relationship. You need wisdom and guidance on a stressful matter. Take a moment and really think before taking action.

DETERIORATING

You have been stunned or hurt through a misunderstanding or miscommunication, and you want to be alone, withdrawn to give yourself time to think and restructure your mind. Aromatherapy would be great for you right now.

3 OF SWORDS

GOLDEN DAWN/ESOTERIC TITLE: Lord of Sorrow
DECAN: 10° – 20°, Saturn in Libra
BINAH IN YETZIRAH: Unhappiness, sorrow, tears

GENERAL INTERPRETATION

When this card appears in a reading, it can signal less than ideal news for any relationship. This card is typically thought of as a breakup card. Being a three, it also suggests interference and is notoriously known to suggest infidelity. While the situation looks gloomy, you know that you love and deeply care for your partner. This is what makes it all so very hard.

NEW

One partner could be barely holding to one relationship while involved in another one. You could have feelings for two people and the emotions of it all are very emotionally complex. An awareness that a love interest is with someone else, but with this knowledge, you date them anyway.

ESTABLISHED

Partners come together mostly likely because of common interests, even though they may not be emotionally attached in the relationship. The relationship does not offer much in way of fulfillment. It is a loveless connection, but you remain together for the sake of not being alone.

EXPANDED AWARENESS

Are you suffering through relationship turmoil because you feel it has something to teach you on a higher level? This card speaks to pain that in buried or denied. Denial. However, as a coping mechanism it is protective, allowing you to move forward in spite of the greatness of sorrow.

DETERIORATING

Thoughts of breaking up are present, and while you think of it as just a fleeting thought, it may happen more often than you want to admit. There may be repetitive issues of anger, hurt, lies, and other complexities that deteriorate your relationship.

4 OF SWORDS

GOLDEN DAWN/ESOTERIC TITLE: Lord of Rest from Strife
DECAN: 20° – 30°, Jupiter in Libra
CHESED IN YETZIRAH: Convalescence, recovery from sickness, change for the better

GENERAL INTERPRETATION

Anxieties are laid to rest. The healing from a time of any sort of hardship is taking place. Isolation. Banishment and/or expulsion. Spiritual retreat.

NEW

After only knowing your new love partner a short while, they stun you by announcing that they need a break from the relationship. On the other hand, you may need a break, too.

ESTABLISHED

You know each other so well, you recognize when you both need a time out. You retreat to separate corners to gain composure in order to have a rational discussion.

EXPANDED AWARENESS

This card suggests some religious or spiritual camaraderie in your relationship in spite of different religious backgrounds. You may be past the stage of taking up bickering as sport; it's not worth arguing when your partner is cranky and tired.

DETERIORATING

Withdrawn and antisocial, you may not feel up to talking with your partner. They are less understanding of your need to hide or avoid tense energy. You need time to think before you say something really inappropriate. Yelling makes your partner bolt like a scared rabbit and you'll have a hard time getting them to come out of their hole.

5 OF SWORDS

GOLDEN DAWN/ESOTERIC TITLE: Lord of Defeat
DECAN: 1° – 10°, Jupiter in Libra
GEBURAH IN YETZIRAH: Defeat, loss, malice, spite, slander, evil speaking

GENERAL INTERPRETATION

The 5 of Swords conveys a circumstance that is often detrimental to a serious relationship. As shown on Waite's version, two people are caused grave pain by another. However, the figure in the foreground may act as instigator to separate the other two, and hangs back to watch the fireworks. Yes, what a jerk!

NEW

Consider the source of the rumor you've heard about your new man/woman. Is it a jealous former girlfriend/boyfriend that doesn't want to see you together?

ESTABLISHED

You find out some important information that you certainly could have used before you rearranged your life to accommodate this relationship. You don't know whom to trust as you partner or his/her friends or others who are close participate in the betrayal or conspire against you. In times of crisis, one or both partners simply turns their back on one another.

EXPANDED AWARENESS

The world is filled with injustices that are witnessed daily. When this injustice comes to our front door, we then know how bad things are and only then do we move to take action. The 5 of Swords coveys an injustice that concerns us on a more intimate level. Life is not fair and triumphant action to overcome these injustices is a never-ending battle. However, in some cases, these injustices act as catalysts that motivates us to be better and to treat our kindred and associates better.

DETERIORATING

Under the worst conditions, this card indicates humiliation, villainy, infidelity, or dealing with unsavory behavior in one or both partners.

6 OF SWORDS

GOLDEN DAWN/ESOTERIC TITLE: Lord of Earned Success
DECAN: 10° – 20°, Mercury in Aquarius
TIPHARETH IN YETZIRAH: Labor, work, journey by water.

GENERAL INTERPRETATION

Communications between members of the relationship are shores apart and require a delicate choice of words so that each understands the other. This card suggests moving away from difficulties either by choice or by force. If it is by choice, then you could still worry if you chose wisely.

NEW

After keeping an interested party at bay while they await your answer for a private weekend trip or possible relationship, you agree and affirm your interest. You get advice or guidance from a trusted friend or leave information about where you are going.

ESTABLISHED

Important emotional and mental changes are happening. You may have to shift your way of thinking and lifestyle patterns for the better in preparation for merging your lives. One or both of you could have a child to bring into this arrangement and look for ways to make the transition a smooth operation. In order to keep your wedding as private as possible, you plan an escape to somewhere (Bahamas, Turks and Caicos Islands, etc.) for your ceremony.

EXPANDED AWARENESS

The 6 of Swords figuratively describes the disintegration or deterioration stage of the relationship. There is still a chance to recover from uproars or recent corruption shown in the 5 of Swords. In difficult situations, it is important to do the right thing and make it a win-win for all involved.

DETERIORATING

The two members of the relationship, while still cohabiting, are emotionally detached. Instead of the fire and brimstone hellish arguing, both decide to pull back, resigning to the idea that separation is imminent.

7 OF SWORDS

GOLDEN DAWN/ESOTERIC TITLE: Lord of Unstable Effort
DECAN: 20° – 30°, Moon in Aquarius
NETZACH IN YETZIRAH: Journey by land, in character untrustworthy

GENERAL INTERPRETATION

Although this card is typically called the thief card, it is just as likely the figure is performing a daring feat as part of an act or the swords represent information or resources gathered as part of research for a project.

The 7 of Swords in a reading that concerns partnerships, from a positive position, indicates mutual efforts for a productive future. Its negative connotations suggest spying, dubiousness, or fraudulent activity. It is also wise to protect your identity when this card appears concerning money or sensitive documents.

NEW

Do you suspect someone of flattering you with the sole intention to pull one over on you? You may feel something isn't right about him/her, and should recognize that flattery is manipulation. Indeed, Lucifer is a beautiful angel; perhaps he also got a bad rap! Trickery thrives through charm.

ESTABLISHED

Members of this union are extremely clever and have strong survival skills. They genuinely love one another, or they call it love at least. Potentially, the products of co-dependent families, they have a tendency to looks past behaviors that are unlawful or contrary to reason.

EXPANDED AWARENESS

Love to faults is always blind, Always is to love inclin'd. Lawless wing'd and unconfin'd, And break all chain from every mind. ~William Blake. The Rossetti Manuscript, (c. 1793-1811). This quote, generally attributed to Shakespeare (incorrectly), expresses the atmosphere of the 7 of Swords in the relationship arena.

DETERIORATING

It may be time for a come-to-Jesus conversation about what's really happening in this apparently not-so-loving relationship. If one member feels used and manipulated, and the other turns to gossip and venting to others, this calls for intervention with a reputable spiritual leader or professional counselor. In some instances, this can represent a jilted lover who stalks.

8 OF SWORDS

GOLDEN DAWN/ESOTERIC TITLE: Lord of Shortened Force
DECAN: 1° – 10°, Jupiter in Gemini
HOD IN YETZIRAH: Narrow, restricted, petty, a prison

GENERAL INTERPRETATION

It takes profound love to remain in a tedious relationship. Stale relationships are fertile ground for members to seek passion outside of the connection.

Self-restraint and impulse control are issues that are relevant to the 8 of Swords. Embarrassment or shame prevents you for asking for assistance.

This card also suggests mental blocks, fogging thinking, or forgetfulness. In spite of distractions, one is able to concentrate, study, or focus on an important project.

NEW

Poor self-image and low-self esteem drives a person to make unhealthy mate choices. Refrain from dating or committing to a relationship until you are emotionally and mentally healthy yourself.

ESTABLISHED

Making the best out of a relationship means that at times we have to think before we act or object to a matter. When the relationship ceases to help an individual grow, they will often describe feelings of being trapped and helpless as to how to fix or leave the relationship.

EXPANDED AWARENESS

Have you ever been irritated by your partner because they were not effective at understanding you or completing something you requested of them? The response to your partner may trigger feelings of your parent's response to you. Find productive ways of curtailing annoyance and irritation through adjusting your patterned response or attitude.

DETERIORATING

A partner keeps close ties to a former mate and claims it is because of money, business, or other unemotional issues. Ostracism is the recourse a member of the coupling has chosen as a solution.

9 OF SWORDS

GOLDEN DAWN/ESOTERIC TITLE: Lord of Despair and Cruelty
DECAN: 10° – 20°, Mars in Gemini
YESOD IN YETZIRAH: Complete destruction, destroyed

GENERAL INTERPRETATION

"Do not worry; it's all in your head" is the modern inference for the 9 of Swords, which seems ironic given that the thing that you are thinking about is the source of feeling worried. Regret, guilt, and despair are also choice words uses to interpret this card.

The questioner or someone close to him or her possibly experiences insomnia and respiratory afflictions.

NEW

You could be anxious about a first date or meeting your partner's acquaintances or parents for the first time. Newly in love, you are not confident that the feeling is mutual. Were you sex-ting your new man/woman and it went to the ex, or worse, your co-worker?

ESTABLISHED

Couples may have different sleep schedules; rising too early or retiring to bed in the middle of the night disturbs one. Someone is overwrought by despair from getting bad news or awaiting tests results.

EXPANDED AWARENESS

Presented with an opportunity that could benefit one individual and betray the other, the weight of the dilemma causes overwhelming despair.

DETERIORATING

Think twice! You could be pulling the wool over your own eyes. When you protest your partner's extreme inappropriateness, they convince you through naturalization in order that you also feel its okay. If a thing doesn't seem right, it could be your imagination and you could unjustly make accusations, The 9 of Swords is a caution to stick only to the facts.

10 OF SWORDS

GOLDEN DAWN/ESOTERIC TITLE: Lord of Ruin
DECAN: 20° – 30°, Sun in Gemini
MALKUTH IN YETZIRAH: Ruin, death, defeat, disruption

GENERAL INTERPRETATION

The 10 of Swords possibly are more dreadful than the Death card. This dread is warranted given the iconic death scene on the Waite version, and in reference to worldly matters, it is quite devastating.

It is not so in terms of high ideals. One clue is the beach scene depicted on Waite's version. It looks serene, and for many, being near the ocean or lake is soothing and helps clear the mind.

The beach symbolizes the state of mind, writes Tony Crisp in *Dream Dictionary: An A-Z Guide to Understanding Your Unconscious Mind* (New York, New York: Dell Publishing, Random House, Inc., 2002). He adds that, in dreams, a beach is the boundary or threshold and our potential in the universal process of life and death.

NEW

Next! That was fun (or not). After one date, you never hear from a person again. The good news is that you are back on the market.

ESTABLISHED

The relationship is on life support at this point. If you are into martyrdom, you'll both stick together because you are motivated to do so by children, finances, or guilt.

EXPANDED AWARENESS

Relationship expert John M. Gottman, PhD. writes about four indicators in which he could predict with about 91% accuracy when a relationship would end. In *The Seven Principles of Making Marriage Work* (New York: Three Rivers Press, 1999) co-authored by Nan Silver, he describes six predictive factors:

1. Harsh Startup
2. The Four Horsemen
3. Flooding
4. Body Language

5. Failed Repair Attempts
6. Bad Memories

The authors explain how these factors include "stonewalling," a term used to describe emotional disengagement from the relationship. This happens mostly in relationships where the partners have been together for a long time and learn to tune each other out. These are occurrences in which the relationship itself feels as if it is slowly dying.

DETERIORATING

The relationship is in trouble based on the above factors. The other nine percent are the ones that hang on for as long as possible. On a personal note: My observation when this card comes up for troubled relationships, it consistently indicates that the couple will "emotionally divorce" instead of an actual legal divorce. The relationship is over but they remain stuck.

Suit of Pentacles (disks)

PSYCHOLOGICAL FUNCTION: Sensing
ELEMENT: Earth
ROMANTIC ATTACHMENT: Secure

TAROT COUPLING KEYWORDS FOR PENTACLES (DISKS)

Positive Qualities: Spontaneous, provokes growth, and idealistic
Impairment/Fear: Fears change, imbalance of masculine energy
Perception of Partner: Risk taker, somewhat needy, and charismatic
Dyadic Interaction: All or nothing attitude, needs space, and shows
enthusiasm about partner's ideas
Challenges: Spaces out, anxious, envy, and recklessness
Complaints of Partner: Impatient, exaggerates, playboy/girl antics
Desires: Connection that offers excitement

ACE OF PENTACLES (DISKS)

GOLDEN DAWN/ESOTERIC TITLE: Root of the Powers of Earth

GENERAL INTERPRETATION

This card suggests value and worth. It represents prosperity and accumulation of goods. Aces are the beginning or first steps, and this card could represent the start of new ways to earn income or to take on new ways of being. For couples, it could mean new money coming in or sometimes a more solid relationship.

NEW

You are finally ready to invest seriously in a relationship. A new relationship gets off to a slow start, but you feel it is worth it and allow it to grow into something which you feel will be beneficial to both of you.

ESTABLISHED

The relationship has a sense of wholeness and security. It is important to the both of you to have financial security for the future, and in doing so, you may decide to live together or get married, if you already aren't. This suggests a secure relationship in which you are comfortable enough to iron out any insecurity without the risks of drama.

EXPANDED AWARENESS

It may be time to look at all sides of a matter and reach a balanced, well-considered solution. Stand up for your rights. Making things official may entail dealings with lawyers or lawmakers.

DETERIORATING

Reason has gone out the window. Rules are made that neither partner can obey. Every mistake is scrutinized and feelings of unfairness and misjudgment surface.

2 OF PENTACLES (DISKS)

GOLDEN DAWN/ ESOTERIC TITLE: Lord of Harmonious Change
DECAN: 1°-10°, Jupiter in Capricorn
CHOKMAH IN ASSIAH: Pleasant change, visit friends

GENERAL INTERPRETATION

In a reading, this card indicates movement, busy times, or managing life as it comes. There could be a stressful period in your life that may take some time to eliminate. The goal here is to make everyone and everything a win-win situation.

NEW

After a dry spell without dating, you are romantically busy, possibly juggling two dates. It feels good to have attention again. Life is not quite settled as it was; you could make changes in your life over a long haul. Try to enjoy it!

ESTABLISHED

You are busy and overwhelmed, but you can manage. There may be changes to your personal life and your career that could leave you with less quality time for yourself or loved ones.

EXPANDED AWARENESS

Prioritizing will help you deal with whatever is thrown at you. You may have added responsibilities at work or household duties that need to be addressed.

An example of a situation in which this card appeared in a reading was that of my client Sam whose wife, Jen, complained about him being a workaholic. This made her feel neglected and less valued. During the reading, Sam recognized that even though it would take some integrating, he needed to be more flexible with his schedule in order to spend more quality time with Jen.

DETERIORATING

Possibly you and your partner have negative traits that you dislike in one another. You have to sort through these negative traits and integrate more positive ones in order to feel more secure in your relationship. Perhaps you are dealing with manipulation by your mate. Sometimes this indicates juggling more than one love interest, which, if is not a pre-agreed term of your relationship, could cause unsettling issues for the relationship.

3 OF PENTACLES (DISKS)

GOLDEN DAWN/ESOTERIC TITLE: Lord of Material Works
DECAN: 10°-20°, Mars in Capricorn
CHOKMAH IN ASSIAH: Business, paid employment, commercial transactions.

GENERAL INTERPRETATION

The 3 of Pentacles indicates a desire for structure and organization. Schemes or plans may be a part of conquering the desire of your heart. It also suggests that you'll need to be clever when it comes to love. Good relationships take work and time.

NEW

There's no wasting time or kissing frogs for you. You have become serious about your future and are only interested in those who want to share it.

ESTABLISHED

Plans for the future are being carefully crafted for maximum success. Couples may seek the advice of a retirement planning specialist or a draw up the details of a will. On an emotional level, couples have great appreciation for each other's inner work as well as the external.

EXPANDED AWARENESS

There is a good sense of structure to the relationship because both members entered the relationship as conscious beings with openness to improve themselves. They build each other up with positive critiques and encouragement.

DETERIORATING

In an ill-dignified position, this card suggests a lack of ambition, unemployment or minimizing the importance of other's advice. You may feel that your partner takes you for granted or is jealous of your achievements. The relationship will not last under a partner's disdain towards progress.

4 OF PENTACLES (DISKS)

GOLDEN DAWN/ESOTERIC TITLE: Lord of Earthly Powers
DECAN: 20°-30°, Sun in Capricorn
CHESED IN ASSIAH: Gain of money or influence

GENERAL INTERPRETATION

Hard economic times cause people to tighten their grip on their funds. Sometimes loans are given to those who lack the financial stability to pay it back. Concerning relationships, an interpretation of the 4 of Pentacles (Disks) that I first heard from Ruth Ann and Wald Amberstone (The Tarot School), is: "Time to meet Dad!"

NEW

Until you have a sense of your partner's true feelings, you avoid revealing how much you love them and suppress the fact that you've hit the jackpot. However, the relation is too new to declare that this is the one.

ESTABLISHED

Resting on each other's laurels is not going to keep the relationship interesting or pay the bill for long. On the other hand, you both earn a decent living and could do a better job at managing your wealth.

EXPANDED AWARENESS

Both members know they have a good thing going and want to keep it as such. Often when a relationship hits a snag, people compensate by trying to buy love with fancy cars, designer handbags, or an impressive home. Perhaps partners have learned that positive reinforcement works best to keep everyone happy. Happy partner equals happy life.

DETERIORATING

A bad investment in the emotional department will cost you more than hurt feelings. This is a caution to guard you assets, both financially and emotionally.

5 OF PENTACLES (DISKS)

GOLDEN DAWN/ESOTERIC TITLE: Lord of Material Trouble
DECAN: 1°-10°, Mercury in Taurus
GEBURAH IN ASSIAH: Loss of profession, loss of money, monetary anxiety

GENERAL INTERPRETATION

Given the appearance on Waite's version, love seems to be far from the mind of the couple. They may have lost everything, but they still have each other. It does seem when down on one's luck, the sense of true love and friendship stands the test of time.

NEW

You fear a new relationship because of past mistakes. Starving for affection or desperately wanting to be in a relationship forces you to hurriedly involve yourself with one who is not worth the drama. Potentially, the relationship may pan out after a really tough start.

ESTABLISHED

Appearances are everything; on the outside, your relationship looks warm, tender, and loving, but on the inside, one or both partners shivers from the lack of warmth behind closed doors. You proceed in your day-to-day activities, but the reality of things, such as maturity, loss of sex drive, and unhappiness leads you to consider going elsewhere to get needs met.

EXPANDED AWARENESS

We rely on those close to us as a source of comfort and support in times of need or difficulties. In a relationship, partners turn to each other as the first source.

A relationship is nourished when partners give and receive a generous dose of affection and pure kindness.

DETERIORATING

Money brought happiness until the well ran dry. Wining, dining, and shopping sprees that were the allurement, no longer happen, so now *you* aren't happening either. Welcome to Loserville, USA – Population: 1.

6 OF PENTACLES (DISKS)

Golden Dawn/Esoteric Title: Lord of Material Success
Decan: 10°–20°, Mercury in Taurus
Tiphareth in Assiah: Success in material things; prosperity in business

General Interpretation

People often think they have a pretty good idea of what they want from life; however, rarely intuit the consequences. For instance, women are far more conditioned to grow up, meet Prince Charming, and live happily ever after. This fantasy of love motivates men and women alike to aspire to this incredible tale. Along with fantasy comes the assumption of an ever generous and giving partner who will fulfill every potential emotional, sexual, and material need. It is possible that the amount of generosity one has to give to a happy relationship is not painted into that white picket fence scenario. The 6 of Pentacles (Disks) expresses charity and generosity. In relationships, it is beyond for richer or poorer in terms of material concerns. It is acceptance and receiving of all parts of a person.

New

Someone holds a secret admiration for you and the kicker is you may already be acquainted with him/her. Pay attention to subtle signs and hints dropped here and there.

Established

Flowers, candy, jewelry, cologne, perfume, gift cards: your partner knows what you like and vice versa. Or perhaps neither has a clue. If this is the case, ask the cards for gift ideas. Refer to suggestions in the Major Arcana chapter.

Expanded Awareness

To dovetail further on the above interpretation, the importance of giving and receiving generosity in your relationship should start by asking your partner what perspectives and beliefs they hold around commitment, as well as roles in a relationship.

As mentioned earlier, we are socialized and raised to understand that men do certain things in a relationship and women have their domestic duties.

In a recent article, on issues in LGBT (lesbian, gay, bisexual, and transgender) relationships, findings shows that LGBT couples have less of a problem with sharing roles and domestic responsibilities. Seems very effective. Bottom line is to be comfortable with receiving and giving.

Deteriorating

Your partner is taken charity a bit too far. In some instances, a partner could be dividing resources or time between you and another person who demands attention.

7 OF PENTACLES (DISKS)

GOLDEN DAWN/ESOTERIC TITLE: Lord of Success Unfulfilled
DECAN: 20°-30°, Saturn in Taurus
NETZACH IN ASSIAH: Unprofitable speculation and employment; little gain for much labor

GENERAL INTERPRETATION

We have all been there, investing or working hard only to get the minimum return on the investment. You hang in because of patience or, better still, hope.

NEW

It may be a while before this new love interest turns into something more substantial. While you wait, it is a good idea to do some inner work.

ESTABLISHED

You had expectation that your partner would change when you got together and you don't see many changes at all. Look around, keep looking, and look even deeper. Okay, now, ask if your partner should be the only one making changes?

EXPANDED AWARENESS

Picatrix's (magical text or grimore) meaning for this decan includes madness, misery, and slavery. You might agree that it is quite drastic.

> *Your emotions are the slaves to your thoughts,*
> *and you are the slave to your emotions.*
>
> ~Elizabeth Gilbert
> *Eat, Pray, Love*

This quote by Elizabeth Gilbert, author the bestseller turned movie *Eat, Pray, Love*, explains why the figure stands waiting for something to happen. This is the hope for a working relationship.

DETERIORATING

You've tried dressing him/her up, sprucing up, propping up, and wash-rinse-repeat. These have all failed. You may have one more try in you and it will take some time to plan your next move.

8 OF PENTACLES (DISKS)

GOLDEN DAWN/ESOTERIC TITLE: Lord of Prudence
DECAN: 1°-10°, Sun in Virgo
HOD IN ASSIAH: Skill, prudence, cunning

GENERAL INTERPRETATION

This card suggest training, or entry-level job in any industry, but most likely in the blue-collar field. I was reading at a party, and when this card appeared in my querent's spread, I said, " This tells me that you win a trophy or are working on educating yourself to run some type of skilled craft." He replied, "Yes, I'm in the trophy business, I make trophies!"

NEW

Perhaps you are interested in a person who is extremely attractive, a.k.a eye candy, arm ornament, trophy wife/husband? Other people think you are shallow; not me! I understand.

ESTABLISHED

Both partners are fully committed to the relationship. Plans to move in together may be made after the completion of school or other major transitions are over. You could both work on ideas or plans for your home, paying attention to fine details to ensure every corner of the house is perfect.

EXPANDED AWARENESS

On the search for love, most of the time the only thing we have to go on is a person's physical attractiveness. Believe it or not, it has to do with biological and psychological processes.

The ideal partner or "imago" (a psychological term used by Jung), is the unconscious better half that we seek. Have you ever noticed that partners seem to resemble each other to the point that they could be siblings or closely resembling parents? That is imago revealing itself.

DETERIORATING

Immaturity and lack of discipline is difficult to someone who needs structure and security. Neither partner is ready to grow up or accept a full commitment.

9 OF PENTACLES (DISKS)

GOLDEN DAWN/ESOTERIC TITLE: Lord of Material Gain
DECAN: 10°-20°, Venus in Virgo
YESOD IN ASSIAH: Inheritance, much increase of goods

GENERAL INTERPRETATION

Financial independence is an issue for the querent. This indicates self-employment, perhaps through a home-based business. You thrive in a relationship, one in which you are well taken care of emotionally and financially.

But has it come with a steep price: the loss of freedom to be with the friends you want to be with or stranded in a place far away from family and loved one?

NEW

You have more time and less restriction on your availability. It is time to call the cutie that's been asking you out for two months.

ESTABLISHED

With a very comfortable lifestyle and comfortable financial stability. Your relationship reflects your fabulous life. One member of this coupling could be living off an inheritance while trying to establish his or her own business. The comforts of your surrounding are no replacement for your lovers arm.

EXPANDED AWARENESS

This is a nature lover's card. You and your partner may own a landscaping business or work in natural settings, Perhaps you both have interest in joining a Zoological Society in your local area.

DETERIORATING

It appears that your partner is only interested in you because of your wealth. This is not so negative if you both are happy. This card could indicate an arranged marriage that is not working out and one partner stands to benefit greatly. Before allowing someone in your inner world, do a background check and watch out for grifters.

10 OF PENTACLES (DISKS)

GOLDEN DAWN/ESOTERIC TITLE: Lord of Wealth
DECAN: 20°-30°, Venus in Virgo
MALKUTH IN ASSIAH: Riches and wealth

GENERAL INTERPRETATION

The 10 of Pentacles (Disks) is emblematic of a successful life. Of course, material prosperity is not the only fulfillment represented by this card. Personal growth and aging gracefully are also visible.

Ten focuses on family matters such as the possibility that a son, daughter-in-law, and grandchild are moving in to help with expenses. Whatever you are inquiring about, this card leans more to a positive solution.

NEW

This one makes up for all the awful dates you've been on in the past. It has all the elements of your dream relationship: interesting conversation, mature adult behavior, and they are gainfully employed.

If you are a single parent back on the dating scene, not to worry; your new love interest will probably love your kids and they may also have children.

ESTABLISHED

It's a cliché; however, you've got it made in the shade, like lemonade! Family members are cooperative and getting along and so are the both of you. You instill strong family values in the younger generation and recognize that your relationship is the model for the ones they will have when the time comes.

EXPANDED AWARENESS

While money is of interest here, it is not so much about the pursuit of material items or financial security in relationships. What's truly sought is peace of mind.

As demonstrated earlier in this book, we seek to repair our past through relationships. The repairs are not easy; however, chances of healing have better odds within the confines of a secure and happy relationship.

DETERIORATING

Couples argue about money and finances no matter how much cash flow there is in their bank account. Thorough planning is a must for budgets and living expenses. However, irresponsibility with someone else's earning makes them super angry. "Wait, it's our money!" I know what you are thinking, but what's mine is mine and what's his is mine is really how it is. Entitlement and lack of respect is what is getting in the way here.

On another note, that great person you met and are so happy to be dating, not only has kids, they are married with children! Yes, I know they are promising to leave their spouse. Are you willing to wait?

CHAPTER 12

THE MINOR ARCANA
Court Cards

In the Golden Dawn tradition, the Court Cards represent people or events and both of these can have personality.

The Court Cards are possibly the most complicated of the Minor Arcana cards to understand because, just like people, they are complex.

For me, it is easier to work with personality characteristics, and by doing so, a single mother is possibly a KING and a single father, both mother and father to his children, may also act as QUEEN.

These have nothing to do with sexual orientations. The same goes for the Knights. Particular to these pairings, the Knights are in some cases paired with a King. Remember, think in terms of personalities and behaviors.

S.L. MacGregor Mathers gave descriptions of the cards in his book *The Tarot*; his research laid the basis for the cards we have today. Each member of the Order were made to copy his drawings of the cards and when they did, members like Aleister Crowley took a bit of creative license with the designs and came up with the *Thoth* deck.

Creating a personal deck was important to the ritualistic process, and ritual affects each person differently, as evidenced in the various decks.

Where I part ways with tradition somewhat is that I have here a system of *Tarot Coupling* Keywords for the Court Cards using the same categories of partner relation used in the Major Arcana.

For those who wish to further the knowledge of the Golden Dawn attributes to Tarot, I recommend Israel Regardie's *The Golden Dawn and OTO's 777 and Other Qabalistic Writings of Aleister Crowley.*

What About the Pages?

In the Golden Dawn tradition, the Pages and the Aces are the "thrones" of their suit. The Pages or Princesses are of the earth element and transition the court cards to the numbered pips.

As personalities, they are traditionally considered adolescent females or young adults, in line for the royal thrown. In a reading, they can clue you into childhood issues that are unresolved, as well as bring news or announce changes in your circumstances.

In my use of the Pages (Princesses), I usually see these as undeveloped/ undiscovered aspects of personalities or immature behavior by an adult querent or partner. The six categories of Tarot Coupling are best used in adult romantic relationships.

I have given traditional attributes with my own suggested keywords for the Pages; all other have *Tarot Coupling* Keywords.

PAGES (PRINCESSES)

Page of Wands

GOLDEN DAWN/ESOTERIC TITLE: The Princess of the Shining Flame, The Rose of the Palace of Fire, Empress of the Salamanders, Throne of the Ace of Wands
QABALISTIC ATTRIBUTION: Malkuth in Atziluth
ELEMENT: Earth of Fire (Specific Earth of Primal Fire)
DECAN: North Pole Quadrant of North Pole
ASTROLOGICAL ATTRIBUTIONS: Cancer, Leo and Virgo
ATTACHMENT: Fearful-Avoidant

POSITIVE KEYWORDS
Smart, simple, naive, guiltless; talkative; immature, bragger, courageous, sociable, busy; charming, talented, athletic, spontaneous

NEGATIVE KEYWORDS
Anxious, uneasy, worry, irritated, edgy; nervous, random, apprehensive, unreliable, easily angered, delinquent, nagging, and ambivalent

GENERAL INTERPRETATION
This Page represents an outgoing and sometime unpredictable personality. Though overly interested in their partners, on the flip side, the Page of Wands can often have illusions around stable relationships. In a relationship with this Page (Princess) you may find yourself having to give them lots of praise and attention. They love to stay busy and have projects. You could be one of those projects or find yourself a "fixer-upper."

NEW
Your new love potential is interesting and you are compatible in many ways. On the outside, they appear very social and confident. You may have some trouble getting close to them in the beginning. They are not easily attached, preferring creative pursuits or careers to a committed partnership.

ESTABLISHED
Friday date nights or going out with friends have become quiet evenings at home. One or both partners may work longer hours and the romance is replaced by a focus on career. You may have some good news to give to your partner that may be a pleasant surprise for them or you may receive surprisingly good news.

EXPANDED AWARENESS

One or both partners begin to explore deeper aspects of their togetherness. There is an interest in mysticism, especially that of other cultures or traditions. One or both partners search for common interests and activities that will draw them closer together while maintaining their individual creative pursuits.

DETERIORATING

Insecure feelings create suspicions that are the underlying cause of snide remarks. The energy in the relationship runs from hot to cold and it becomes hard to discern what one partner wants from the other.

Page of Cups

GOLDEN DAWN/ESOTERIC TITLE: The Princess of the Waters, Lotis of the Palace of the Floods, Empress of Nymphs and Undines, Throne of the Ace of Cups
ELEMENT: Earth of Water (Specific Earth in Primal Water)
Decan: SECOND QUADRANT
ASTROLOGICAL ATTRIBUTIONS: Sagittarius, Scorpio. Libra
ATTACHMENT: Anxious – Preoccupied

POSITIVE KEYWORDS

Artistic, creative, gentle, imaginative; dreamer; pensive, elegant, effeminate, graceful; tender.

NEGATIVE KEYWORDS

Untruthful, liar, harsh, critical, overly emotional, whiner

GENERAL INTERPRETATION

Page (Princess) of Cups often brings succor and ease to any situation. They are delightful and are often well-liked; however, they are not usually comfortable in their own skins. If your relationship takes on the personality of the card, it would most likely be very dreamy and ideal, lots of romance, but somehow it seems too good to be true. It also represents a relationship that is more like a never-ending roller coaster ride.

NEW

You are the hopeless romantic. You never give up on love. You don't mind starting over again, as this new potential partner seems to be exactly what you have been looking for and you are certain of it.

ESTABLISHED

There is a lot of certainty about the direction of the newly established connection. Both partners are comfortable with each other and plans are in the making to relocate or start a family.

EXPANDED AWARENESS

Partners highly appreciate the honesty, love, and insights gained from one another the longer they stay together. The relationship may have reached a level where one or both partners feel comfortable enough to venture out and follow once-abandoned passions. Partners also review what can be realistically accomplished in their lives, including fulfillment of prior dreams and goals.

DETERIORATING

No one wants to show weakness and and so they exhibit external toughness, but it only comes off as heartless and uncaring. Complaints and requests fall on deaf ears further complicating an already tense situation. Imaginary situations are conjured up only to get a rise out of a partner.

Page of Swords

GOLDEN DAWN/ESOTERIC TITLE: The Princess of Rushing Winds, Lotus of The Palace of Air, Empress of The Sylphs and Sylphides, Throne of the Ace of Swords
ELEMENT: Earth of Air Specific Earth in the World of Primal Earth
DECAN: Third Quadrant
ASTROLOGICAL ATTRIBUTIONS: Capricorn, Aquarius, and Pisces
ATTACHMENT: Fearful Avoidant

POSITIVE KEYWORDS

Clever, skills, severe, stern; fast; whirlwind, beautiful, strong, canniness; astute, finessed, street smart, talented

NEGATIVE KEYWORDS

Skittish, empty-headed, absent-minded, crazy, flip; flaky, petty, abrupt, brash, unannounced

GENERAL INTERPRETATION

Seemingly immature and inexperienced, the Page of Swords is probably just the opposite. Smart, adventurous, and independent, this is someone who actually knows what they want and often obtains it by relying on their intellectual resources. They want to know about their partners, yet sometimes are not keen to emotional nuances. One or both partners are willing to try anything once.

New

Tired of the same boring partners, you change course and seek out potential mates who are not typical boy/girl-next-door types. This could indicate that you have hooked up with someone who feeds your intellect, but is a bit socially awkward.

Established

One of the things that work in this partnership is that you do things together, even if you have to sacrifice and do something you may not want to do, but you do it because your partner enjoys it. The secret is to continue to learn new things and always try to find something new and interesting about your partner.

Expanded Awareness

Did you know that the biggest sex organ we have is our brain? The key to positive experiences in relationships don't begin "below" but above, in our minds. When things seems stale or romance is *blah*, try stimulating both yours and your partner's intellect.

Deteriorating

Partners learned negative ways to manipulate long ago. Linear thinking is a way of resisting and respecting the viewpoint of your partner. In order to reach or maintain a solid footing, couples must reach a level of understanding and respect.

Page of Pentacles (Disks)

Golden Dawn/Esoteric Title: The Princess of Echoing Hills, Rose of the Palace of Earth, Princess and Empress of the Gnomes, Thrones of Ace of Pentacles (Disks)
Element: Earth of Earth
Decan: Fourth Quadrant
Astrological Attributions: Aries, Taurus, Gemini
Attachment: Secure

Positive Keywords

Fertile, strong, diligent, solid, stern; serious, grounded; persistent, charitable, altruistic, big-heartedness; pupil, learned, rich, wealth

NEGATIVE KEYWORDS
Stingy, mean, bad news, complex, workaholic, wasteful, overspends, reckless

GENERAL INTERPRETATION
In Qabalistic terms, this is literally as down to earth as you can get. This card indicates someone who keeps it real and pulls no punches, if they are operating in their positive aspects. For love seekers, this could represent a very feasible approach to emotional fulfillment.

NEW
Physical attractiveness counts right now. You are searching for romance and love by starting at the top of the gene pool. This also says that a new relationship will not move fast enough for your taste or you may need to slow it down.

ESTABLISHED
Partners encourage each other to be sensible and careful about all the necessities of living, such as money, food, etc. The focus may be on investing in the future of your children or grandchildren. Your concerns go beyond the superficial. This indicates both are conscientious partners who would like to do nothing more than have a conscious and functioning relationship. Both partners offer continuing support to each other and all those concerned.

EXPANDED AWARENESS
Partners are very gentle and take their promise of commitment very seriously. It may be the case here that both partners have dutifully worked to stabilize their connection. The Page of Pentacles may suggest an obsession with an individual. This card also points out that you may see a partner through rose-colored glasses, falling in love not with the real person, but projected qualities of the person.

DETERIORATING
Perhaps this relationship has been awful for a long time but devotion to children and the fear of failure causes you to not make changes. Neither partner has resources that will improve the connection. Even if there are resources, you may not be able to rely on your partner to properly put them to use.

KNIGHTS (PRINCES)

Knight of Wands (Male or Female)

SEQUESTER

GOLDEN DAWN/ESOTERIC TITLE: Prince of the Chariot of Fire, Prince and Emperor of the Salamanders
DECAN: Last Decan of Cancer – first two Decans of Leo
QABALISTIC ATTRIBUTION: Tiphareth in Atziluth
ELEMENT: Air of Fire (Specific Air of Primal Fire)
ATTACHMENT: Fearful Avoidant

TAROT COUPLING KEYWORDS

Positive Qualities: Private, can be social butterfly and yet private

Impairment/Fear: Cuts people off emotionally, distances, fears smothering, avoids humiliation

Perception of Partner: Too easily led, overly dependent, tendency to be insecure, dull, overbearing lacks spontaneity

Dyadic Interaction: Limits togetherness, distances through work, travel, projects, egotistical, non committal, acts irrationally, runs from anything too demanding, spontaneity

Challenges: Sharing feelings, staying involved, closeness, and integration of partner's positive and negative traits

Objection of Partner: Avoidance, indifferent to others, no time for closeness, distracted, not serious

Desire: Participate is major areas of life

GENERAL INTERPRETATION

Waite's Knight of Wands appears in a desert where he may have been sequestered. This may be by personal choice. This card suggests someone who is very attractive and accustomed to getting his or her way. I have called this card The Sequester as this Knight often represents someone who desires to be in a relationship, but is also very skittish when it comes to settling with a partner. They may feel isolated by their partner or they themselves are prone to avoiding solid relationships.

NEW

This could be the one, but not so fast! This one will have what feels like a good thing, and it is, up to a point. If you can keep them interested long enough, it could turn out to be a hot connection!

ESTABLISHED

Other people don't see what you see in each other. Your friends and family may have doubts about the longevity of your relationship and fear its collapse. What they don't see is how you motivate each other and how you feed each other's soul.

EXPANDED AWARENESS

This connection is perplexed by the paradox of attachment and detachment. While both partners truly desire a fulfilling and committed relationship, if only in theory, it is difficult to really feel settled. You may find that the moment one feels intimately connected, the desire to be chased or longing for attention from another interest pops up in your mind. Perhaps absence does make the heart grow fonder, you may need to give each other a little space.

DETERIORATING

You may have come to realize that your lover is not the settling kind. Perhaps they have already left and you are struggling to find out what went wrong. This may have happened right when things were going well. Fearful-avoidant types often are reluctant to become deeply involved because of this reason – abandoned at the drop of hat.

Knight of Cups (Male or Female)

RESOLVER

GOLDEN DAWN/ESOTERIC TITLE: Prince of the Chariot of the Waters, Prince and Emperor of Nymphs and Undines
DECAN: Last Decan of Libra – first two Decans of Scorpio
QABALISTIC ATTRIBUTION: Tiphareth in Assiah
ELEMENT: Air of Water (Specific Air of Primal Water)
ATTACHMENT: Anxious-Preoccupied

TAROT COUPLING KEYWORDS

Positive Qualities: Compromises, solution-oriented, mannerly
Impairment/Fear: Lost self, uncertainty, resists self-assertion, fragmented self-image, runs emotional scale of highs and lows, feels unnoticed, feels ignored or invisible, unloved

Perception of Partner: Lacks sensitivity, control freak, full of criticism, selfish, detached, severe, hurtful

Dyadic Interaction: Being a pleaser, being submissive, idealist, exaggerates emotional responses, confused

Challenges: Become assertive, form boundaries, desires to feel special, consistency in relationships, stay present in relationships, and secretly wants control

Objection of Partner: Dreamer, unmotivated, manipulates emotions, lacks independence, needs to be noticed, and attention getting tactics, and rejects rational ideas

Desires: Harmonious partnership, romance, grows old together

GENERAL INTERPRETATION

A Knight of Cups is quite a dutiful and well-mannered individual, often placing the needs of others before him/herself. Similar to the younger member of the court of Cups, this romantic-at-heart is often preoccupied with love interests. Many find the Knight of Cups an alluring, albeit elusive, prospect. If you are only interested in a casual, romantic partner, this Knight is your best bet.

NEW

An intriguing encounter has caught you off guard and you have been hit with Cupid's arrow. Awed by this powerful attraction, you are seeing moons, stars, and hearts!

ESTABLISHED

Under the influence of this Knight, partners are best friends. Both partners try to help each other and resolve issues providing a sense of normalcy in times of stress. This is a partnership in which loyalty means a great deal.

EXPANDED AWARENESS

The underlying thread to any relationship that helps us maintain it is how well we are valued and how much we can compromise on the things that do not match our needs. Socialization helps us to learn consideration and value through friendships. It is amazing to see how many long-term partners relay that they started out as friends and the friendship blossomed into romance.

DETERIORATING

Disheartened and disappointed, you may not be able to muster up any enthusiasm about a future. One or both partners feel taken for granted and do not understand how things have become so muddled. Hearts are aching, words are minced, and emotions are high. Losing this person will be extremely painful, should it hit the ending stage.

Knight of Swords (Male or Female)

RESISTOR

GOLDEN DAWN/ESOTERIC TITLE: Prince of the Chariots of the Winds, Prince and Emperor of Sylphs and Sylphides
DECAN: Last Decan of Capricorn – first two Decans of Aquarius
QABALISTIC ATTRIBUTION: Yesod in Yetzirah
ELEMENT: Air of Air (Specific Air of Primal Air)
Attachment: Dismissive Avoidant

TAROT COUPLING KEYWORDS

Positive Qualities: Planner, decisive, advocate
Impairment/Fear: Fear of being limited or controlled, doesn't want to grow up, fears domination, rule breaker
Perception of Partner: Overbearing, rigid, self-governing, perfectionist, authoritative, persuasive, persistent, filled with contradictions
Dyadic Interaction: Confrontational, hot-tempered, impatient, rebellious, mental games, sarcastic, takes for granted, flighty
Challenges: Stay focused, learn discernment, learn to value others, trust others, responsibility to self and others, establish feeling connections within self and others
Objection of Partner: Hasty, directionless, confused in ambitions, unclear on motives, infatuated, anger
Desires: Change the world with partner

GENERAL INTERPRETATION

As a Resistor, this Knight wants to go against the grain and resists anyone trying to control his/her world. He/She wants to be in control of emotional entanglements, as they do not like complicated emotional exchanges. They want to be the ones who decide that they are in love and they need love to make sense because they take commitment seriously.

Alternatively, they jump into relationships feet first, fearlessly at full throttle, resisting rules and boundaries.

NEW

This may be a time of second chances. Perhaps a decision was made too quickly to break up with your lover. This card suggests that you could be thinking about an ex and are resisting the opportunity to begin another relationship because you think you need closure.

ESTABLISHED

A great contributor to the success of this connection is the capacity for both partners to be flexible, but also able to plan and abide by decisions. It is also important that when the dominate partner is in the driver's seat that the other relinquishes control – at least temporarily.

EXPANDED AWARENESS

This is a connection with a lot of energy and sometimes one or both partners can seem larger–than-life. Because of the high energy, partners have to be able to go with the flow and know that the only thing constant in this relationship is change.

DETERIORATING

Partners have really bad attitudes and are complete jerks to each other, although one of them feels justified for their bad behavior. The relationship has been on again/off again, but this time you are thinking it is over for good. Should you close this door, think long and hard about why you would open it again.

Knight of Pentacles (Disks) (Male or Female)

LONE WOLF

GOLDEN DAWN/ESOTERIC TITLE: Prince of the Chariot of Earth, Prince and Emperor of the Gnomes

DECAN: Last Decan of Aries – first two Decan of Taurus

QABALISTIC ATTRIBUTION: Tiphareth in Malkuth

ELEMENT: Air of Earth (Specific Air of Primal Earth)

ATTACHMENT: Secure

TAROT COUPLING KEYWORDS

Positive Qualities: Health conscious, dependable, detail-oriented

Impairment/Fear: Never included, desires disapproved, overprotected, stagnation, discouraged, ostracized, rejected

Perception of Partner: Imposing, nosey, flirty, too sociable, too much activity, never leaves them alone, people are intrusive

Dyadic Interaction: Exploitive, stubborn, resentful, reserved, makes own plans, exclusive

Challenges: Don't alienate others, willing to work at relationships, share resources, build social skills

Objection of Partner: Detached, materially focused, lacks imagination, doesn't respect privacy, workaholic no time for charity or socializing, escapes to work or hobby
Desires: Build a nest egg for the future

General Interpretation

The Knight of Pentacles is generally a very independent and private person. Although they are very personable, social beings, they do not rely on others to validate them. This is what makes them a Lone Wolf. Wolves are pack animals whose survival depends on their social bonds. However, when a mature wolf desires a suitable mate, this (and other reasons) are why they must disperse from the core pack. The Knight of Pentacles is conscious of the need for a circle of close friends and family. This makes it their decision to commit a careful and time-consuming task.

New

Things will start out absolutely fantastic! You will seem to not be able to get enough of your fresh love mate. Because you enjoy each other so much, you can look forward to lots of dates or simply hanging out together, just lounging. You are potentially unsettled by times when your partner seems to suddenly need space or isolates him or herself.

Established

While there are periods when there seems to be a gap in your connection, these may not last for very long – for instance, when a partner stops calling you or disappears for a weekend. There is no reason to be alarmed; perhaps they are feeling secure in the relationship and feel you are, too.

Expanded Awareness

The Knight of Pentacles is traditionally considered the type that is very reserved and responsible. As a Lone Wolf in this system, it does not negate from being a responsible individual, but comes with an understanding that their "detachment" is not a careless act. When you are in a secure relationship, there is no need for anxiety when your partner is away. This Lone Wolf is ironically interested in exclusivity, but may take their time finding the right relationship partner.

Deteriorating

No one wants to stay where they are neither wanted, nor feel accepted. You or your partner may feel ostracized due to any number or differences and may find it easier to just abandon the relationship. Important matters that range from household duties or financial obligations have been neglected and are now cause for unrest.

QUEENS

Queen of Wands

CONFORMIST

GOLDEN DAWN/ESOTERIC TITLE: Queen of the Thrones of Flame, Queen of the Salamanders or Salamandrines
Decan: Last Decan of Pisces – first two Decans of Aries
QABALISTIC ATTRIBUTION: Binah in Atziluth
ELEMENT: Water of Fire (Specific Water in Primal Fire)
ATTACHMENT: Fearful-Avoidant

TAROT COUPLING KEYWORDS

Positive Qualities: Strong leader, great manager, goal-oriented
Impairment/Fear: Guilt-stricken, pride, uniqueness, disapproval of parent, self-promotion, always want to be different, must conform to the rules
Perception of Partner: Timid, angry, take things literally, cannot adapt, detached, arrogant, headstrong, bratty child
Dyadic Interaction: Critical, emotional, carried away, manipulative, fits or rage, drives away, controlling and condescending, imposes rules
Challenges: Relaxation, loosen up, take risks, develop and accept identity, accept being different
Objection of Partner: Strict, lacks vision, all or nothing attitude, wants to be center of attention, mood swings, quick to anger
Desires: Executive or jet-setting lifestyle; pleasure

GENERAL INTERPRETATION

Contrary to common interpretation of the Queen of Wands as a loose, fun-loving, hothead, The Queen of Wands, more often than not, is very conservative. While they are visionaries, they are paradoxically very respectful of established approaches and ways of doing things. These conformists are competent individuals who do not want to be boxed in just because of strong values. They just prefer to know where they come from and to know where they are going. Interestingly, many of them are very kind and often feel taken for granted.

NEW

Is romance in the air at your place of work? You may find it hard to downplay the attraction to someone who works with you or visits your workplace. This suggests that a relationship has progressed into physical intimacy before one or both partners are emotionally connected.

ESTABLISHED

While you and your partner manage to hold together the relationship, it may seem that something or someone else throws it out of balance. You may also have demanding jobs or work schedules that challenge spending time together, but work together to manage the situation.

EXPANDED AWARENESS

Conformists may or may not recognize that they often adjust their attitudes to please others. They are, however, very independent and not much can dissuade them once they make up their minds that there is a time and place for everything, and they have great patience for letting things fall into place. For the most part, they are deeply spiritual people, but their partners may not be aware of this aspect. One reason is because their spirituality acts as a private escape for them.

DETERIORATING

The bane of the relationship is basically that one or both partners straddle the fence on commitment. Also, this card usually indicates that there is an issue with an outside party who interferes with the relationship.

Queen of Cups

PERSISTER

GOLDEN DAWN/ESOTERIC TITLE: Queen of the Thrones of the Waters, Queen of Nymphs and Undines
DECAN: Last Decan of Cancer – first two Decans of Leo
QABALISTIC ATTRIBUTION: Briah in Binah
ELEMENT: Water of Water (Specific Water in Primal Water)
ATTACHMENT: Anxious-Preoccupied

TAROT COUPLING KEYWORDS

Positive Qualities: Psychic, aware, sweetheart and very nice
Impairment/Fear: Extreme sensitivity to abandonment, unpredictable nurturing, lost contact of caretaker
Perception of Partner: Unavailable, cold, unfeeling,
Dyadic Interaction: Demanding, extreme closeness

Challenges: Separation anxiety, needs constant reassurance or affection, lacks patience, cries easily
Objection of Partner: Too needy, overly sensitive, unstable, unable to be consoled, fluctuate between rage and anger, indecisiveness, moody
Desires: Love, marriage, soul mate

GENERAL INTERPRETATION

The Queen of Cups wins the title as the most perfect partner, at least in theory. When this Queen appears in your reading, there is an enormous attraction either for you or from the object of your desire. As a Persister, this Queen has an intoxicating effect. You'll find yourself wanting to cling to her or vice versa.

NEW

You want to fall in love with someone who shares the same spiritual pursuits and interest that are aligned with your own. You desire a partner who is in touch with their emotions and will tolerate yours.

ESTABLISHED

The intensity of emotions that are evoked by your partner's presence makes it difficult to find any of their faults. As their faults persists, when problems arise it becomes difficult to address certain negative behaviors because of overpowering emotional reactions.

EXPANDED AWARENESS

The Queen of Cups is the Aphrodite of the Tarot deck. It is not easy to escape her enticing pull. This pull is what we feel when we experience attraction to someone. We develop a longing for them and persistently want to spend every waking moment with them. On Waite's version, the Queen seems obsessed as she glares at the cup she holds. This cup has obvious spiritual connotations symbolizing a yearning for a relationship with the Divine. This is the ultimate purpose of relationship, that being to discover the divine in each other.

DETERIORATING

No matter how reassuring you have tried to be, your partner insists on challenging your feelings. This also suggests temperamental disputes in the relationship.

Queen of Swords

REGULATOR

GOLDEN DAWN/ESOTERIC TITLE: Queen of the Thrones of Air, Queen of the Sylphs and Sylphides
DECAN: Last Decan of Virgo – first two Decans of Libra
QABALISTIC ATTRIBUTION: Briah in Yetzirah
ELEMENT: Water of Air (Specific Water in Primal Air)
ATTACHMENT: Dismissive Avoidant

TAROT COUPLING KEYWORDS

Positive Qualities: Discipline, rational, sharp
Impairment/Fear: Loss of control, loss of love, no voice, shame, guilt, can't be me, lacks confidence, anger
Perception of Partner: Too scattered, unfocused, too emotional, wishy-washy, not serious, lacks organization
Dyadic Interaction: Cynical, critical, domineering, invasive, know it all, outbursts of anger, punisher, fault finder
Challenges: Develop sensitivity, considerate of partner's feelings, let go control, value other's opinion, lacks passion
Objection of Partner: Imposing, controlling, overbearing, rigid, egocentric, intolerant, constant criticism, only thinks of self, bossy
Desires: Honest and clear communication from partner

GENERAL INTERPRETATION

This Queen has earned the title of Regulator because of astute disciplinary abilities and a capacity to regulate emotional compulsions in order to clearly assess almost any situation. This suggests a relationship that is based on intellectual stimulation and is for those who are attracted to strong independent Athenian types.

NEW

You want to know more about a person who is on your "love radar." You may investigate them through mutual friends. They also want to know more about you; however, you may only feed them little bits of information at a time.

ESTABLISHED

One of the partners in this relationship has to be the one with a cool head. Should this Queen show up in an established connection, it is probable that both partners are extremely intelligent and have been able to sustain a long-term relationship. Partners also have individual interests to keep them occupied. This Queen is often an enigma to her partner.

EXPANDED AWARENESS

One of the most difficult challenges for this dismissive-avoidant Queen is being open when a partner desires closeness. Traditional interpretations for this card include widowhood, head of household, and privacy. Should your resonate with the Queen of Swords, despite of having a relationship partner, you may still feel somewhat alone and detached. This card also suggests a divorcee or single parent.

DETERIORATING

One or both partners hunger for affection and may use excuses to avoid intimacy. Perhaps he/she is angry and withholds affection. You may want to communicate with your partner but they are inaccessible either by choice or circumstance.

Queen of Pentacles
MODIFIER

GOLDEN DAWN/ESOTERIC TITLE: Queen of the Thrones of the Earth, Queen of the Gnomes
DECAN: Last Decan of Sagittarius-first two Decans of Capricorn
QABALISTIC ATTRIBUTION: Briah in Malkuth
ELEMENT: Water of Earth (Specific Water in Primal Earth)
ATTACHMENT: Secure

TAROT COUPLING KEYWORDS

Positive Qualities: Generous, practical, mature
Impairment/Fear: Fears competition, rejection, feelings of discomfort, fears success, hates not being accepted or approved, helpless, must be cooperative
Perception of Partner: Always in competition, overly aggressive, never satisfied, must be center of attention, bad sense of value
How Partner Relates as: Ambitious, keeping up with the Jones, user, sabotages partner's efforts, deliberately cripples

Challenges: Directness, Unwilling to adapt, Develop vision and creativity, raking risks
Objection of Partner: Stressing, rigid, self-indulgent, no energy for partner
Desires: Large family, manage a household, secure love

General Interpretation

This card often represents prosperity and stylish living. It suggests the main caretaker in the home or the nurturer in the relationship. The Queen of Pentacles is a modifier who can be cooperative and a people pleaser. They take great pains in demonstrating their worth and to be praised for their accomplishments. The Queen of Pentacles modifies any surroundings for comfort and is an expert at turning a house into a home.

New

You've worked very hard to present yourself as a person of substance. You want a serious relationship and will take steps to ensure you attract exactly the most satisfying mate. You recognize that you may have competition for this new partner and intend to win them over. Your strategy for this new connection is using your emotional reserves practically.

Established

Partners are proud of each other's successes and in a very secure place in their relationship. They make sure that each other's needs are met and will sometimes go overboard with their affections. Generally, when this card appears in a reading an established relationship is high functioning and runs relatively smooth.

Expanded Awareness

Modifiers will often do things that they really don't want to do because they hate to disappoint their loved ones. They understand the importance of saving face at critical times. This does not means they don't act as their authentic selves; it is just an old habit of making everything okay, so that everyone gets along.

Deteriorating

The thing that impressed you in the beginning was how your partner could manipulate situations for their own advantage. It was this demonstration of power that was part of the attraction. Somewhere along they way, they have lost that edge and have resorted to the "damsel in distress" mode. You are unsure if you should rescue your partner or save yourself.

KINGS

King of Wands

CHRONIC CHALLENGER

GOLDEN DAWN/ESOTERIC TITLE: Lord of the Flame and of the Lightning, King of the Spirits of Fire, King of the Salamanders
DECAN: Last Decan of Scorpio – first two Decans of Sagittarius
QABALISTIC ATTRIBUTION: Chokmah in Atziluth
ELEMENT: Fire of Fire (Specific Fire in Primal Fire)
ATTACHMENT: Anxious, pre-occupied

TAROT COUPLING KEYWORDS

Positive Qualities: Great advisor speaks eloquently, visionary
Impairment/Fear: Lacks empathy, fear of failure, numbs conscious, guilt, unappreciated, loss of power, disapproved
Perception of Partner: Incompetent, lazy, compromises, unaggressive, doesn't take initiative, non-attentive, saboteur, hard
Relates to Partner as: Negative critic, dominating, rude, attention seeker, oblivious, competitive
Challenges: Cooperation, Being a know it all, value effort of partner, notice details, acceptance
Objection of Partner: Impulsive, quick to judge, ignores feelings, doesn't value competence, no time for comforting, does not recognize value of partner, sadistic
Desires: To be number one in partner's heart

GENERAL INTERPRETATION

The members of the Court of Wands are generally known as charismatic and larger-than-life aggressors. This King is the head aggressor, often acting on impulse and always up for a challenge. This suggests someone who is focused on career and business, and balances it with concern for home life.

NEW

Here is someone who is a serial dater. They are very skilled at dating because they understand how others vie for attention and there is no way they could lose. So, if it appears that they are doing and saying all the right things, it is mostly because they have had lots of practice.

ESTABLISHED

Once you get your partner to settle down, they may become quite the stick-in-the-mud. Weekends, once reserved for revelry and passionate sex, are now about watching television and lounging on the couch. Actually, this is not as bad as it sounds. The King of Wands enjoys being at home. Once they have settled down with a perfect partner they adore, they may use their competitive edge for work or business.

EXPANDED AWARENESS

A relationship under this influence is no bed of roses. One or both partners bring to the relationship their constant striving to be the absolute best. If there is an inkling of any lack, and they are not accomplishing this, then they work diligently to strive for perfection. They fear their partner's disapproval, and should they become emotionally vulnerable, are prone to acting out of character.

DETERIORATING

This suggests a partner or circumstance that is out of control. The competition for having the upper hand makes harmony in the relationship difficult. Partners can put each other down with unkind remarks.

King of Cups

CRUSADER

GOLDEN DAWN/ESOTERIC TITLE: Lord of the Waves and of the Waters, King of the Hosts of the Sea, King of Undines and Nymphs
DECAN: Last Decan of Aquarius- first two Decans of Pisces
QABALISTIC ATTRIBUTION: Chokmah in Binah
ELEMENT: Specific Fire in the World of Primal Water
ATTACHMENT: Anxious-Preoccupied

TAROT COUPLING KEYWORDS

Positive Qualities: Good-natured, considerate, loyal
Impairment/Fear: Fear being alone, needs constant sympathy and love, feels excluded, excessively interested in welfare of others, overly accommodating, afraid to express needs; clingy
Perception of Partner: Selfish, Offensive, acts without reason, negligent, intolerant, lazy, uncaring, materialistic
Dyadic Interaction: Relentless attention, resentful, unrealistic expectations, critical of performance

Challenges: Time for self, live in real world, express own needs, be firm and learn to say no

Objection of Partner: Depressed, intrusive, insecure, too shy, taken advantage of by others, drained by others, hypersensitive and distracted

Desires: Cohabitation, strong emotional bond, lots of children

GENERAL INTERPRETATION

The King of Cups is an emotionally complex individual who is delightful and considerate of others. Like his counterpart the Queen of Cups, he too is alluring, captivating, and considered an "ideal" relationship partner.

NEW

You may go for the shy sensitive types or may attract someone who dotes on you, smothering you with affection and attention. You will certainly "drink the Kool-aid" from this King's cup.

ESTABLISHED

When the King of Cups appears for an established relationship, partners often comment that they are each other's soul mates. Many think this is the most marriageable personality in the deck. You may not be able to avoid falling deeply in love with this King.

EXPANDED AWARENESS

The King of Cups has entered your life to help you further your emotional self and to truly understand love. Love, far from being only a feeling, is also about expression, sharing, and communication. You'll have an interesting time discovering your intuition, sensitivities, and depths of you or your partner's emotional well.

DETERIORATING

You are uncertain if you can stand your partner's clinginess and smothering. You may feel guilty about wanting time for yourself because your partner's or your own emotions overtax you. This card in an unfavorable position suggests alcoholism or depression.

King of Swords

Avoider

Golden Dawn/Esoteric Title: Lord of the Winds and Breezes, King of the Spirit of Air, King of Sylphs and Sylphides
Decan: Last Decan of Taurus-first two Decans of Gemini
Qabalistic Attribution: Chokmah in Yetzirah
Element: Specific Fire in Primal Air
Attachment: Dismissive -Avoidant

Tarot Coupling Keywords

Positive Qualities: Brave, wise and honest
Impairment/Fear: Emotional and physical rejection, loss of self through contact with parent (partner)
Perception of Partner: Demanding, smothering, over emotional, gullible
Dyadic Interaction: Detached, avoidant
Challenges: Has to be right. Difficulties initiating contact emotionally and physically, lacks expression of deep feelings, being aware of physical body and surroundings, cold and distant
Objection of Partner: Lacks Passion, Sexual Difficulties, Manipulative, Turns words around, quick to argue
Desires: Relationship with same values and morals

General Interpretation

This King has low tolerance for those who don't share his intellectual superiority. Emotional whims have no place in this King's life. He thrives on structure almost as militaristic in his approach to relationships. The King of Swords values integrity and seeks the same in partners.

New

Your new love interest is an especially skilled communicator. It is refreshing to have such a great conversationalist who can hold your attention, which is difficult to do, given their striking looks and amazing charm.

Established

The King of Swords in an established connection suggests partners who have gone through many battles together and are willing to stick up for each other no matter what. Partners can act as the voice of reason for each other. Because of their rigid views and being a sort of "know-it-all," your partner can be the difficult one in the relationship.

EXPANDED AWARENESS

You are lucky to have a partner who means what they say and will also do what he/she says they will do. It is their honor that is on the line and they need you to trust them, and they want to trust you.

DETERIORATING

This relationship may be too difficult to stay in because you may feel like you are contantly are walking on eggshells, never knowing when your partner will have an outburst. Selfishness and untrustworthiness are seeping into the foundation that holds the relationship together.

King of Pentacles (Disks)

CHASER

GOLDEN DAWN/ESOTERIC TITLE: Lord of the Wild and Fertile Land, King of the Spirits of Earth, King of the Gnomes
DECAN: Last Decan of Leo – first two Decans of Virgo
QABALISTIC ATTRIBUTION: Chokmah in Malkuth
ELEMENT: Specific Fire in Primal Earth
ATTACHMENT: Secure

TAROT COUPLING KEYWORDS

Positive Qualities: Business-oriented, distinguished, giving
Impairment/Fear: Pushed away by caretaker, fearful and dependent, vies for attention, ambivalent behavior, abandonment
Perception of Partner: Indifference, distant, can't rely on partner
Dyadic Interaction: Demanding, extreme closeness, predictable, stuck, possessive
Challenges: Initiate distance, infringing on partner's friendships, independency
Objection of Partner: Dull, pursues then pulls back, chasing, devalues, petty-minded, unadventurous, deaf to reason
Desires: Relationship of value and substance

GENERAL INTERPRETATION

The King of Pentacles has accomplished many things this lifetime. They are experts at manifestation. Whatever they desire, they usually get. They also rarely have trouble finding suitable partners. They tend to work hard and are often entrepreneurs. They are interested in all the pleasures and good things life has to offer and will go any means necessary to have them.

NEW

You may no longer wish to be the one that is always taking care of the needs of others and want to seek a partner who will take care of you, and this usually pans out as financially. You may treat your dating life like it is a business deal. Some things will have to be off the table and others will make or break a deal.

ESTABLISHED

You could not ask for a more focused and responsible partner. This card typically represented the breadwinner or head of the household. These types are often great providers and have excellent dispositions.

EXPANDED AWARENESS

"Love is patient, love is kind" (1 Corinthians 13:4-8). This perfectly applies to one of the principles that the King of Pentacles would live by. They are patient partners, but can also have demands of their own. They rarely take their loved ones for granted. They have possibly entered your life to teach you how to appreciate yourself and the world in which you exist.

DETERIORATING

In a reading, this card suggests a partner who is stingy with resources and affection. They also may be fickle and jealous of their partner's achievements. It may appear that they no longer care about the relationship, or anything else for that matter.

CHAPTER 13

CORE VALUES SPREAD

I developed this spread in order to be able to utilize what I've learned about attachment theory.

It is wonderful to use for exploring what your parents modeled for you, if only to have an "aha" about your choices in dating or patterns in your relationships. It is not a diagnostic tool per say, but provides food for thought.

Position 8 is optional. This means that if your reading feels complete, let's say at Position 7, then you would skip laying out an eighth card. The *Who* or *What* makes a difference, meaning that if your are using this spread to find out how to improve communication with your girl/boyfriend (for instance), this position could offer the next step or suggested plan of action.

Another thing to mention for this spread is that people may or may not want to use both parents for whatever reason. You can substitute Parent 1 or 2 for any caretaker or just the primary. This could have been your grandmother or your uncle who were among your primary caretakers. Yes, it will work for those raised in single parent situations.

1. Current Issue/ Focus
2. Parent 1 – Masculine
3. Parent 2 – Feminine
4. Their Relationship
5. What You Learned/Unconscious – Trauma
6. Ideal/Current Partner
7. You
8. Who/What Makes the Difference – (Optional)

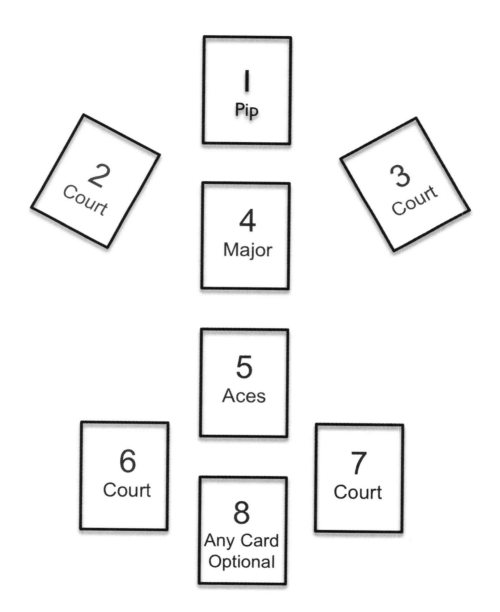

ENDNOTES

CHAPTER 1

1. From Charles Homer Haskins, *Renaissance of the Twelfth Century*, (Cambridge, Harvard University Press, 1927) cited in *The Arts of Intimacy: Christians, Jew and Muslims in the Making of Castilian Culture* by Jerrilynn D. Dodds, María, Rosa Menocal and Abigail Krasner Balbale (New Haven: Yale University Press, 2008), 202.
2. Quote found in Keith Thomas, *Religion and the Decline of Magic*, (Weidenfeld & Nicholson Edition 1997, New York, Oxford University Press, 1971), 212.
3. Stuart R. Kaplan, *The Encyclopedia of Tarot, Volume 1* (New York, New York, Noble Offset Printers, Inc., 1971), 53.
4. Antoine Court de Gébelin, *Le Monde Primitif, anayles et compare avec le monde moderne, Volume VIII* (Paris, 1175-1784). As cited in *The Encyclopedia of Tarot, Volume 1,* by Stuart R. Kaplan (Noble Offset Printers, 1971).
5. Helen Farley, *A Cultural History of Tarot: From Entertainment to Esotericism* (New York, New York, I.B. Tauris & Co. Ltd., 2009), 14.
6. Markus Kattstein & Peter Delius, Editors, *Islam: Art and Architecture* (Koningswinter, German, Konemann, 2004), 170.
7. Darius A. Spieth, *Napoleon's Sorcerers: The Sophisians*, (Cranbury, New Jersey, Rosemount Publishing & Printing Corp., 2007).
8. Paul Huson, *Mystical Origins of the Tarot*, (Rochester, Vermont, Destiny Books, 2004), 5.
9. Nassar D. Khali *Islamic Art and Culture: Timeline and History*, (Cairo, Egypt, The American University in Cairo Press, 2008), 9.
10. From Michael Dummett and Sylvia Mann, *The Game of Tarot*, cited by Helen Farley, *A Cultural History of Tarot* (New York, New York, I.B. Tauris & Co. Ltd., 2009), 13.
11. Nassar D. Khali *Islamic Art and Culture: Timeline and History*, (Cairo, Egypt, The American University in Cairo Press, 2008), 27.
12. White Knuckle Playing Cards website, Brett A. Jones, *The Origin of Playing Cards and their Introduction to European Culture A Brief Timeline of Theories & Facts*, http://whiteknucklecards.com/history/originofcards.html).
13. See Kaplan, Dummett, et al.
14. Ronald Decker, Thierry Depaulis and Michael Dummett, *A Wicked Pack of Cards – The Origins of the Occult Tarot* (New York, St. Martin's Press, 1996), 41.
15. Stuart Kaplan, *The Encyclopedia of Tarot* Volume II (New York, New York, U.S. Games Systems, Inc. 1986), Preface, xiii.
16. Ronald Decker, Thierry Depaulis and Michael Dummett, *A Wicked Pack of Cards – The Origins of the Occult Tarot* (New York, St. Martin's Press, 1996), 39.
16a. Michael Dummett, *Twelve Tarot Games* (London, Gerald Duckworth & Co. Ltd., 1980), 2.

16b. Stuart R. Kaplan, *The Encyclopedia of Tarot: Volume II* (New York, U.S. Games Systems, Inc., 1986), 105.

16c. Ronald Decker, Thierry Depaulis and Michael Dummett, *A Wicked Pack of Cards – The Origins of the Occult Tarot* (New York: St. Martin's Press, 1996), 243.

17. Keith Thomas, *Religion and the Decline of Magic* (New York, Oxford University Press, 1971, 1997), pp.118-119.

18. Ibid.

19. Richard Cavendish, *The Tarot* (New York, Crescent Books, 1986).

CHAPTER 2

1. *The Merriam-Webster Dictionary*, http://www.merriam-webster.com/dictionary/divination.

1a. Serge Sauneron, *The Priest of Ancient Egypt*. Translated by Ann Morrissett (New York: Grove Press, Inc., 1960), 71.

1b. Ibid, 95.

1c. Ibid, 100.

2. Various writers have compiled list integrated here. Clifford A. Pickover, *Dreaming the Future: The Fantastic Story of Prediction,* (Amherst, New York, 2001) 24, and Mary K. Greer, *Tarot Mirrors: Reflections of Personal Meaning* (North Hollywood, California, Newcastle Publishing Co., 1988).

CHAPTER 3

1. Arthur Rosengarten, Ph.D, *Tarot and Psychology: Spectrums of Possibility* (St. Paul Minnesota, Paragon House, 2000).

2. Ronald Decker, Thierry Depaulis and Michael Dummett, *A Wicked Pack of Cards – The Origins of the Occult Tarot* (New York, St. Martin's Press, 1996), 37.

CHAPTER 4

1. John Scheid, *Religions of the Ancient World*: *a Guide*, general editor Sarah Iles Johnson (Cambridge, Massachusetts, 2004) 112.

1a. Ibid. 114.

2. Daniel V. Papero, *Clinical Handbook of Couples Therapy,* edited by Neil S. Jacobson, Alan S. Gurman (New York, New York, The Guilford Press, 1995), 12.

2a. Frank S. Pittman III and Tina Pittman Wagers, *Clinical Handbook of Couples Therapy,* edited by Neil S. Jacobson, Alan S. Gurman (New York, New York, The Guilford Press, 1995), 295.

3. Ibid.

4. Ibid.

CHAPTER 5

1. Harville Hendrix, PhD., *Keeping The Love You Find*, (New York, New York, Pocket Books, 1992).

2. Ibid, 11.

2a. About.com Guide; Education-Psychology. What is Motivation? Entry by Kendra Cherry, (http://psychology.about.com/od/mindex/g/motivation-definition.htm).

2b. Drew Westen, *Psychology: Mind, Brain & Culture*, 2nd Edition (New York, New York, John Wiley & Sons, Inc, 1999), 437.

2c. Ibid., 449.

2d. Ibid., 821-824.

3. Mayer Resnick, *Love's all in the brain: fMRI study shows strong, lateralized reward, not sex, drive* (http://www.eurekalert.org/pub_releases/2005-05/aps-lai053105.php, May 31, 2005).

4. Ibid.

4a. Harville Hendrix, PhD., *Keeping The Love You Find*, (New York, New York, Pocket Books, 1992), pg. 52.

4b. Anson Alex, Statistics for Online Dating in 2013 [Infographic] by Anson Alex, February 25, 2013, http://ansonalex.com/infographics/statistics-for-online-dating-in-2013-infographic/.

5. Drew Westen, *Psychology: Mind, Brain & Culture*, 2nd Edition (New York, New York, John Wiley & Sons, Inc, 1999).

6. Ibid.

7. Harville Hendrix and Helen LaKelly Hunt, *Receiving Love: Transforming You Relationships By Letting Yourself Be Loved* (New York, NewYork, Atria Books, 2004), 5.

8. George Levinger *A social psychological perspective on marital dissolution,* (Journal of Social Issues,1976), 32 (1), 21-47 Quoted on: http://changingminds.org/explanations/theories/stage_theory.htm.

9. Thomas Moore, *Soul Mates: Honoring the Mysteries of Love and Relationship*, (New York, New York, HarperCollins, 1994), 24.

9a. "Types of Intimacy: What is Intimacy?" Last accessed June 21, 2013, http://www.counseling.ufl.edu/cwc/types-of-intimacy.aspx.

10. Thomas Moore, *Soul Mates: Honoring the Mysteries of Love and Relationship*, (New York, New York, HarperCollins, 1994).

11. Ibid.

CHAPTER 6

1. Arthur Rosengarten, Ph.D, *Tarot and Psychology: Spectrums of Possibility*, (St. Paul Minnesota, Paragon House, 2000), 64.

2. Drew Westen, *Psychology: Mind, Brain & Culture*, 2nd Edition (New York, New York, John Wiley & Sons, Inc, 1999),10.

2a. Ibid.

2b. Ibid.

2c. Ibid.

2d. Arthur Rosengarten, Ph.D, *Tarot and Psychology: Spectrums of Possibility*, (St. Paul Minnesota, Paragon House, 2000).

2e. Drew Westen, *Psychology: Mind, Brain & Culture*, 2nd Edition (New York, New York, John Wiley & Sons, Inc, 1999).

2f. Arthur Rosengarten, Ph.D, *Tarot and Psychology: Spectrums of Possibility*, (St. Paul Minnesota, Paragon House, 2000).

3. Drew Westen, *Psychology: Mind, Brain & Culture*, 2nd Edition (New York, New York, John Wiley & Sons, Inc, 1999)

4. Thomas Moore, *Soul Mates: Honoring the Mysteries of Love and Relationship*, (New York, New York, HarperCollins, 1994), 29.

5. Harville Hendrix, PhD. tells us in *Keeping the Love You Find: A Personal Guide* (1992, Simon &Schuster, Inc.), 54.

5a. Drew Westen, *Psychology: Mind, Brain & Culture*, 2nd Edition (New York, New York, John Wiley & Sons, Inc, 1999), 634.

5b. Ibid.

6. Erik Erikson, *Childhood and society*, (New York, W. W. Norton, 1963 cited by Drew Westen, *Psychology: Mind, Brain & Culture*, 2nd Edition (New York, New York, John Wiley & Sons, Inc, 1999), 661.

7. Ibid., pp. 471, 625.

7a. Drew Westen, *Psychology: Mind, Brain & Culture*, 2nd Edition (New York, New York, John Wiley & Sons, Inc, 1999), 626

8. Your Tango Experts Blog; *"What's Your Attachment Style?"* Entry by Sheila Robinson-Kiss, October 20, 2001, http://www.yourtango.com/experts/sheila-robinson-kiss/what-attachment-style-reveals-about-your-compatibility.

9. Harville Hendrix, PhD., *Keeping The Love You Find*, (New York, New York, Pocket Books, 1992), 54-55.

9a. Ibid.

9b. Caitlin Goossen, *The Master's College, The Perceived Influence of a Father on His Daughter's Development*, (Undergraduate Research Journal for the Human Sciences, Volume 8, 2009) http://www.kon.org/urc/v8/goossen.html, last accessed on July 16, 2013.

Chapter 7

1. The website of eHarmony; www.eHarmony.com.
2. C.G. Jung, *Psychological Types*, trans. H.G. Barnes, revision R.F.C. Hull, Collected Works, Volume 6, Bollingen Series XX (Princeton, New Jersey, Princeton University Press, 9th Printing, 1990, 1976, 1974.
3. Alexander Avila, *Love Types: Discover Your Romantic Style and Find Your Soul Mate*, (HarperCollins eBooks for Kindle, 2007).
4. The website of The Myers-Briggs Foundation; "MBTI® Basics" http://www.myersbriggs. org/my-mbti-personality-type/mbti-basics/.
5. Mary K. Greer and Tom Little *Understanding the Tarot Court*, (Woodbury, Minnesota Llewellyn Publications, 2004), 67.

Chapter 8

1. Harville Hendrix and Helen LaKelly Hunt, *Receiving Love: Transforming You Relationships By Letting Yourself Be Loved* (New York, New York, Atria Books, 2004).
1a. *Epistemology, introduction,* http://pespmc1.vub.ac.be/EPISTEMI.html
2. Erwin Panofsky, *Studies in Iconology: Humanistic Themes in the Art of the Renaissance*, (New York, New York, Icon Editions, 1939,1962, 1967,1972), 3.
2a. Biddingtons.com. *Pedigree & Provenance*, http://www.biddingtons.com/content/ pedigreeicon.html
2b. Jack Tresidder, *The Watkins Dictionary of Symbols*, (London, Watkins Publishing, 2008), 135.

Chapter 10

1. Paul Carus, *The History of The Devil and The Idea of Evil from The Earliest Times to The Present*, (np1900) http://www.sacred-texts.com/evil/hod/index.htm.
1a. Amber Jayanti, *Living the Qabalistic Tarot: Applying an Ancient Oracle to the Challenges of Modern Life*, Revised Edition, (Boston: Weiser, 2000, 2004), 26.
2. Ami Ronnberg and Kathleen Martin, eds., The Archive for Research in Archetypal Symbolism, *The Book of Symbols: Reflection on Archetypal Images*, (Cologne, Germany, Taschen, 2010), 522.
3. Richard Cavendish, *The Tarot*, (New York, Crescent Books, 1986), 34.
4. Ami Ronnberg and Kathleen Martin, eds., The Archive for Research in Archetypal Symbolism, *The Book of Symbols: Reflection on Archetypal Images*, (Cologne, Germany, Taschen, 2010), 296.
4a. Gareth Knight, *A Practical Guide to Qabalistic Symbolism*, (York Beach: Weiser, 1993), 201.
4b. Ibid., 202.

4c. Ibid., 204.

5. Amber Jayanti, *Living the Qabalistic Tarot: Applying an Ancient Oracle to the Challenges of Modern Life,* Revised Edition, (Boston, Massachusetts, Weiser Books 2000, 2004).

5a. Ibid., 26.

5b. Robert Wang, *The Qabalistic Tarot,* (York Beach, Maine, Samuel Weiser, Inc.), 250.

6. Ibid.

7. Sandor Konraad, *Numerology: Key to the Tarot,* (West Chester, Pennsylvania, Whitford Press,1983), 29.

7a. Ronald Decker, Thierry Depaulis and Michael Dummett. *A Wicked Pack of Cards – The Origins of the Occult Tarot.* (New York: St. Martin's Press, 1996).

7b. Carl Gustav Jung, *The Archetypes and the Collective Unconscious,* trans. R.F.C. Hull, 2nd Edition, Volume 9 part i, Bollinger Series XX (New York, New York, Princeton University Press, 9th Printing, 1990, 1976, 1974). 255

7c. Ibid.

7d. Ami Ronnberg and Kathleen Martin, eds., The Archive for Research in Archetypal Symbolism, *The Book of Symbols: Reflection on Archetypal Images,* (Cologne, Germany, Taschen, 2010), 162.   7e. Ibid., 156.

7f. Christopher Knight and Robert Lomas, *The Hiram Key: Pharaohs, Freemasons and the Discovery of The Secret Scrolls of Jesus,* (New York, New York, Barnes & Noble, Inc. 1996, 1998). 7, 8.

7g. Christopher Knight and Robert Lomas, *The Hiram Key: Pharaohs, Freemasons and the Discovery of The Secret Scrolls of Jesus,* (New York, New York, Barnes & Noble, Inc. 1996, 1998). 7, 8.

7h. Duncan Moore, *A Guide to Masonic Symbolism,* (Hersham, Surrey, Lewis Masonic, 2009), 46. ndon: Watkins Publishing, 1997).

7j. Amber Jayanti, *Living the Qabalistic Tarot: Applying an Ancient Oracle to the Challenges of Modern Life,* Revised Edition, (Boston, Massachusetts, Weiser Books 2000, 2004).

7k. Gary Walters et al., "Sexual Objectification", http://outoft hefog.net/CommonBehaviors/SexualObjectification.html.

7l. Serge Sauneron, *The Priest of Ancient Egypt,* translated by Ann Morrissett, (New York: Grove Press, Inc. 1960, pg. 34

8. Andrew Collins, *Beneath the Pyramids: Egypt's Greatest Secrets Uncovered,* (Virginia Beach: 4th Dimension Press/ARE, 2009).

9. Robert Wang, *The Qabalistic Tarot* (York Beach, Maine Samuel Weiser, Inc., 1987), 206.

9a. Ibid., 207.

9b. Ibid., 207.

9c. Richard Cavendish, *The Tarot,* (New York, Crescent Books, 1986), 99.

9d. Jack Tresidder, *The Watkins Dictionary of Symbols,* (London: Watkins Publishing, 1997), 129.

9e. Robert Wang, *The Qabalistic Tarot* (York Beach, Maine Samuel Weiser, Inc., 1987), 199, 200.

9f. Richard Cavendish, *The Tarot*, (New York, Crescent Books, 1986), 104.

9g. Robert Wang, *The Qabalistic Tarot* (York Beach, Maine Samuel Weiser, Inc., 1987), 194.

10. Ami Ronnberg and Kathleen Martin, eds., The Archive for Research in Archetypal Symbolism, *The Book of Symbols: Reflection on Archetypal Images*, (Cologne, Germany, Taschen, 2010), 512.

11. Wikipedia, s.v. "Pittura infamanti," last modified May 8, 2012, http://en.wikipedia.org/wiki/Pittura_infamante.

12. Barbara G. Walker, *The Woman's Dictionary of Symbols and Sacred Objects* (San Francisco, California, Harper, 1988).

13. Andrea Vitali, Card 12 – The Hanging Man, last accessed on September 25, 2012 http://trionfi.com/0/i/v/v12.html.

14. The Book of Enoch, Translated from the Ethiopian by R.H. Charles, 1906. English E-text edition scanned by Joshua Williams, Northwest Nazarene College, 1995. Edited by Wolf Carnahan, 1997 http://www.ancienttexts.org/library/ethiopian/enoch/index.html.

15. Philip Coppens, *The Stone Puzzle of Rosslyn Chapel,* 3rd Edition (Enkhuizen, Netherlands, Frontiers Publishing, Adventures Unlimited Press, 2004).

16. Ibid., 109.

17. Robert Wang, *The Qabalistic Tarot* (York Beach, Maine Samuel Weiser, Inc., 1987), 185.

17a. Judd Burton, About.com, Ancient/Classical History, "Dagon was the Chief God of the Philistines", http://ancienthistory.about.com/od/godsmyth/a/Dagon.htm.

18. Barbara G. Walker, *The Woman's Dictionary of Symbols and Sacred Objects* (San Francisco, California, Harper, 1988), 379.

18a. Amber Jayanti, *Living the Qabalistic Tarot: Applying an Ancient Oracle to the Challenges of Modern Life,* Revised Edition, (Boston, Massachusetts, Weiser Books 2000, 2004), 185.

18b. Tony Crisp, *Dream Dictionary: An A to Z Guide to Understanding Your Unconscious Mind.* 10th Anniversary Edition. (New York: Dell, 200).

19. Robert Wang, *The Qabalistic Tarot* (York Beach, Maine Samuel Weiser, Inc., 1987) 180.

20. Ibid., 179.

21. Stuart Kaplan, *The Encyclopedia of Tarot* Volume II (New York, New York, U.S. Games Systems, Inc. 1986), 11.

22. Robert Wang, *The Qabalistic Tarot* (York Beach, Maine Samuel Weiser, Inc., 1987), 171.

23. Ibid.

23a. Ami Ronnberg and Kathleen Martin, eds., The Archive for Research in Archetypal Symbolism, *The Book of Symbols: Reflection on Archetypal Images*, (Cologne, Germany, Taschen, 2010), 18.

24. Tallay Ornan, "The Bull and Its Two Masters: Moon and Storm Deities in Relation to The Bull in Ancient Near Eastern Art" Israel Exploration Journal 51 no. 1 (2001): 3-9, http://www.academia.edu/864897/Ornan_2001_The_Bull_and_Its_Two_Masters_IEJ_51_1-26.

BIBLIOGRAPHY

Amberstone, Ruth Ann and Wald and Gina Thies. *Tarot Tips Newsletter*, http://www.tarotschool.com/Newsletter.html.

Avila, Alexander. *LoveTypes: Discover Your Romantic Style and Find Your Soul Mate.* HarperCollins eBooks for Kindle. 2007.

Bartholomew, Kim and Leonard M. Horowitz. "Attachment styles among young adults: A test of a four-category model." *Journal of Personality and Social Psychology.* no. 61(2), (1991): 226-244. doi:10.1037/0022-3514.61.2.226.

Begg, Ean. *The Cult of the Black Virgin.* London: Penguin, 1996.

Budge, Wallis E. A. *An Egyptian Hieroglyphic Dictionary.* Vol. 1, New York: Dover, 1978.

------. *The Gods of The Egyptians: Studies in Egyptian Mythology.* Vol. 2. New York: Dover, 1969

Camille Michael. *The Medieval Art of Love: Objects and Subjects of Desire.* New York: Harry N Abrams, 1998.

------ and Julian of Norwich. "The Book of Symbols: Reflection on Archetypal Images" in *The Archive for Research in Archetypal Symbolism.* Editors Ami Ronnberg and Kathleen Martin. Cologne: Toschen, 2010.

Camp, Robert. *Love Cards: What Your Birthday Reveals About You & Your Personal Relationships.* Naperville: Sourcebooks, 1997.

Carnahan, Wolf., ed. 1997. *The Book of Enoch,* Translated by R.H. Charles. NP: 1906. English E-text edition scanned by Joshua Williams, Northwest Nazarene College, 1995. http://www.ancienttexts.org/library/ethiopian/enoch/index.html.

Carpenter, Edward. *The Origins of Pagan and Christian Beliefs.* London: Senate, 1996.

Carus, Paul. *The History of The Devil and the Idea of Evil from the Earliest Times to the Present.* NP: 1900. http://www.sacred-texts.com/evil/hod/index.htm.

Cavendish, Richard. *The Tarot.* New York: Crescent Books, 1986.

Cicero, Chic and Sandra Tabatha. *The New Golden Dawn Ritual Tarot: Keys to the Rituals, Symbolism, Magic, & Divination.* St. Paul: Llewellyn, 1996.

Collins, Andrew. *Beneath the Pyramids: Egypt's Greatest Secrets Uncovered.* Virginia Beach: 4th Dimension Press/ARE, 2009.

Coppens, Philip. *The Stone Puzzle of Rosslyn Chapel,* 3rd Edition. Enkhuizen, Netherlands: Frontiers, 2004.

Crisp, Tony. *Dream Dictionary: An A to Z Guide to Understanding Your Unconscious Mind.* 10th Anniversary Edition. New York: Dell, 2002.

Daniels, Kooch and Victor Daniels, *Tarot D'Amour: Find Love, Sex, and Romance in the Cards,* York Beach, ME, Red Wheel/,Weiser. LLC, 2003.

Day, Laura. *Practical Intuition™ in Love: start a journey through pleasure to the love of your life.* New York: HarperCollins, 1998.

de Gébelin, Antoine Court, *Le Monde Primitif, anayles et compare avec le monde moderne, Volume VIII.* Paris, 1175-1784.

Decker, Ronald, Thierry Depaulis and Michael Dummett. *A Wicked Pack of Cards – The Origins of the Occult Tarot*. New York: St. Martin's Press, 1996.

Docters van Leeuwen, Onno and Rob. *The Complete New Tarot*. Translated by Robert A.W. Docters van Leeuween. New York: Sterling Publishing, 2004.

Dodds, Jerrilynn D., María, Rosa Menocal and Abigail Krasner Balbale. *The Arts of Intimacy: Christians, Jew and Muslims in the Making of Castilian Culture*. New Haven: Yale University Press, 2008.

Dummett, Michael A. E. *The Visconti-Sforza Tarot Cards*, New York: George Braziller, 1986.

-----. *Twelve Tarot Games*. London: Duckworth, 1980.

----- and Sylvia Mann, *The Game of Tarot: From Ferrara to Salt Lake City*. London: Duckworth, 1980.

Erikson, Erik. *Childhood and society*. New York: W. W. Norton, 1963.

Esposti, Carlo Degli. *La Cappella Dei Re Magi Nella Basilica Di San Petronio*. Bologna, Italy: Basilica di San Petronio, 2007.

Farley, Helen. *A Cultural History of Tarot: From Entertainment to Esotericism*. New York: I.B. Tauris & Co. Ltd., 2009.

Fideler, David, ed. *Alexandria: Cosmology, Philosophy, Myth and Culture*. Grande Rapides: Phanes Press, 2000.

Gad, Irene. *Tarot And Individuation: A Jungian Study of Correspondences with Cabala, Alchemy and the Chakras*. Lake Worth: Nicolas-Hayes, Inc. 2004.

Giles, Cynthia. *The Tarot: Methods, Mastery, and More*. New York: Fireside, 1996.

Gilbert, Adrian. *Magi: Uncovering the Secret Society that Read the Birth of Jesus in the Stars*. Montpelier: Invisible Cities, 2002.

Graves, Robert. *The White Goddess*. Amended and Enlarged Edition. New York: The Noonday Press, 1966.

Greer, Mary K. *Tarot Mirrors: Reflections of Personal Meaning*. North Hollywood: Newcastle, 1988.

------. and Tom Little. Little *Understanding the Tarot Court*. Woodbury: Llewellyn, 2004.

------. *The Complete Book of Tarot Reversals*. St. Paul: Llewellyn, 2002.

Hall, Manly P. *The Secret Teachings of All Ages: an encyclopedic outline of Masonic, Hermetic, Qabbalistic and Rosicrucian symbolical philosophy: being an interpretation of the secret teachings concealed within rituals, allegories and mysteries of all ages. Readers Edition*. New York: Jeremy P. Tarcher/Penguin, 2003.

Haskins, Charles Homer. *Renaissance of the Twelfth Century*. Cambridge: Harvard University Press, 1927.

Hazan, Cindy and Phillip Shaver. "Romantic Love Conceptualized as an Attachment Process." *Journal of Personality and Social Psychology*, Vol. 52 (1987) DOI: 10.1037/0022-3514.52.3.511

Hendrix, Harville *Keeping the Love You Find: A Personal Guide*. New York: Simon &Schuster, 1992.

----- and Helen LaKelly Hunt. *Receiving Love: Transforming You Relationships By Letting Yourself Be Loved*. New York: Atria Books, 2004.

Huson, Paul. *Mystical Origins of the Tarot*. Rochester: Destiny Books, 2004.

Jacobi, Eleonore. *Tarot for Love & Relationships*. New York: Sterling, 2003.

Jacobson, Neil S. and Alan S. Gurman. eds. *Clinical handbook of Couple Therapy*. New York: The Guilford Press, 1995.

Jayanti, Amber. *Living the Qabalistic Tarot: Applying an Ancient Oracle to the Challenges of Modern Life,* Revised Edition, Boston: Weiser, 2000, 2004.

Johnston, Sara Iles, ed. *Religions of the Ancient World: A guide*, Massachusetts, The Belknap Press of Harvard University Press, 2004.

Jung, Carl Gustav. *Psychological Types,* Vol. 6, Bollingen Series XX. Translated by H.G. Barnes, Revision by R.F.C. Hull. Princeton: Princeton University Press, 9th Printing, 1990, 1976, 1974

-----. *The Archetypes and the Collective Unconscious,* 2nd Edition, Volume 9 Part I, Bollinger Series XX. Translated by R.F.C. Hull. New York: Princeton University Press, 1990, 1976, 1974.

Kaplan, Stuart R. *The Encyclopedia of Tarot,* Vol. 1 New York: Noble Offset Printers, Inc., 1971.

------. *The Encyclopedia of Tarot* Vol. II (New York: U.S. Games Systems, Inc., 1986.

Kattstein, Markus and Peter Delius, ed., *Islam: Art and Architecture*. Koningswinter, German: Konemann, 2004.

Kennedy, Eugene and Sara C. Charles, MD. *On Becoming a Counselor: A Basic Guide for Nonprofessional Counselors and Other Helpers,* 3rd edition New York: The Crossroad Publishing Company, 2001.

Khali, Nassar D. *Islamic Art and Culture: Timeline and History,* Cairo, Egypt: The American University in Cairo Press, 2008.

Knight, Christopher and Robert Lomas. *The Hiram Key: Pharaohs, Freemasons and the Discovery of the Secret Scrolls of Jesus*. New York: Barnes & Noble, Inc., 1998.

Knight, Gareth. *A Practical Guide to Qabalistic Symbolism*. York Beach: Weiser, 1993.

Konraad, Sandor. *Numerology: Key to the Tarot,* West Chester: Whitford Press, 1983.

Laurence, Theodor. *The Sexual Key to the Tarot*. New York: Signet/The New American Library, Inc. 1971.

Leavitt, Judith. *Common Dilemmas in Couple Therapy*. New York: Routledge/Taylor & Francis Group, 2010.

Levinger, George. "A social psychological perspective on marital dissolution." *Journal of Social Issues* (1976), 32 (1), 21-47. http://changingminds.org/explanations/theories/stage_theory.htm.

Léon, Dai. *Origins of the Tarot: Cosmic Evolution and the Principles of Immortality*. Berkeley: Frog Books, 2009.

Lewis, James R. and Evelyn Dorothy Oliver. *Angels A to Z*. Edited by Kelle S. Sisung. Canton: Visible Ink Press, 1996, 2002.

Mathers, S.L. MacGregor. "The Tarot: Its Occult Signification, Use In Fortune-telling and Method of Play, Etc." *The Tarot and The Key of Solomon*. Reprint. York Beach: Weiser/Kessinger Publishing.

Maunder, Bob and Jon Hunter. "Chalkboard Talks: Patterns of Adult Attachment," http://www.youtube.com/watch?v=GHHCy1IHTUc.

Moore, Duncan. *A Guide to Masonic Symbolism*. Hersham: Lewis Masonic, 2009.

Moore, Thomas. *Soul Mates: Honoring the Mysteries of Love and Relationship*. New York: HarperCollins Publishers, 1994.

Mueller, Ph.D., Robert, Signe E. Echols and Sandra Thomson. *The Lovers' Tarot*. New York: Avon Books. 1993.

Nichols, Sallie. *Jung and Tarot: An Archetypal Journey*. York Beach: Samuel Weiser, Inc., 1980.

Ordo Templi Orientis. *777 and Other Qabalistic Writings of Aleister Crowley*. York Beach: Samuel Weiser, Inc., 1973,1998.

Otto, Beatrice K. *Fools are Everywhere: The Court Jester Around the World*. Chicago: University Press, April 2001.

------. Crowley, Aleister (The Master Therion). "The Book of Thoth: A Short Essay on the Tarot of The Egyptians." Stanford: U.S. Games Systems, 2002.

Panati, Charles. *Sacred Origins of Profound Things*. New York: Arkana/Penguin Group, 1996.

Panofsky, Erwin. *Studies in Iconology: Humanistic Themes in the Art of the Renaissance*. New York: Icon/Harper & Row, 1972.

Papero, Daniel V. "Bowen Family Systems and Marriage." *Clinical Handbook of Couples Therapy* Edited by Neil S. Jacobson, Alan S. Gurman (New York: The Guilford Press, 1995.

Pemberton, John. *Myths and Legends: From Cherokee Dances to Voodoo Trances*. New York: Chartwell Books, 2010.

Picknett, Lynn. *The Secret History of Lucifer: The ancient bringer of light revealed*. London, England: Robinson, 2005.

Pickover, Clifford A. *Dreaming the Future: the Fantastic Story of Prediction*. Amherst: Prometheus Books, 2001.

Pittman III, Frank S. and Tina Pittman Wagers, *Clinical Handbook of Couples Therapy* Edited by Neil S. Jacobson, Alan S. Gurman. New York: The Guilford Press, 1995.

Place, Robert. *Alchemy and the Tarot*. Saugerties: Hermes Publications, 2011.

RavenWolf, Silver. *Solitary Witch: The Ultimate Book of Shadows for the New Generation*. St. Paul: Llewellyn Publications. 2003, 2005.

Regardie, Israel. *The Golden Dawn: A Complete Course in Practical Ceremonial Magic*. 6th Edition. Edited by Carl Llewellyn Weschcke. St. Paul: Llewellyn, 2002.

Resnick, Mayer *Love's all in the brain: fMRI study shows strong, lateralized reward, not sex, drive*. (May 31, 2005). http://www.eurekalert.org/pub_releases/2005-05/aps-lai053105.php.

Richert, Scott. P. "The Cardinal Virtues: The Four Hinges of the Moral Life." *About.com Catholicism*. (2012) http://catholicism.about.com/od/beliefsteachings/tp/Cardinal_Virtues.htm

Ronnberg, Ami and Kathleen Martin, ed. *The Book of Symbols: Reflection on Archetypal Images*. The Archive for Research in Archetypal Symbolism. Cologne, Germany: Taschen, 2010.

Rosengarten, Arthur. *Tarot and Psychology: Spectrums of Possibility*. St. Paul: Paragon House, 2000.

Sauneron, Serge. *The Priest of Ancient Egypt.* Translated by Ann Morrissett. New York: Grove Press, Inc., 1960.

Scheid, John. "Religions in Contact." *Religions of the Ancient World: a Guide,* General Editor Sarah Iles Johnson. Cambridge: Belknap Press of Harvard University Press, 2004.

Seznec, Jean. *The Survival of the Pagan Gods: The Mythological Tradition and Its Place in Renaissance Humanism and Art.* Translated by Barbara F. Sessions. Princeton: Princeton University Press/ Bollingen, 1953, 1981.

Shumaker, Wayne. *The Occult Science in the Renaissance: A Study in Intellectual Patterns.* Berkeley: University of California Press, 1972.

Spieth, Darius A. *Napoleon's Sorcerers: The Sophisians,* Cranbury: Rosemount Publishing & Printing Corp., 2007.

Sterling, Stephen Walter. *Tarot Awareness: Exploring the Spiritual path.* St. Paul: Llewellyn, 2000.

Struthers, Jane. *Tarot for Life & Love: Using the Tarot to Get the Most Out of Relationships.* London, England: Kyle Cathie Limited, 2002.

Thomas, Keith. *Religion and the Decline of Magic.* New York: Oxford University Press, 1971, 1997.

Tognetti, Arlene and Lisa Lenard. *The Intuitive Arts on Love.* Indianapolis: Alpha Books, 2003.

Townley, John. *Composite Charts: The Astrology of Relationships.* Woodbury: Llewellyn, 2000.

Tresidder, Jack. *The Watkins Dictionary of Symbols,* London: Watkins Publishing, 1997

Tyson, Donald. *Portable Magic: Tarot is The Only Tool You Need,* Woodbury: Llewellyn Publications, 2006.

Wynne M.A., Katrina. *An Introduction to Transformative Tarot Counseling: The High Art of Reading.* Newport: Sacred Rose Publishing, 2010.

Vega, Phyllis. *Romancing the Tarot: How to Use Tarot to Find True Love, Spice Up Your Sex Life, or Let Go of a Bad Relationship.* New York: Fireside/Simon & Schuster, 2001.

Vitali, Andrea. *Card 12 The Hanging Man,* last accessed on September 25, 2012 http://trionfi.com/0/i/v/v12.html.

------. and Terry Zanetti. Il Tarocchino di Bologna: Storia, Iconografia, Divinazione dal XV al XX secola. Bologna, Italy: Edizioni Martina, 2005.

Waite, Arthur Edward. *The Pictorial Key to The Tarot.* London: W. Rider, 1911.

Walker, Barbara G. *The Woman's Dictionary of Symbols and Sacred Objects* (San Francisco: Harper & Row, 1988).

------. *The Secrets of the Tarot: Origins, History and Symbolism.* New York: Harper & Row, 1984.

Walters, Linda Gail, http://www.lindagailwalters.com/Tarot-Court-Cards.html.

Wang, Robert. *The Qabalistic Tarot.* York Beach: Samuel Weiser, Inc., 1987.

------. *Perfect Tarot Divination Through Astrology. Kabbalah, and Principles of Jungian Interpretation.* Vol. 3 The Jungian Tarot Trilogy Practical Studies. Canada: Marcus Aurelius Press, 2007.

------ *Tarot Psychology: Handbook for the Jungian Tarot.* Connecticut, U.S. Games Systems, Inc., 1992.

Webster, Richard. *Communicating with the Archangel Michael for Guidance & Protection*. St. Paul: Llewellyn, 2004.

Westen, Drew. *Psychology: Mind, Brain & Culture*, 2nd Edition. New York: John Wiley & Sons, Inc, 1999.

Wirth, Oswald. *The Tarot Of the Magicians*. Translated by Samuel Weiser, Inc. York Beach: Samuel Weiser, Inc, 1985.

ADDITIONAL RESOURCES

Canadian Online Resource: http://www.child.alberta.ca/home/documents/familyviolence/doc_opfvb_booklet_women_colour.pdf

eHarmony; www.eHarmony.com.

Internal Website of The Vatican. http://www.vatican.va/siti_va/index_va_en.htm

Melanie Klein, http://www.melanie-klein-trust.org.uk/projective-identification.

Out of The Fog: Information and support for those with a family member or loved one that suffers from a personality disorder, http://www.outofthefog.net/index.html

The Merriam-Webster Dictionary, http://www.merriam-webster.com/dictionary/divination.

The Myers-Briggs Foundation; "MBTI® Basics" http://www.myersbriggs.org/my-mbti-personality-type/mbti-basics/.

USA Online Resource: WomensHealth.gov; Office on Women's Health; U.S. Department of Health and Human Services; http://www.womenshealth.gov/violence-against-women/types-of-violence/domestic-intimate-partner-violence.html